10

JAPANESE CULTURE

in the

MEIJI ERA

Volume IV

Manners and Customs

Published by
Ōbunsha
with editorial offices in
Yokodera-chō, Shinjuku-ku, Tokyo.

all rights reserved

first impression, March, 1957

JAPANESE MANNERS & CUSTOMS

in the

MEIJI ERA

Compiled and Edited by

Yanagida Kunio

Translated and Adapted by

Charles S. Terry

ŌBUNSHA

TOKYO JAPAN

A RICE DEALER

A primitive, simple " cleaning rice " tool was seen in front of the shop.
A rice-cleaner was hulling rice.

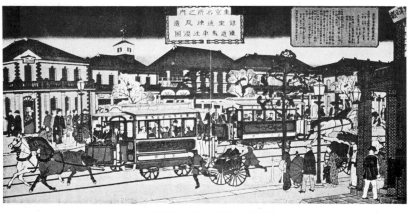

HORSE-DRAWN BUSES

In 1892 horse-pulled buses began operating between Shimbashi and Asakusa,
later between Shinagawa and Shimbashi

THE COSTUME OF GIRL STUDENTS

The young girls wore beautiful hakama to go to school. It had until then been strictly to masculine use but it was adopted by girl students.

すらりとならんだ丸の内の三菱
ビルディング（明治40年代）
三菱カ原とよばれた丸の内に、三菱は1894
年（明治27年）第1号館をたてたのを
かわきりとして、つぎつぎとたて
ましてゆき、ついに「一丁
・ロンドン」とまでいわれ
るようになった。

MITSUBISHI BUILDING STREET AT MARUNO-UCHI

Red brick buildings were built one after another by Mitsubishi and called " A miniature London."

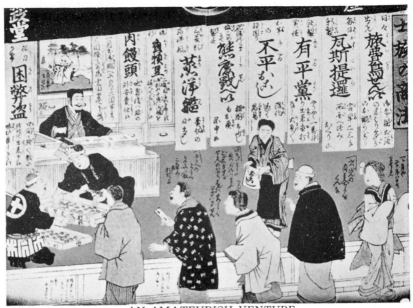

AN AMATEURISH VENTURE

A samurai was not free from conventionalism. He opened a shop, not knowing how to sell merchandise, nor how to treat customers.

THE MARRIAGE CEREMONY

The bride and groom, go-betweens, and attendants are seen. The principal feature of the wedding was a ceremony in which the bride and groom each took three sips of sake from each of a set of three sake cups.

PROMOTING MEAT EATING

It was not until Meiji period that people in Japan had not eaten beef. In and after 1871 people promoted meat eating as a sign of culture.

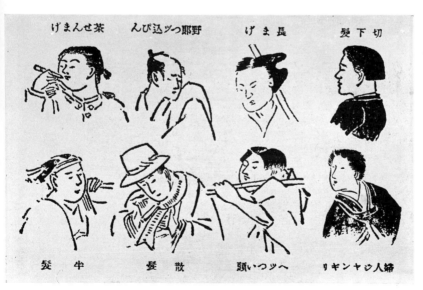

VARIOUS KINDS OF HAIR STYLE

At the beginning of Meiji Period.

A RICE DEALER

A primitive, simple "cleaning rice" tool was seen in front of the shop.
A rice-cleaner was hulling rice.

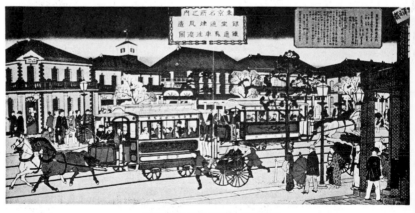

HORSE-DRAWN BUSES

In 1892 horse-pulled buses began operating between Shimbashi and Asakusa,
later between Shinagawa and Shimbashi

THE COSTUME OF GIRL STUDENTS

The young girls wore beautiful hakama to go to school. It had until then been strictly to masculine use but it was adopted by girl students.

すらりとならんだ丸の内の三菱
ビルディング（明治40年代）
三菱ケ原とよばれた丸の内に、三菱は1894
年（明治27年）第1号館をたてたのを
かわきりとして、つぎつぎとたて
ましてゆき、ついに「一丁
ロンドン」とまでいわれ
るようになった。

MITSUBISHI BUILDING STREET AT MARUNO-UCHI

Red brick buildings were built one after another by Mitsubishi and called "A miniature London."

PROMOTING MEAT EATING

It was not until Meiji period that people in Japan had not eaten beef. In and after 1871 people promoted meat eating as a sign of culture.

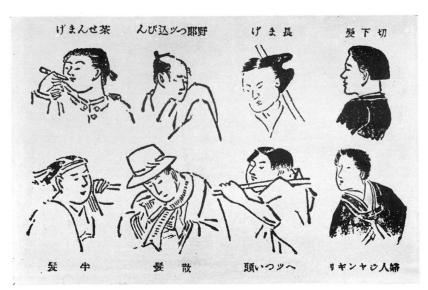

茶せんまげ　　野郎ッ込びん　　長まげ　　切下髪

半髪　　散髪　　へッつい頭　　婦人ヤシンギリ

VARIOUS KINDS OF HAIR STYLE
At the beginning of Meiji Period.

AN AMATEURISH VENTURE

A samurai was not free from conventionalism. He opened a shop, not knowing how to sell merchandise, nor how to treat customers.

THE MARRIAGE CEREMONY

The bride and groom, go-betweens, and attendants are seen. The principal feature of the wedding was a ceremony in which the bride and groom each took three sips of sake from each of a set of three sake cups.

TRANSLATOR'S PREFACE

AT the request of the Centenary Cultural Council, I have tried, in preparing this volume, to produce a text that not only Japanologists but non-specialists can understand. This has unfortunately involved many deviations from the original, because the subject dealt with is intrinsically obscure to anyone who has not lived in Japan and become comparatively familiar with the Japanese language. To have supplied all or even the larger portion of the information presupposed by the authors, who were of course writing for Japanese readers, would have meant not only to write a book twenty times as long as this, but also to have obscured the authors' main theses. I have therefore adopted the only alternative, to explain where this can be done simply and to omit or revise where it cannot.

One particular omission is so serious as to require special comment. The last chapter of the original was a discussion by Professor Yanagida of changes in the Japanese language during the Meiji period. This being a most important subject and one in which the authors are especially interested, I worked long and hard to put it into English, only to come to the conclusion that the task was impossible, an opinion in which the Centenary Council concurred. The difficulty was primarily that the discussion revolved about differences between speech and writing and between dialects and standard Japanese, and the nuances of the examples cited could not be expressed in English without adding reams of explanation.

Professor Yanagida holds that the Meiji government's attempt to standardize Japanese was based largely on urban prejudices against provincial dialects, and that it indicated far too little concern on the part of education authorities for the actual linguistic needs of the people at large. In the schools, he argues, young people, instead of being taught to speak their own tongue clearly and effectively, were crammed full of scholarly words adopted from Chinese and curious phrases translated literally from European languages. What Japanese the children were exposed to was not, he believes, a well thought out standard language, but the dialect of the Tokyo upper class, which was more often than not useless to them in their everyday lives. The result, he contends, was that they rarely mastered "standard" Japanese, or their own dialect, or anything else, and that for this reason the Japanese language as it is used today is apt often to be vague or garbled. The details of Professor Yanagida's argument would be of interest to Westerners who have a reasonably thorough knowledge of Japanese, but incomprehensible to anyone else.

I should perhaps add, though I fear it superfluous, that I was asked to make this translation not because of any special understanding of the subject on my part, but merely because of a dearth of translators. The authors have often employed methods of research and presentation that are quite novel to me, and I can only pray that I have done them justice.

Charles S. Terry

Tokyo, Japan
September, 1956

CONTENTS

Chapter One

INTRODUCTION

CHANGING WAYS OF LIFE

AS even the most unobservant individual knows, manners and customs change over the course of time. This is not to say, however, that the rate of change is constant. During the three centuries of the Tokugawa period, when Japan loitered in peaceful isolation from the rest of the world, changes in the general mode of living were nearly imperceptible, but after the coming of Commodore Perry, the transformation in everyday life was virtually revolutionary. The political conflict surrounding the Meiji Restoration of 1868 to some extent concealed the cultural implications of the new government's policies, but by around 1887, political authority was stable, and people began to notice the vastness of what had occurred in the previous two decades. The strict class system of the Tokugawa period had been abolished, and now young men, far from being bound to minute plots of ground in rural districts, might hope to become successful entrepreneurs, renowned scholars, or even ministers in the government. The nation looked forward with surprise and pleasure to a new life.

Everything was novel and wonderful. There were new schools which anyone might attend. Railway trains traveled between the cities. Fine modern buildings lined the streets of the capital. Communication facilities were so convenient that one could leave the farm and go to the city without fear of being completely separated from one's family. Change was the keynote of the era, and those who could not keep up with the pace were ridiculed or scorned. There was a joke about a farmer who, desiring to send a package to his son in the city, went out and hung it on a telegraph wire. " Old-fashioned " was for some time the most dreaded adjective in the Japanese language.

Manners and customs, however, do not change completely overnight, and in the new age certain relics of the past became very conspicuous. If one looks beyond the new surface one finds a substratum of tradition that remained virtually constant. Our task in this book is to examine this substratum. We shall find surprisingly many ancient cultural elements that were preserved not only throughout Meiji, but into contemporary times. Political and economic changes over this period were cataclysmic, but they do not tell the whole story of Japanese life—government bureaus and large corporations may be housed in modern reinforced concrete buildings, but the houses in which most Japanese eat, sleep, and raise their children have retained many of their basic features down to the present.

Having been born and educated in the Meiji period, I am constantly amazed at the speed with which life has changed, but at the same time often startled to find old, old customs that have not disappeared. The forty-five years of the Meiji period witnessed the great leap from a feudalistic social system to one based on capitalism and competition. The past, however, was not completely discarded, and in many areas ancient practices which throw light on the substratum of Japanese life continued to be observed. Still, during this youthful lively era, the tendency was ever toward the new, and sometimes ancient customs that might better have been guarded were lost in the rush. I hope that in this volume my colleagues and I have succeeded not only in clarifying the basic, change-resisting features of the Japanese mode of living, but also in pointing up a number of Meiji failures and shortcomings that remained to be dealt with.

The various phases of life in Meiji Japan are discussed in

the ensuing chapters, and there is no need for my going into them in detail at this point, but I would like briefly to recapitulate a few of the broader trends.

In the structure of the houses we live in, the grip of the past on our lives is far stronger than we customarily suppose. During the early years of Meiji, when Lafcadio Hearn made his journeys around Japan, the cities he saw were agglomerations of small wooden houses, as charming perhaps as a row of delicate old Japanese lanterns—and very little more substantial. The social conditions that had formed the little cottages in the cities of those times had a long history. Even in the provincial castle towns, houses were of much the same form. But while the front roofs were low and the view from the outside unimpressive, there were frequently a number of fine white-walled storehouses about the houses and large handsome rooms within them. One thing about houses in the villages was that while the owner might think of his home as his castle, there were certain indefinable restrictions on his freedom. Aside from the dwellings of the village head-man and certain antique buildings, houses were built by cooperative effort, and in many instances the material came from community stock-piles. A prospective builder could not therefore always do just as he pleased. Whether he was erecting a new house or rebuilding on the remains of one that had burned, he could not build without the approval of his fellow villagers. Even in the Meiji period such conditions persisted in farming communities. They had long been part and parcel of Japanese custom.

Despite the great earthquake of 1923 and the ravages of the late war, a few ancient houses are still standing. A comparison of them with modern houses reveals not only alterations in the outside form, rearrangement of rooms, and a shift from paper to glass doors, but what is more significant, a spiritual change in the Japanese attitude toward the home. We shall try in a later section to determine what sort of change this was.

As for the question of food, it is commonly believed that

3

the Japanese have all eaten rice since ancient times. A Meiji-period song went like this:

> Though born in the Land of Abundant Reeds
>   and Beautiful Rice Plants,
> I cannot eat rice.
> What a strange story!

Of course, the song is metaphorical, but it was sung on the supposition that the Japanese had been eating rice since ancient times. Such, however, is not the case. In 1874, the Tax Revision Bureau in the Ministry of Finance submitted a report to the effect that the amount spent in the provincial areas for rice was less than one third of the total amount spent for food. Afterwards, as soldiers and other travelers who visited the rice-eating towns carried urban customs back to their little villages, sales of rice increased. However, it would be no exaggeration to say that throughout the Meiji period, Japanese farmers ate rice only on special occasions. This was true not only in the mountain villages. An 82-year-old farmer from what is now Suginami Ward in Tokyo avows that until the Taishō era (1912–1926) his everyday diet consisted of wheat, barley, and tares. During World War II, when the women in the villages heard the government's propaganda in favor of substitute foods, they looked at each other and laughed, since what was described as "substitute foods" was what they had been living on since birth. Country people were also startled by the wartime rice ration. Some of the authorities were aware that inhabitants of the villages did not as a rule eat rice, but they had been told to issue rice, and issue rice they did. As a result, many of the farmers had more of the grain during the war than they had ever had before.

That be as it may, however, the number of people who based their diets on rice increased tremendously during and after the Meiji period. Foreign rice had to be imported, and one first began to hear the now common saying that highly polished white rice was a source of disease. Simultaneously with the shift to a rice diet, the consumption of sugar grew rapidly, and meat, hitherto exceedingly rare, appeared even on the tables of ordinary folk. In short, eating habits underwent revolutionary changes during the Meiji period and in turn produced changes in the other facets of daily life.

During the early years of Meiji, the work clothes as well as the everyday dress of the rural population consisted even in winter only of layers of unlined hemp garments. People of today can but be astonished at the robustness with which the farmers and fishermen of yesteryear faced the cold. However, although cotton and cotton cloth had become somewhat widespread as early as the middle Edo period (that is, around the eighteenth century), they do not seem to have affected working clothes or everyday wear outside the towns. It was only with the sudden development of spinning and weaving techniques during Meiji that the hemp garment began to fall rapidly out of use.

The replacement of hemp brought about great changes in the everyday chores of women. In older times, thread was spun and cloth woven and bleached by hand. Then the material was either taken to the dyer's, known picturesquely as the "blueing shop," or dyed at home. To provide only the requisite single garment for each member of the household was no mean task. The extreme difficulty involved in spinning hemp is the basis for a number of jokes that survive today concerning rivalry between wives and mothers-in-law, but today we find it difficult to laugh at the severe labor taken for granted in these stories. They give us a pitiful picture of village girls gathered together on the long winter nights and trying with laughter or gossip to distract themselves from their boring and time-consuming work. To make matters worse, the loom on which hempen thread was woven was of a very primitive type that made it necessary for the weaver to wrap the cloth about her as it came off the machine.

At first cotton thread was spun by means of a small bamboo tube and woven by hand. The loom, however, was of a design that allowed the weaver to sit and work merrily along with a small reed. The effort required was less than that needed to run the loom employed for hemp, and, incidentally, the weaver at her work made quite a graceful picture. Eventually, however, thin foreign yarn known colloquially as "Chinese thread" was imported, and, since the government for a time abolished the customs duty on it, it sold for surprisingly little. Women no longer needed to spin cotton, and while aware that cloth made from the new thread was of relatively poor quality, they used it.

With the development of textile factories, the thin pliant cotton turned out on machines replaced the stiff homespun that had been almost tiresomely durable. The new cloth took dyes easily and made more attractive clothing. It was no mere fashion that made women fond of it, however, but a matter of strict practicality, and after the new material had been introduced, the history of the hand-loom came to a hasty end.

Silk has been used in Japan since time immemorial, but throughout premodern history, it belonged exclusively to the non-working class. Not until the Meiji period did it slowly spread, like rice, among the common people. As this was going on, muslin also became so fashionable that the famous Yūzen Dye-works of the Tokugawa period became the Muslin Dye-works. Neither silk nor muslin, however, was used for work clothes. Both were treasured for gala dress, and in that sense usage differed from present-day practices among women in the cities.

During the Tokugawa period, a few warriors, priests, and women of pleasure spent much of their time in travel, but the vast majority of the population lived in the same house from the time they were born until they died, and considered themselves lucky for being able to do so. After old Edo became the thriving metropolis of Tokyo, an ever-increasing number of persons left home to make their living in the city or on the road. Still, at the first of the era there were practical restrictions that hindered individuals from going to new areas.

To set up a residence in most places it was necessary to have a guarantor or at least the support of a landlord. This rule was particularly rigid in small villages. Moreover, a young person could not very well move without his parent's permission, for if he did, he was likely to be disinherited. In some places, this situation exists even today.

One of the great accomplishments of Meiji period was that people throughout the country gained the privilege of living where they wished. Young boys left the farms for city schools; officials were transferred from place to place; and soldiers came from the country to bases in urban areas. Travel ceased to be unusual or dangerous, and people began to regard it with a hitherto unknown equanimity. Still, however, rural areas continued to make rather a large to-do when people went off on journeys.

With the development of industries, the cities became melting pots filled with people from all different areas, and many of these were converted in a generation or two into bonafide city dwellers, who harbored no intentions whatever of returning to the country.

The whole scenery changed. Factories sprang up in the mountains and along the rivers, and the former castle towns began to expand into large urban centers. The population shot up, and there ceased to be room on the farm for second or third sons. Some of these became officials—pure consumers supported by taxes—but many more set out in the world as laborers, thus giving birth to a class that had never before existed in Japan and at the same time creating the labor supply necessary to further modernization. All these external changes were based on a change in spirit, a general will to do away with the old and discover the new.

One of the important features of Meiji life was the widespread adoration of the emperor. As a matter of actual fact, the imperial government had considerably greater true stature than it had had during any of the centuries since the establishment of the Kamakura shogunate in the twelfth century, and the people were proud to consider themselves children of an august ruler, living in the age of progress. Japan's great modern tragedy was that the genuine affection of the people for their emperor was later misused by politicians.

Chapter Two

CLOTHING, FOOD, AND HOUSING

1. CLOTHING

a. The Loss of Distinction Between Everyday and Occasional Dress

ONE great principle to be observed in the mores of pre-modern Japan was a clear distinction between ordinary routine days and festive occasions. The attitude of the people toward life was in a sense dominated by this distinction.

It is evident from many old verbal expressions that in the minds of our ancestors everyday clothing was a completely different thing from fancy occasional dress, and the same applied to food. We find, for example, expressions such as " everyday rice " and " everyday rice container," which were clearly distinguished from words that referred to the food used on festive days. The latter was in many places called literally " different food."

Sechi, the old term for ceremonial days, appears to be etymologically related to the word that signifies the joints of a bamboo stalk. Festive days thus were probably thought of as dividing the year into seasons, just as the joints divide a stalk of bamboo into sections. The usual yearly festival days were spoken of collectively as the " annual activities " (*nenjū-gyōji*). They were by no means determined by accident. In general, the basis for them lay in agrarian life, and most of them fell at the beginning or end of some phase of the annual farm work, when it was considered necessary to pray to the gods for a good crop. In addition to the " annual

9

activities" there were personal days of celebration, such as the days of birth, of marriage, of coming to manhood, and of attaining a propitious age (*e.g.* sixty). These events were to a person's life what the annual activities were to the year.

Since the distinction between ordinary and special days had religious connotations, it was rigidly forbidden to conduct oneself on routine days in a manner appropriate to festive days, or vice versa. Modern Japanese still speak of " a lazy fellow who works only on holidays." This expression was originally a term of scorn for persons who failed to observe the days when it was proper to rest and make offerings to the gods. In Okinawa there is a popular superstition that such a person will be bitten by a poisonous snake, and in various other locations it is said that in the past the young men of the community tore the roof off the house of a person who committed this offense. It is precisely because at one time there was a religious prohibition against work on such days that now, when their religious significance is no longer deeply felt, it is considered all right not to work on them.

Despite religious prohibitions, however, there must have always existed an instinctive desire to carry the gaiety and pleasure of festive days over into ordinary life. In the Meiji period, this became in many instances financially feasible, and what with a loss of faith in the old gods, the ancient distinction began to fade. This phenomenon began in the cities, where ideas founded on agricultural life did not have a strong hold. It gradually spread, however, to the rural areas, thanks both to a strong Japanese tendency toward adulation of urban life and to increased population movements.

After the end of the Tokugawa period intercourse with foreign countries became active, and imitation of foreign manners and customs added to the general trend. A new life in which all days were in principle the same spread throughout the country.

Clothing is said to be the most direct indication of a people's general frame of mind. Certainly the ancient distinction between regular and festive days was evident in popular dress, and the loss thereof was equally visible in the changing styles of the Meiji period.

b. Festive and Everyday Dress

Japanese clothing may be divided broadly into three classes, according to whether it is worn at work, during leisure hours on ordinary days, or on festive occasions. From the beginning festive dress was quite distinct in form, the sleeves and skirts being entirely too long for wear while working. This remained largely true in the Meiji period, despite decreasing emphasis on the distinction between special and routine days. The usual name for such clothing was " festival dress " (*matsurigo*), "annual-holiday dress " (*setsugo*), " New Year dress " (*shōgatsugo*), or " All Soul's Day dress " (*bongo*), dependent on the dialect. These terms are all connected with annual celebrations, but in many areas there were also colloquial expressions like " go-to-shrine dress " (*miyamairigo*), " coming-to-womanhood dress " (*kanetsukego*), and " bridal dress " (*yomerigo*), which are based on the main events of an individual's lifetime. All the words mentioned, incidentally, are very old.

There were many variations in the material and cut of festive dress at the beginning of the Meiji era, and the government, bent on " enlightenment," took a number of measures to encourage uniform modern standards. Decrees were issued from time to time, but few of them had much effect among the common people. Still, since festive dress was worn only rarely and had little to do with the requirements of everyday life, it was comparatively easy to change, and it began rather quickly to show the influence of the new culture.

The first Meiji regulation concerning clothing is found in a proclamation of the chancellery dated November 12, 1872. This ordered the substitution of Western dress for the ceremonial robe and crown hitherto worn by noblemen at court. Of course, there were reactions among the more conservative against the adoption of Western styles, and a famous prince, Shimazu Hisamitsu, made an official protest, but the tendency toward imitation of the Occident was irresistible. There were even people who argued that Japanese clothing ought to be generally prohibited.

Outside the court, Western dress first appeared in the form of uniforms for soldiers in the new army, but in the early seventies the more fashionable men in society adopted more suitable versions for formal wear about town. The gentleman dressed in a Western suit and sporting an unruly head of hair only recently deprived of its traditional topknot was for a time the symbol of enlightenment. Some women appreciated Western clothes too, and in the eighties ladies in European dress were to be seen constantly at the Rokumei-kan, a Western-style restaurant and ballroom erected in Tokyo in 1882 and considered for a number of years thereafter the very center of all that was chic. The age of Westernization for the sake of Westernization passed, however, and while Western clothes grew increasingly popular, it was not because they were smart, but because they were suitable as working apparel.

Despite the wishes of the court, strict ceremonial dress could hardly have been expected to give way all at once to foreign clothing. Even in the proclamation of 1872, referred to above, it was stated that traditional dress might be worn on ceremonial occasions in the event that the wearer did not yet possess the newly ordained attire. Also, in 1874 various types of Japanese-style dress were specifically approved for officials in charge of religion as well as for Shinto and Buddhist priests. In September, 1877, the chancellery designated for low-ranking nobles and ordinary officials a ceremonial attire consisting, in addition to a kimono, of a loose cloak called a *haori* and very full pleated trousers (*hakama*) that appear at a glance to be a skirt. The *haori* was to be black and to bear the family crest of the wearer. This outfit became the usual formal dress for men and with variations has remained so until the present.

It appears that in very early times festive dress and work clothing were the only types distinguished, but as time went on the need for an intermediate style was felt, first in the towns and later in the countryside as well. In farming and fishing villages people usually wore their work clothes all day long during busy seasons, but otherwise changed to a more comfortable everyday garment in leisure hours. It was said in many places that when the harvest was in, one might begin to wear "long clothing," as opposed to work clothes, which came only to the thigh. Thus everyday dress, like ceremonial dress, was distinguished by length. In the Kantō area fisherman not at sea wore a dark blue garment with sleeves that tapered down to a close fit at the wrists (*tsutsusode,* or "tubular sleeves"). This was called a *nagatoba,* and it is interesting to note that the state of being ill (and hence not at work) went by the same name. In places where it was very cold in winter, the everyday dress for village women had a long skirt, but when there was housework to be done, they wore over this a type of baggy trousers.

At first both hemp and cotton were used for everyday clothes, but gradually the former was displaced by the latter. Until the Meiji era, the women in farming villages made thread and wove clothing for their entire families, but with the development of the textile industry and the importation of cheap cotton from abroad, the production of Japanese short-fiber cotton and fabrics made therefrom tended to die out. In many locales the change to manufactured goods came around the middle of the Meiji period. An interesting side effect was that the old practice of starching cotton fabrics until they were stiff—a remnant of the age of hemp—fell into disuse. From about this time, as oldsters recall, women began to look soft and gentle even from a distance.

In the urban areas it was only a step from the confusion of special and routine days to the loss of distinction between festive and everyday clothing, but certain adjustments had to be made before formal dress could be worn on ordinary occasions. Kimonos with long sleeve-pockets (about to the waist with arm outstretched) were adopted for everyday wear, but women and men both found the sleeves cumbersome, and women created a new style by tying them up with a cord, while men often abandoned them later for sleeves that tapered to a manageable size.

Commoners of the Tokugawa era were subject to many limitations as to color and quality of clothing, primarily because the shogunate was forever bolstering its system of strict social distinctions. Regulations differed to some extent in the divers provinces, but in general silk was prohibited to the lower classes, as were the colors red and purple, along with loud ornamental designs. Consequently, everyone, man or woman, old or young, wore a kimono of dark blue, gray, or orange material, the only variation being that the material might be either plain or striped.

After the Restoration the restrictions were abolished, and in theory people might have worn the gaudiest clothes within their means, but in the earlier half of the Meiji period kimonos were surprisingly conservative. Styles changed from time to time, but there was no concerted attempt to take advantage of the new freedom. Men and women alike preferred dark blue or brown silks, usually with a quiet stripe or plaid. The emancipation of color first became visible in the summer cotton kimono. Traditionally this had been a very plain garment, but at summer festivals, when everyone dressed alike and there was safety in numbers, a bold design had often been selected. Gradually individuals gathered the courage to venture out alone in such costumes, and the style spread. In 1905 the Mitsukoshi Clothing Store introduced ladies' silk kimonos with "*genroku*" designs, so called because they resembled the bold, flashy patterns popular in the Genroku Era (1688—1703), and this proved to be a milestone. By the next year styles that suggested the dazzling gold and silver paintings of the Momoyama period were in favor, and brilliance had become the main feature in women's fashions. It is worth noticing that women began to allow the border of the undergarment to show at the collar of the kimono, and this seemingly small touch came to be considered a very important part of their attire. The material was ordinarily silk crepe, and the colors employed were red, purple, blue, or yellow, the shades varying according to the age of the wearer.

The *haori* also underwent great changes. Around 1885 it was usually made of black silk crepe, and then for a time colors became fashionable, but from about 1890 to 1902 black was again favored. Afterward color once again came into vogue and remained so until the end of Meiji. After around 1901 thin figured satin also became popular. Until around 1890, the lining of the *haori* was almost always made of lustring, but later a soft satin like that used for lining Western clothing was substituted. After 1905 the *haori* became more and more elegant. Whereas it had originally been worn for warmth, it now often took on a purely ornamental aspect and was sometimes made of ultra-thin silk gauze for summer wear.

The above changes were largely confined to Tokyo, and, for that matter, to only a segment of the population there. Rural areas were inclined to imitate city life in many respects, but they held rather stubbornly to traditional apparel. Still the shifting fashions of the metropolis, kaleidoscopic though they were, reflect important cultural trends. In the first place, they illustrate graphically that the people were slow to take advantage of the new freedom resulting from the rout of the Tokugawa shogunate. This very probably means that colorful or luxurious clothing was so closely associated with festive days that it was not considered proper for ordinary wear until the distinction between special and routine days had well nigh disappeared Second, the confusion between Western and Japanese clothing was at its height during the late eighties, the very period when the government was trying to decide between monarchy on the democratic plan and Kaiserism *à la japonaise*. After the Russo-

Japanese War, styles, like public sentiment, reverted to tradition. Extreme Westernization came in for a general reappraisal and there was a strong trend toward clothing resembling that of the Momoyama period, possibly the most thoroughly Japanese of all epochs in the nation's history.

The most pronounced change, however, was the collapse of the distinction between the festive and the ordinary, which had hitherto amounted to a strict rule of life. The mingling of these two concepts even began to spread from the cities to the provinces, though not rapidly.

c. Work Clothes

Work clothing is apparently not subject to rapid changes. In the Meiji era, other types of Japanese apparel began almost immediately to show the influence of the Occident, but farmers and fishermen, whose working methods remained largely what they had been for centuries, continued to wear much 'the same garments as before, and to a surprising degree they took them along when they moved to the city and began working in factories. Even now the clothing worn by tradespeople and laborers in Tokyo, though Westernized, differs little in color or over-all design from traditional farm clothes.

Long after cotton was adopted for festive dress, work clothes, the prime requisite for which was strength, continued to be made of hemp. This was especially true in remote areas, and in a number of districts hemp or even coarser materials, such as wisteria fiber and bark, were used until the end of the Meiji period. In Shūchi County of Shizuoka Prefecture, work clothes were actually called "wisteria kimonos" (*fujigimono*), and truthfully so since the cloth for them was woven from the fiber of a type of wisteria growing wild in the local mountains. People said that such clothing could be worn summer and winter for ten years, and that when a person wearing it walked through mountain brambles, the thorns broke off without tearing the material. Such fabrics were heavy, and they must have irritated the skin, but they were economical and suitable to all climes.

A prominent feature of farm clothes was that they were divided into upper and lower parts. The coat usually came down to the hips and had close-fitting sleeves, while the trousers were in one of two general styles. One type fitted tightly and was fastened underneath the upper garment, while the other was loose around the hips so that the upper garment could be tucked in. Both were tight around the legs, and this facilitated work. There were many variants, and seemingly even more local words for them. In some of the central areas the looser variety was called "monkey pants" (*sarubakama*), a very apt description.

Various types of protective covering for the arms and legs have been used with work clothes since early times. Arm coverings usually extended from the elbow to the wrist, and often they were attached to gloves. The latter, incidentally, were as a rule fingerless and often covered only the backs of the hands. Leggings were very important, particularly for the many who worked in wet paddy fields. Formerly they seem to have been fashioned of water-resistant rushes and leaves or woven from the fibers of sage or brush, but these materials were gradually replaced by hemp and cotton. In the Kantō area women formerly wore arm coverings, but eventually switched to tight-fitting long sleeves. Tied or fastened along the forearm, these made the working outfit easier to get in and out of, but they did not allow as much freedom of movement as separate coverings.

After the Western jacket and trousers proved to be an efficient outfit for soldiers, they were accepted by many farmers. The change was relatively small, however, since the traditional two-piece work clothing was similar in many ways. It would be an overstatement to describe this development as an instance of Occidental "influence" in the rural areas, though it was possibly due in part to more or less conscious aping of city people.

In the middle years of the era, officials both major and minor were strongly urged to wear Western dress to work, and gradually teachers and students began to take to it too. The change did not occur all at once. One frequently encountered school boys attired in Western suits, but wearing wooden clogs. More likely than not, the trousers would be tied up with an obi from which a hand towel was suspended in the rear. In rural areas the postmen wore uniforms, but retained their straw sandals. Even farmers who wore Western shirts and trousers apparently considered shoes a mere accessory and only hesitatingly adopted them.

In the Meiji period Occidental dresses for women were fashionable only for formal attire. Women at work, either on the farm or elsewhere wore more traditional clothing. In 1872, when the first Japanese textile mill was set up (in Tomioka, Gumma Prefecture), the young girls employed as reelers wore men's striped *hakama* to work. This was a little strange to behold, but it was difficult to work in long kimonos, and it would hardly have done to dress in farming apparel. Subsequently, the *hakama*, which had until then been strictly limited to masculine use, was adopted by girl students as well as factory women. By 1900 a type of *hakama* that had no division between the legs had become very popular among women. In 1907 the following instructions were issued to the teachers in the schools of Hiroshima Prefecture:

The female instructors in primary schools will engage in physical training just as male instructors, and both in and out of school they will be expected to be quick and alert. Accordingly, on the school ground they will wear narrow-sleeved kimonos and *hakama*.

This, incidentally, is the first example of clothing regulations for women teachers in the rural districts. During the last years of the Meiji period, urban school women, instructors and students alike, more often than not wore *hakama*.

In urban areas, ordinary housewives at work tied up the

long sleeves of their everyday kimonos with cords and either tucked the lower parts of their skirts into their obis or wore aprons. In the closing years of the Taishō era puffed sleeves were added to the full-length Western apron to form the work garment now used by Japanese housewives.

Work clothes in farm villages were almost same for men and women of all ages. The colors were dull, and even the names for the garments sounded old. Modern women would not accept them, but it took some time for a more suitable outfit to be found. Finally women realized the value of Western clothes in this respect, but a number of rather curious combinations of old and new were tried and discarded before this occurred.

The apron was used as a part of the work garment for both men and women throughout the country. There were various forms, but the most usual one hung from the waist down to around the shins. In some areas women took great pride in the aprons they made and put considerable craftsmanship into them. The material was originally hemp, but this was gradually replaced by cotton. Aprons still form a customary part of the garb worn by grocers, butchers, fishmongers, sake merchants, and many others.

d. Headdress and Footgear

Some form of headdress was ordinarily employed by farm workers as a protection against sun, wind, dirt, and insects. Styles varied from place to place, but they proved very impervious to change during the Meiji era, since the methods of farm work remained very much the same as ever. Often the head covering formed an important element in what we think of today as local color. In Yuri County of Akita Prefecture, for instance, women working outdoors wore a black cloth tied around the head in such a way as to leave only the eyes, nose, and mouth exposed. Young girls substituted green, blue, or pink for black. Wash towels were and are used for covering in many areas and in a multitude of different styles. In Satsuma (southern Kyūshū) men tied the ends of the towel behind their heads, whereas women did not tie them at all. In the islands around Yamaguchi and northern Kyūshū, on the other hand, young women tied their headcloths on their foreheads so that the backs of their heads were covered. This was a particularly common style among the girls engaged to watch children. The same style is still found in the islands off Izu, and it appears to have been more universal there in the past. In warm weather a headband, tied either in front or in back, was used to keep perspiration out of the eyes.

Headdress was also a protection against cold, and many varieties were devised for winter wear. In the Kariwa district of Niigata Prefecture a hat, at times lined with cotton, was sewn to the collar of the working garment. Since this was worn inside as well as outside, it appears to have been looser than the ordinary headcloth. In the Aizu district of Fukushima Prefecture a primitive hat made of sage or straw seems to have been used since early times as a part of the winter outfit.

During the second decade of the Meiji period a number of people in Tokyo began to use shawls, and after 1903 it became the fashion to wear thin striped-silk scarfs. Although it was usual to drape these around the shoulders, in cold weather they were sometimes worn over the head. During the last years of Meiji large shawls resembling blankets became fashionable, the style being to fold them in two lengthwise and hang them about the shoulders. This type of shawl spread gradually to rural areas, and country people still consider it convenient for travel today. In the cities, however, it has disappeared, and, as a result the term *akagetto* (red blanket), as used by urban residents, is now roughly equivalent to the American " hick."

Headdress was an important part of ceremonial clothing, especially that used for religious services, marriages, and funerals. Originally, in fact, it was considered proper always to wear something on the head on all special occasions, but nowadays people most often uncover before superiors as well as in temples and shrines. A white or nearly white wash cloth was usual for ceremonial wear. What has now become the common headband, or *hachimaki*, was originally a sort of shellcap, which could also be used with formal dress. Other old styles are preserved in a number of modern types. A broad-fronted hat (*tsunokakushi*) made of unspun cotton and worn by brides almost everywhere is an example. We might note, however, that in the Nobe region of Aomori, brides drape a short unlined kimono from their heads instead. In the same area women cover themselves with the left sleeve of a kimono at funerals.

When babies were taken to the local shrine for the first time their heads were covered with a cotton headdress, and in some places it was considered necessary to use a diaper for this purpose. All of these practices are based on the ancient habit of the wearing headdress on festive days.

In 1871 military caps were adopted for the army, and somewhat afterward, when modern haircuts had become the rule, men began to wear Western hats. These were known at first by a name derived from the French *chapeau*, but the modern word is *bōshi*. The latter comes from Chinese, but resembles the old Japanese words *botchi* and *boshi*, which have a similar meaning. Straw hats began to be manufactured in 1878, and around 1905 the panama and napoleon, as well as the hunting cap, appeared. Many men even wore Western hats with kimonos, and the school cap with kimono and *hakama* was virtually a uniform for students.

Changes in footgear also reflect the shifting condition of the age. In May, 1901, the following order was issued from the central police :

> As a precaution against the plague, it is forbidden
> to walk barefoot outdoors in the city of Tokyo. Violators
> of this order will be arrested and punished in accordance

with Article Four, Section 426, of the penal code.
This command was put into effect in the following month.
Sanitation was the main reason for it, but the idea that going
barefoot was barbarous and would bring shame to the nation's
capital must have furnished part of the hidden motive. Until
now ricksha men, grooms, laborers, and in fact anyone engaged
in hard labor as a rule had worn no footgear, except perhaps
for simple straw sandals.

The wooden clogs known today as *geta* are seen in picture-
scrolls of the middle ages, and remains of a similar footgear
have been found in ancient archeological sites, but this was
not originally the footgear of laborers, and its use was quite
limited. Toward the end of the Tokugawa period, however,
geta of the modern type came into rather wide use, and after
the beginning of Meiji, they were produced in ever-increasing
quantities. As a result, paulownia trees, from the wood of which
they are made, were planted on a much larger scale than
previously.

Even in the Tokugawa period *tabi*, cotton socks with the
great toe separated from the others, were fairly common. It
appears that they were worn because of the rareness of cotton
material, as well as its pleasant soft feel, rather than because
they were a good protection from cold feet. At first they
were used only by the old or the infirm, but later ordinary
people began to wear them when making calls or when dressed
in holiday clothing. White was considered the proper color.
Tabi were tied on with strings until around 1882 or 1883,
when they were first furnished with catches. A special type of
thick-soled *tabi*, intended for wear while working became widespread among the lower classes during the Meiji period. These
too were fastened first with cords, but later with buttons or
catches. Their adoption probably reflects the influence of
Western shoes.

Shoes were introduced to Japan together with Western clothing as a part of the military uniform. The Tokugawa government

ordered a large number of them for its soldiers, but the order was delivered during the civil war that accompanied the Restoration, and the new government received it instead. Unfortunately, the shoes were of a narrow foreign last, and not a single Japanese foot could be found to fit them. They were finally thrown away, but the need for military shoes led in 1870 to the establishment of a shoe factory in the Tsukiji district of Tokyo. It was the first of its kind.

A magazine in 1871 listed nine types of footgear worn in Tokyo. Among others, they included *geta*, wooden slippers, a variety of straw sandals, and Western shoes. In effect, instead of switching suddenly to foreign shoes, the Japanese simply added them to the types of footgear already in use. It does not appear that shoes invariably went with Western clothing. A magazine of 1872 speaks of men dressed in traditional clothing and carrying swords, but at the same time wearing Western footgear. This was typical of the confusion that characterized the age.

One large factor tending to prevent foreign shoes from becoming everyday wear in Japan was the Japanese habit of removing footgear upon entering houses. This, on the other hand, encouraged the widespread adoption of *geta*, which are still extremely popular. Along with shirts and dresses, shoes did eventually become a part of the work clothing of many people, but even today they are considered too much a nuisance to bother with when going out on a short errand, and some profess even to find *geta* more comfortable for outdoor activities like mountain climbing.

With the spread of *geta* and shoes, the straw sandal has tended to fall out of use, but since it can be made at home for little or nothing, it is still common in rural districts. There are many types of straw footwear, and certain areas have developed the techniques for producing them to a high level.

The adoption of Occidental clothing and shoes appears to have brought changes in Japanese posture and carriage, notably the disappearances to a large degree of the broad square shoulders and swaggering walk of men.

e. Cosmetics

Originally lip rouge and face powder were used only for religious ceremonies, marriages, and other festive occasions. However, either because people desired to carry the gala spirit of festivals over into routine days or because elaborately made-up women in religious service came to be employed often as dancers and singers at secular affairs, make-up became a fashion among ordinary women. In the towns the ceremonial significance of cosmetics was lost at a relatively early date, but it was preserved into the Meiji period in some rural areas. Perhaps the most striking customs in this respect were those of blackening the teeth and of using artificial eyebrows instead of the real ones, which were shaven off. Tooth black was in early times associated with puberty rites for girls, but gradually it came to be thought of as proper for all married women. The stain was made by heating iron scraps and plunging them in strong tea, often sweetened with rice wine or candy. The powder of gall nuts was added to make the mixture adhere, and the whole mess was applied with a brush. Later it was touched up every now and then.

In 1868 a proclamation issued to the nobility stated that since blackening the teeth and shaving the eyebrows were not really ancient practices they needed no longer to be continued and after 1871 there was a great deal of talk about abolishing them generally. The following appeared in a publication of 1875: " What could be more tasteless than for women to blacken their teeth and shave their eyebrows ? By doing so they lose their natural beauty and make themselves appear deformed.... We believe that if such evil customs are not prohibited by law, the chance for a brand new era will be lost." In the same year Fukuzawa Yukichi published a satire called " The Deformed Maiden " in which he chided women for these man-made deformities, but in a book entitled *The*

Clever Women of Today, which had come out only two years before, it had been argued that while it was all right to be modern and enlightened, women should not go so far as to discard the traditional methods of enhancing their charm. The maintainers of tradition, however, eventually had to bow before the policies of the Restoration. On March 3, 1873, the empress herself appeared in public with white teeth and real eyebrows, and the general public soon began to follow suit. In Tokyo tooth black was before long a thing of the past, but it lingered on for some time in the provinces. A report written in August, 1883, on the manners and customs of Asaake County, Mie Prefecture, stated as follows: "The age for staining the teeth is not fixed, but it usually comes around the time of marriage. In some places there is a tooth-blackening ceremony for young girls when they reach the age of thirteen. On this occasion the staining is secured from seven different places, and a pretense is made of applying it." However a report of 1899 on the customs of the Nishiei district, Kawakita County, Ishikawa Prefecture, said: "Formerly when women married they immediately blackened their teeth, but in recent times this custom has fallen into disuse."

Soap was known in the Tokugawa period under the name of *shabon*, from the French *savon*, and in 1874 manufacture of it was begun in Tokyo. Perfume came out in 1872, when a Tokyo shop named the Arame-ya put on sale a Japanese version under the name "fragrant oil of enlightenment" (*kaika kōyu*). A non-metalic face powder made by Western methods replaced the traditional leadbased product, which came to be regarded as physically harmful. By the end of the Meiji period, Club Face Powder and a variety of other brands were on sale. The first beauty parlor was opened in Tokyo in 1906, and a few years later electro-therapy and plastic surgery, as well as manicuring and the other more common Western beauty treatments, were being administered.

In the early years of Meiji, women's coiffures remained more

or less in the old tradition. Eventually, however, Western styles
of hairdress came into fashion, at least with Occidental clothing.
In July, 1871, a ladies' hairdressing society was organized, and
it published a pamphlet called " An Illustrated Explanation of
Japanese Coiffure " which stated firmly that since numbers of
heavy or cumbersome ornaments were placed in traditional
Japanese coiffures, they were bad for the health. On the other
hand, the Western bun was desirable since it was at once
thrifty, healthy, and convenient. In the following months the
society published another pamphlet entitled " Foreign Styles in
Ladies' Hairdressing," in which it again propagandized in favor
of Occidental modes. The little book contained a statement
of the purposes of the society together with patterns for four
types of Western hairdress. The rule of the organization stated
in particular : " The ladies of the society must abandon heavy
hair oil along with ornamental combs and bodkins. They may,
however, use a light oil, and when they are not wearing hats,
they may at their own discretion decorate their hair with flowers
or simple flowered hairpins." The four types of hairdo were
called the " up-swept roll," the " down-swept roll," the " English
tie," and the " Margaret." All of them immediately became
fashionable in Tokyo, especially among the ladies who frequented
the Rokumei-kan. By 1898 it was estimated that one fifth of the
women in Osaka were using Western hairdos. We should add,
however, that during the late 1880's when a general trend toward
conservatism had appeared, the traditional Japanese coiffures
had for a time eclipsed the Western styles. Still it was not
long before the latter again became fashionable, this time in the
form of a loose pompadour popular among girl students around
1902 and 1903. During the Russo-Japanese War there appeared
a coiffure which was aptly called Hill 203 after the name of a
famous battleground in Port Arthur. It enjoyed a great vogue
for a time, but after 1907 was replaced by a number of new
styles. When Western coiffures first became popular, it was
fashionable to substitute a rose for the large elaborate hairpins

of the past. Later the various hair clips and ribbons used by Western women were put on sale. The new styles fashionable in Tokyo gradually spread to the provincial cities and towns, but women in the farming villages remained entirely free from their influence. In such rural areas it had long been the custom to distinguish between the hairdos of married women and single women, and it was therefore difficult to accept coiffures from the cities, where no such distinction was made. The most common hairdo among country women was very simple. The hair, which was allowed to grow long, was wound into a ball and held up with small hairpins or tied with a cloth or headband. In some areas women attending funerals wore a special hairdress called a "mourning" or "abstinence" hairdress.

The wide sash, or obi, worn by Japanese women has been classed with the Western corset and Chinese foot-binding as one of the three great wonders of the world. People are prone to believe that the obi has always been much as it is today, but in fact the modern obi first appeared in cities in the Tokugawa period and is therefore relatively new. Obviously unsuitable for work, it was from the first used with festive clothing. In the beginning it was tied in the front, and this is true today on the islands of the Izu area and in Okinawa, but in general it is now tied in the back. In the Meiji period the obi was the main ornament in the typical Japanese attire for women, and after 1900 it became particularly important. It was about that time that the Mitsukoshi Clothing Store first sold material with the so-called "*genroku*" designs, and as the decorative patterns on kimonos grew more brilliant, the obi did so too. Large designs in blazing colors came into fashion, and what with the prosperity that followed the Russo-Japanese War, luxurious gold and silver brocades and other expensive materials were often used.

The obi fashionable in the cities exerted some influence on rural women's fancy dress, but as one would suppose, it had no effect on working apparel. Farm women tied their work garments with the cords of their aprons or narrow sashes.

The most notable innovation among men was cropped hair, which was first seen on the heads of soldiers by the Tokugawa shogunate during its last days. As we shall see, not all Japanese men were quick to part with their topknots and sidelocks, but eventually the Western style prevailed. A magazine of 1871 carried a song to the following effect : " If you tap a shaven and topknotted head you will hear the sound of retrogression ; if you tap an unshaven head you will hear the sound of the Restoration ; but if you tap a closecropped head of hair you will hear the sound of culture and enlightenment." While the translation can only roughly approximate the meaning, it will perhaps convey the idea that by this time the traditional hair styles were considered passé. In the same year the trend was spurred on by a now famous proclamation concerning hairdress and the carrying of swords by samurai. In 1869 only 13% of the men in Tokyo had short haircuts, but by 1876 the proportion had increased to 60%, and by 1890 a man with a traditional hairdo was hardly to be found in the cities. The new style spread to rural districts, and it is said that in some cases local officials went to the extent of placing a fine on men who did not cut their hair short. Some village mayors appear to have been given certificates of merit by the government for having successfully promoted the haircut in their jurisdictions. Regardless of official efforts, however, it took a great deal of resolution for a man to cut off his gallant topknot, and in some areas the traditional styles lingered on for quite a long time. In Okinawa they were forbidden by law in 1895, but when a teacher in a local primary school on Ishigaki Island took his pupils off on an overnight picnic and gave them all haircuts, the male relatives of the boys were so incensed that they forced the school to shut down for a time and prevented the local administration from working for three days. The new haircut was not universal in Okinawa, in fact, until after 1903.

In the cities, the old-style hairdressers gave way to the

Occidental barber shop. Clippers were first imported in 1885 or 1886, and by 1891 they were in wide use.

For a time in Tokyo it was stylish for women to cut their hair short like men. In the March, 1872, edition of a magazine called *Shimbun Zasshi* (*Newspaper Journal*), there appeared the following comment : "Recently in the city we have seen women with close-cropped hair. Such is not the Japanese custom and furthermore nothing of the sort is seen among the women of the West. The sight of this ugly fashion is unbearable." In April of the same year a proclamation banning short haircuts for women was issued by the Tokyo government, and the practice ceased.

Overcoats were considered ornamental as well as useful. A cloak resembling the Inverness cape was popular in the early Meiji period and continued to be so in slightly altered form until the early 1890's. During the third decade of the era the overcoat as such appeared, and in the following decade the Inverness itself was popular. A woman's overcoat for use with kimono, developed from the ample flannel cloak of earlier times and called the Azuma coat, became stylish around 1892, and in a magazine for November, 1897, there appeared the following remark : "The Azuma coat has been popular for five years and nowadays old and young women alike feel they must wear it just as men wear the Inverness. The shawl has been discarded, its only present-day use being to cover the legs when riding in a carriage."

Watches, rings, handkerchiefs, and other accessories were widely used after the beginning of Meiji. Pocket watches quickly became the pride and joy of the gentlemen of fashion, but were too highly priced for most men. It was reported in December, 1871, that in Nara Prefecture the only persons carrying watches were public officials. The wrist watch began to gain in popularity around 1902. Rings were fairly common, though most of the earlier ones were cheap imitations of Occidental models with false sets. After about 1897 gold rings were stylish among those who were considered real ladies and gentlemen.

2. FOOD

a. Food for Festive Occasions

The ancient distinction between routine and festive days was particularly pronounced in matters concerning food, and the special dishes served on festival days had an even greater significance than the fancy clothing worn. Not only the ingredients, but the methods of heating and cooking were different, and for that reason holiday food went under such dialectical names as "something different" (*kawarimono, shinagawari*) and, literally, "sometimes" (*tokidoki*).

One cardinal distinction was that grains, ordinarily eaten whole, were ground into flour for special occasions. This involved more work, but it permitted molding the food into various attractive shapes, and the very labor involved made the result seem more important. The most typical dish was a type of cake called *shitogi*, made from rice flour and molded into various forms. Originally it was considered proper to eat this uncooked, but later it became the practice to boil, steam, or fry it before serving it to people, although it was still left raw when offered to the gods. Modern forms include the cake made of steamed glutinous rice and called *mochi*, which is served on great occasions, and a variety of rice dumplings many of which are connected with religious services.

While many people today assume that the Japanese people as a whole have always eaten rice as their principal food, it was formerly reserved for special days. On such occasions, however, it was essential. Macaroni, buckwheat noodles, and other foods made from flour of various sorts were also considered unusual fare in the past. This testifies to the tremendous changes in eating habits in modern time, since dishes of this sort are now regarded as mere substitutes for rice.

Curiously, an opposite change also took place, namely that grain prepared whole came in some cases to be regarded as special food. Actually, this is not difficult to explain. Until the Meiji period, rice, when cooked whole, was ordinarily steamed, but afterwards people began to use the simple method of boiling. Consequently, steamed rice tended to become a luxury. Nowadays a dish called "red rice" (*sekihan*), which is made by adding red beans to the rice, is served on congratulatory occasions, although in general rice containing other vegetables is considered rather inferior.

Fish was originally an invariable part of the festive food, but was not considered proper for routine days. Before the Meiji era, it would have been unavailable for ordinary fare anyway, since transportation facilities were so poor that fish dealers rarely appeared in country villages.

On some festival days the members of each family gathered together to eat before, or rather with, their gods and the spirits of their ancestors, but more often the feasts were cooperative affairs in which all the families in the community participated. Our forefathers saw a great significance in eating and drinking together, and occasional cooperative feasts were considered necessary to the unity of the group. In festivals dedicated to tutelary deities there were ceremonies in which the celebrants received portions of the food presented to the god. This signified a belief that by sharing the god's food man established an invisible bond with him. Persons who were particularly intimate were described as "friends who ate rice from the same pot," and there was a strong feeling that two persons could not converse pleasantly together unless they had first dined together. An interesting result of these ideas concerning the sharing of food was the practice, still rather common today, of preparing at each meal a token portion for members of the family who were absent on long journeys.

Rice wine, or sake, was an indispensable item in festive dinners, and the latter component of the modern word for drinking party, *sakamori* originally signified specifically the cooperative feast. In modern towns it is possible for individuals to drink together whenever they want to, but in the old life of rural villages sake was thought of only in connection with celebrations, and people had few chances to drink at all. On the other hand when the time came they seem to have done a thorough job. The beverage was brewed at home for each occasion, and if any was left over after the festival, it was passed around again the next day and the next until not a drop was left.

Mochi, fish, wine, and most other festive foods or drinks are intrinsically pleasant, and there was a natural desire to have them even on non-festive occasions. In the towns, therefore, there appeared shops where one might purchase such delicacies at any time and in any quantity, provided of course one had the money. The resulting confusion of routine and festive foods gradually spread, as in the case of clothing, to rural areas.

b. Everyday Food

In general the main dish in an everyday meal was whole grain prepared in a variety of ways. As we have remarked, rice, though cultivated and loved since early times, was too luxurious even for those who produced it to eat often, certainly not in pure form. It was the chief item in the land tax, and the amount remaining after the annual tribute had been taken would never have sufficed for the regular diet. In 1873 the tax was reformed and thereafter was paid in money, but to the farmer this merely meant selling the rice to obtain the money instead of paying in kind. There was in effect little change in the burden borne by the agricultural population, and no change at all in the case of tenant farmers, who continued to pay rent in kind. Until recently even in places where management was technically advanced, farmers were almost never able to eat rice three times a day.

The chief item in the diet of farmers, who made up the majority of the nation's population in the Meiji era, was in some cases rice mixed with other cereals or even merely the other grains minus the rice. *Keshine*, which literally means "ordinary rice," was the word for routine food in many areas, but its meaning varied according to the location. In Iwate Prefecture it signified a cheap type of millet, while in certain central regions as well as in northern Kyūshū it referred to mixed grains exclusive of rice.

In a report written in 1901 on the eating habits in Biwakubi-mura of Aizu, it was stated that the main dish consisted of one part millet and rice mixed and two parts finely grated radish (*daikon*). In more remote villages of the same area the main food was nothing more than leafy vegetables with a small quantity of rice added. Ordinarily rice was eaten only on the first three days of the year, during the New Year celebration. In Himagashima, Aichi Prefecture, the usual everyday dish contained ten parts barley and three parts rice, and millet was often eaten even in the best houses. Around 1874 only four or five bushels of rice were needed to last an entire family a year. In Nibukawa-mura, Ono-gun, Gifu Prefecture, the more fortunate people ate a mixture of one part fodder-like grain and two parts rice, while some poor people had to reduce the proportion of rice to one fifth of the total. Until about 1877 in Gogō-mura, Kagawa Prefecture, it was said that seven parts of barley were used to three parts of rice, but in fact the mixture was almost entirely barley. Often people ate a plain rice or millet gruel to which vegetables were added. In spring the latter were usually dried *daikon*, sweet potatoes, and dried rape, while in the summer eggplants were common, and from fall through winter *daikon* or sweet potatoes. Gruel was valuable since it did not take much rice and since vegetables were not really necessary. It is still used as an everyday food in a large area around Kyoto.

Sweet potatoes became popular about two hundred years

ago. They are particularly common on islands where there are few wet paddy fields, and they constitute the main food in Aogashima, off the shore of Izu, the Gotō Archipelago in Nagasaki Prefecture, and various islands off the shore of southern Kyushu.

The rice diet, which had been fairly common in cities since somewhat earlier times, spread far and wide during Meiji. Several reasons might be given, all of which add up to the basic fact that the country developed an economy that made this possible. It should not be overlooked, of course, that military conscripts and other persons who were exposed to city life played a large part in carrying urban habits to the country-side. In the army it was the practice at the outset to mix a quantity of ground barley with rice as a protective against beriberi, but the proportion of barley gradually decreased, and the rice grew gradually whiter. Young men who learned the flavor of rice during their military service took a yearning for it back home with them, and the grain came to be transported even to remote parts of interior. People who had attached almost religious importance to white rice were now able to buy it on a large scale and to eat it regularly. Unfortunately, the number of those who did increased so greatly as to create a serious problem in national food supply.

Nowadays people use an expression which means " to like something even better than three square meals of rice a day," and in general it is thought that three is the proper number of daily meals. As can be seen from Heian and Tokugawa period writings, however, it appears to have been the custom until comparatively recent times to eat only twice daily. Actually, the sources count only the meals for which the family gathered together around the caldron. There were also in-between meals eaten out of doors. That women performing the difficult work of pounding rice were given a midday lunch is recorded in the most ancient texts. The word used for this meal, incidentally, is employed today for between-meal eating.

One may assume that the term, which originated in the Kyoto region and spread to other areas, took on its present meaning when the midday lunch became a regular meal, a phenomenon that occurred during the Tokugawa period in the cities and the Meiji period in the country. Later, farmers began to eat at various other intervals during the busy seasons, sometimes when they arose in the morning and often at the mid-morning rest periods. Today, work-time refreshments are called "small lunch" in eastern Japan, while in the west they are spoken of as "tea," and in areas along the Japan Sea as "in-betweens" or "between-chopsticks." Farmers who work into the night stripping rice ears or hulling the grain, usually have a late supper in addition to the regular night meal. Foods appropriate for between-meal snacks are sweet potatoes, coarse rice cakes, and leftovers. The gradual increase in numbers of meals probably reflects an increase in work per person.

Rice being the principal dish in an ordinary Japanese meal, meat, fish, and vegetables are considered auxiliary foods. They are usually called by the names *okazu* or *osai*. The former seems to derive from the word *kate*, which implies mixing with the principal food, while the latter is probably a variant of *soe*, which means "following."

Secondary foods have changed over Japanese history, but never so rapidly as in the Meiji period. Let us first consider the case of fish. In modern times, Japan has become famous for her marine industries, but she has not always been a great fishing nation. Of course, in the areas along the seacoast and the rivers, fish and shellfish were important foods even in early times, and with the development of transportation facilities they became so in towns, but, as we have stated before, in inland farming villages they were reserved for special occasions, amounting to only a few days out of the year. Even in the early part of the Meiji era it was almost impossible to obtain anything better than salted fish in the rural areas. Canned seafoods were put on sale around 1874, but years were required before they reached the ordinary farm household, and refrigerated foods did not become available until the 1920's. In most farming districts vegetables were the ordinary accompaniment to the principal food, and before the Meiji period, when numerous foreign plants were imported, the principal varieties were those growing wild in the fields or forests, together with a few garden products such as beans, melons, and eggplants. No doubt the scarceness of cultivated legumes was due to the fact that Japan is blessed with many edible wild plants, among them rhubarb, bamboo shoots, starwort, spikenard, and mushrooms. These vegetables were usually pickled, boiled with soy sauce, or used as ingredients for soup.

One of the most important secondary foods was *miso*, a paste made of partially fermented soybeans. This was sometimes eaten plain, but usually put in soup with vegetables and seasoning. *Miso* has been an ordinary item in the Japanese diet since early times, and even today there are few households in which *miso* soup is not served at least once a day. In the northeast and several other districts it is said that even in the leanest years, one can live on the wild plants, provided there is *miso* to go with them. In farming villages the paste was invariably prepared in the home, and it was commonly referred to by a term that meant literally " our own *miso*." It was a matter of pride not to eat it until the third year after the beans had been put up, and if they had spoiled or become distasteful during that time the housewife was considered incompetent. Spoiled *miso* was also considered a portent of misfortune, while the day for cooking the beans was considered an appropriate time for divination. People were extremely finicky about the flavor and color. In the Meiji period large-scale manufacture of *miso* was commenced in various locales, and gradually it came to be sold in shops rather than produced at home. Until quite recently, however, the farm house that was forced to use " store-bought " *miso* was held somewhat in disregard.

Japan consumes more salt pickles than any other country

36

in the world. They are known as "fragrant things" (*kōnomono*), and, indeed, together with bean paste they contribute much to the distinctive odor of Japanese villages. The original method of preserving vegetables appears to have been simply to dry them and bury them in the ground, but working on the analogy of salted fish, people soon began to add salt. In the winter when there were no fresh vegetables, the preserves were taken out of the ground and boiled to remove the salt. Eventually, however, someone stumbled across the fact that they were good uncooked and since then salt pickles have occupied a very important place in the rural diet, constituting in many areas the principal secondary food. Women worked hard at their pickling and considered it a test of their merit. To say that the pickling in a certain house tasted good was to praise the virtues of the housewife who had made them. In addition to pickles preserved for long period of time, there are others which can be prepared in a day or two, but these are a later development. The basic process of pickling was discovered in colder areas, where winter vegetables are rare.

Since early times a great deal of effort has been expended on assuring a plentiful supply of salt for pickling. It is probably not too much to say that the appearance of wholesale houses in the cities and commercial warehouses in the villages resulted from the need for salt, and the principal roads linking the coast with the interior were the salt trade routes. Toward the middle of the Meiji period, the government monopolized the sale of salt at considerable profit to itself, but there were few complaints, since people were happy to have a dependable supply.

Nishime, a boiled mixture of vegetables flavored with various seasonings was especially common as an everyday dish in the towns, but in the villages it was usually served only during festivals or when guests were present. One of the main ingredients today is soy sauce, which itself was imitated from a foreign product only shortly before Meiji and used at the time primarily by priests in Buddhist monasteries. Before its introduction, there were somewhat similar liquids known as *tamari*, which was produced by clarifying the residue from *miso*, and *sumashi*, which was made by wrapping *miso* in a rag and squeezing out the juice. The latter had existed since ancient times. Both *tamari* and *sumashi* were primitive forms of soy sauce, and when it became available they virtually disappeared. At first the sauce was made in the home, but large-scale manufacure was soon begun, and thereafter even country people switched to the commercial product. The Meiji period was one of rapid developments in the production of this form of seasoning, and its availability probably contributed to the growth in popularity of sliced raw fish, which is seasoned with it, and which is now a favorite delicacy.

Aside from the traditional secondary foods mentioned above, the period of enlightenment witnessed the adoption of meat into the normal diet, but we should observe in this connection that meat dishes were not entirely new. In the age when wild birds and beasts were abundant, they were frequently caught and eaten. Diaries of the Ashikaga period, for instance, make it quite clear that some people ate fowl, deer, rabbits, and perhaps other meats. Nevertheless, from ancient times animal husbandry was thought of as existing primarily for the purpose of raising beasts of burden, and people preferred not to eat these. Furthermore, there were Buddhist prohibitions against eating the meat of quadrupeds. During the Tokugawa period of isolation, in Nagasaki, where all trade with foreign countries was carried on, Japanese ate beef, pork, and chicken in imitation of the foreigners, and with the importation of Dutch medical knowledge, the nutritional value of meat was recognized to the extent that some people in other parts of the country took it up for medicinal purposes. Toward the end of the Tokugawa period the ancient taboos against eating animals became lax in the cities, and beef became somewhat popular. Fukuzawa Yukichi wrote the following of his student days in the Ogata School in Osaka (1854–6): "In those days there were only two houses that served beef. One was in Minamizume, near Namba-bashi, and the other was near the wall at Shimmachi. They were of the lowest class, and ordinary people would not be seen in them. The clientele consisted of liberally tattooed ruffians and students from Ogata. No one cared where the meat came from, or for that matter whether the cow had been slaughtered or had died of an illness. For fifteen cash one was served a plentiful quantity of beef, sake, and rice, but the meat certainly was tough and smelly."

Though there were a few daring souls like Fukuzawa, there remained a strong tendency to shun the flesh of animals. The early visitors from foreign countries found that one of the greatest inconveniences of living in Yokohama was the difficulty of locating beef. In 1865, however, a slaughterhouse was set up near Yokohama, and cows imported from America and China. A year or so later cows began to be sent from Kōbe to meet the need. In the last years of the Tokugawa period an enterprise called the Nakagawa-ya attempted, on the recommendation of Fukuzawa, to set up a slaughterhouse in Edo, but no one would rent land for it. Eventually the interested merchants secured a plot of land in the village of Shirogane (now Shiba Shirogane in Tokyo), which belonged to the shogunate, but to guard against religious defilement, a rope from which white strips of paper were suspended was hung across the entrance in the same manner as at Shinto shrines. It is said that one person received permission from his landlord to open a restaurant and serve meat dishes, but was hindered by the objections of his neighborhood association.

There was nevertheless evidence not merely of a desire to find some way around the traditional injunctions against eating meat, but also of a strong urge to do everything that was being done in more advanced countries. After the Meiji Restoration, therefore, meat became very fashionable, more or less as a step toward cultural enlightenment. In about 1870

39

or 1871 butcher shops carrying banners or signs which read "meat for your health", or "government-approved meat," began to spring up all over Tokyo. In 1871 Kanagaki Robun published a book called *Aguranabe* in which he gibed at those who promoted meat eating as a sign of culture. In the preface he said sarcastically, "Anyone—warrior, farmer, craftsman, or merchant, young or old, male or famale, clever or stupid, rich or poor—I repeat, anyone who does not eat beef is an unmitigated boor." It is interesting to note that beef was served at first in the form of *gyūnabe* or, as it is better known, *sukiyaki*. This was prepared just as today by either frying or pre-boiling the meat and adding scallions, bean curd, and *shirataki* (a noodle-like food made from the paste of the devil's tongue root). The dish was prepared at the dinner table and eaten as it cooked.

In the first month of 1872, the emperor first partook of beef, and the custom thereafter spread rapidly. In the fourth month of same year even Buddhist priests were permitted to eat it (and, incidentally, to marry). Around the same time, pork and chicken were added to the diet, and in the late 1880's horse meat was put on sale. In a book called *Tōkyō Shin-hanjō-ki* (*Record of Tokyo's New Prosperity*) the following passage appeared: "At present the eating of beef is very fashionable, and butcher shops all over the city are prospering. We are happy that the consumption of beef has increased and that more and more households are paying attention to its nutritional value. However, since the supply is limited and the price high, some shops mix horse meat and pork with their beef or even substitute the meat of unclean animals. Everyone must be careful to eat only at reliable restaurants." This was written shortly after the middle of the Meiji period. Afterwards meat continued steadily to become more and more popular in Tokyo and other cities and towns, but remained uncommon in farming villages.

c. Luxury Items

The custom of drinking sake has existed in Japan since ancient times. In the Meiji period consumption of it rose tremendously, the principal reasons being that the occasions for drinking became more frequent, and that the beverage itself was improved. It was originally drunk only on festive days, when everyone drank together from the same jug, more or less to fire the general spirit. Some, however, apparently liked to carry the spirit, or spirits, of the festival over into ordinary life, and this gradually led to the fashion of drinking apart from the group, which became widespread during the Meiji era. In various regions breweries were established by large capitalists, and aside from meeting the growing needs of the cities, these led to the appearance of the village tavern and to the practice of buying sake by the bottle instead of making it at home, as the farmers formerly had done. In effect sake became one of the delights available to anyone who could pay for it.

The first solitary drinkers were probably servants who were rarely able to join in group celebrations. Later ordinary people in the towns began to peer through the curtains of street stands and ask for a nip, and many took up the habit of drinking at home in the evening, no doubt due partially to nostalgia for the holiday drinking parties, but primarily to the simple fact that in the convenient new world sake was always to be had. Another Meiji phenomenon was the practice of drinking just to be sociable. In the Meiji cities a man often had to work among total strangers, and drinking together was a tried and true method for strangers to break the ice. Even today there remains a feeling that two people cannot talk freely to each other unless they have once got drunk together. This is an unconscious projection of the old idea that feasting together improved spiritual contact. In the Meiji period more and more people would " have one if you will," and one began to hear that such-and-such a person had shortened his life by drinking.

Intellectuals objected that people had become indiscriminate drinkers, and there arose a movement in favor of restricting or prohibiting sake. In 1884 the Japan Temperance Society was organized, with the approval and support of such famous men as Nishi Amane, Katō Hiroyuki, and Mishima Tsuyoshi. Then, in 1890 the Japan Prohibition League was created, and this was followed by the appearance of many similar organizations, whose membership gradually increased. A bill to prohibit drinking by minors was introduced into the Diet in 1900, but it was opposed in various quarters and did not become law until 1922.

Tobacco, another favorite luxury, is said to have been introduced into Japan at the end of the middle ages, since when it has been in common use by women as well as men. The usual practice in the past was to smoke cut tobacco in pipes, but in some areas the tobacco leaves were simply rolled. Farmers habitually grew the plant in their front gardens and often kept instruments for cutting it, although there were professionals who traveled about with cutting equipment. If one carried one's pipe with him, one was sure of being furnished tobacco in any house on which one happened to call. The fact that the rest period in many areas was called " tobacco " testifies to the importance of smoking to farm workers of the past. Cigarettes were first manufactured in about 1877 and toward the middle of the 1890's there was a notable increase in the number of cigarette smokers and manufacturers. The first tax on tobacco was enacted in 1876, and in 1897 its sale was monopolized by the government. The government tobacco factories produced three untipped brands of cigarettes, Lily, Cherry, and Star, along with four paper-tipped brands, Shikishima, Yamato, Asahi, and Yamazakura. In Western countries most smokers do not seem to inhale deeply, but many Japanese take long deep drafts, and the effect to tobacco on Japanese nerves is probably greater. The damage done by nicotine was recognized at an early stage, but many failed to notice that smoking also caused a decline in nasal sensitivity. At first, to be sure, the strong smell of tobacco produced such a close atmosphere that people often sought to avoid it, but eventually they ceased to be aware of it or of the fact that it blocked out other odors, just as a number of spices block out other flavors.

Today tea has become so much a part of Japanese life that the ordinary diet is sometimes referred to as " daily tea and rice." The tea-drinking habit seems to have spread among the common people as a result of the influence of the tea ceremony, which developed in the middle ages. For a long time, the beverage was one of those treasured items reserved for festival days, and Meiji customs testify to its former scarcity. There were for instance localities in which tea was one of the important betrothal presents, and in a few areas the betrothal itself was called " the exchange of tea." Also popular beliefs, such as that drinking tea will give children a cold or that drinking it out of a bowl in which yam soup has been served without first washing the bowl will poison the system, arise out of the fact that tea was formerly not drunk every day. *Chazuke*, or " tea and pickles," in modern times is virtually a pronoun for a simple meal, but the dish referred to is something that farmers of old rarely got to taste. They usually drank only hot or cold water.

Farming families usually supplied their own needs for tea by planting a few tea bushes in their gardens or around their houses. The gathering and processing of the leaves were the work of women. Since the housewife in a farming family performed the function of serving tea, there were many areas in which her seat at the hearth was referred to as the " tea-steeping " or the " tea-boiling " seat (*chasen-za, chani-za*). When women nowadays have a favor to ask of the gods or the Buddhas, they " give up tea " (*chadachi*) for a number of days as their husbands on similar occasions give up sake, and it is probable that tea is even more important to women than sake to men. When drinking Japanese tea, it is customary to eat something salty, such as pickled green plums or vegetables, or even a little spoonful of salt.

The food served with tea has gone under a number of different names, such as *chanoko* (literally, "the child of tea"), and *oke-cha*, or *uke-cha*, both of which terms are compounded from the words for "receive" and "tea." After sugar came into wide use, it frequently took the place of salt, either in its usual form or in cakes, dried sugared persimmons, sugar dumplings, or the like. The main reason for drinking tea in agricultural villages seems to have been simply a desire for something to please the tongue between meals. There are many places in which the mid-morning or mid-afternoon snacks are referred to as "tea," "little tea," or something on that order, and even in Tokyo, in-between meals given to workmen are called "tea." In the villages around Kyoto and Osaka the pre-noon tea was called "early tea" (*zencha*), "morning tea" (*asacha*), or "fourth-hour tea" (*yotsucha*), while the afternoon tea was called "eighth-hour tea" (*yatsucha*), "seventh-hour tea" (*nanatsucha*), or "second tea" (*nibancha*)." The spread of tea in the Meiji period led to an increased number of short rest periods in farming villages, and at times even people who were not working at all began to drink cup after cup out of boredom. So again, as in the case of sake, an item that had been reserved for special occasions came to be used indiscriminately.

As is suggested by the common term "tea cakes," (*cha-gashi*) the consumption of cookies or cakes arose in response to the growing love for tea. The word for cookies and similar confections (*kashi*) originally referred to nuts, and in olden times chestnuts, papania acorns, torreya nuts, and beans were the principal "confections." In ancient Kyoto there were "cake shops," which sold fruits, nuts, beans, tangles, or potatoes prepared in some delicious fashion. After the appearance of sugar in the Tokugawa period confections took on new forms, but sugar was for a long time sold only at medicine shops, and the price was so high that even in the cities only houses that were well off could afford it. For ordinary people it was a rare and marvelous elixir. In the Meiji period, when it became available on a large scale, consumption reached prodigal proportions. Merchants helped this tendency along by advertising that individual consumption of sugar was an index to a country's cultural development. The confections of the Meiji period were virtually all made with sugar, and there were many varieties. Children were fond of a hard candy made from brown sugar and later of caramels, but the latter did not appear until 1914. Western pastries were sold in Tokyo at the beginning of the Meiji period, and there were several new inventions, such as a type of bun filled with bean jam, that had both Western and Eastern features. English biscuits were issued to soldiers at the end of the Meiji period and gradually became popular among civilians. Cheap brands were manufactured in large quantities for sale in the rural areas, where consumption of sugar had also increased, though not so rapidly as cities. Farming families did not really obtain a fair supply of sugar until a system of rationing was introduced. Differences in taste between city and country people led to some variations in the degree to which they took to sugar, but it is undeniable that during the Meiji period all food and drink consumed by the Japanese tended to become sweeter.

In the Tokugawa period the various indigenous fruits were improved, and after the beginning of Meiji a number of new ones, such as the peach, the pear, the apple, and the navel-orange, were brought from foreign countries. Even considering government encouragement, the improvement in fruits and the increased production thereof are astonishing. They became sweeter as consumption increased, but this development apparently did not hurt the sugar market. On the contrary, the consumption of sugar and that of fruits seem to have stimulated each other. People simply demanded more and more sweet food of all kinds. As trade increased, foreign fruits, such as bananas and pineapples, were imported, and they contributed to the general interest in foreign countries. The practice of canning fruit gradually spread.

Aside from luxury items already mentioned, milk, coffee, black tea, beer, soft drinks, and the like also attained a degree of popularity during the Meiji era. People remained relatively ignorant of milk for a time after the Restoration but what with government promotion of milk-drinking after 1872, the demand for it gradually increased. In October, 1873, something called "Rules for the Information of Cow-milkers" was published, and one gathers from this that there were a fair number of milk-drinkers around and about.

A statement by the Tokugawa period writer Ōta Shokuzan to the effect that he had drunk coffee on a Dutch ship and had found it unpleasant is often quoted as an indication that the Japanese did not care for the beverage, but by around 1887 the Western-style restaurants were offering after-dinner coffee, and a few families were drinking it at home. In an astonishingly short time, the stimulating drink became an indispensable item for city people.

Black tea is very different in flavor from Japanese tea, and it is produced and drunk differently. When it was adopted, complications were introduced into Japanese etiquette for receiving guests. Hitherto Japanese tea had been served to callers as well as to the family, but since the new tea was exotic, it came to be regarded as a more polite refreshment for the honored visitor. Curiously, some people served green tea alongside it.

The consumption of beer and other Occidental spirits was spurred on by increasing familiarity with Western cooking. The first newspaper advertisements for beer appeared in the summer of 1872. In 1877 breweries were established, and subsequently the demands of beer drinkers became louder and louder. The Ebisu Beer Hall, which was opened in Kyōbashi in 1899, is thought to have been the first Japanese beer parlor. Bottled lemonade and a similar Japanese imitation called *ramune* appeared on the market in the early Meiji years along with other soft drinks. They furnished some competition to bottled spirits, but it was not until the First World War that there appeared a large variety of them or, for that matter, a special fondness for them.

d. Dining Out

In former times the rule was for members of the family to gather together at meal times to eat food that had been pre- pared over the hearth fire, but during the Tokugawa period people began to eat out occasionally, and after the onset of the Meiji era this practice became common. It had always been the custom for people to carry a packaged lunch for the noon meal and on trips, but the appearance of tea-houses in the Meiji period led to many changes. People began eating their boxed lunches in such places, and gradually many of the shops started to sell various cooked foods on order.

Some even added full meals, that is to say rice, to their menus, and the practice of eating alone became more usual. Differences in individual food preferences became more numerous, and conversely the element of family coherence that had resulted from eating as a group grew thinner. Eating a meal alone on a separate tray had been a practice connected with funerals, and had consequently had connotations that rendered it distaste- ful to the superstitious. In the Meiji era, however, few people could be found who paid much attention to such superstitions.

The lunch shops served meals at fixed prices, and, of course, could not afford to let the customer eat all the rice he might happen to want. Consequently means were devised for serving him a fixed quantity at once instead of letting him have a new bowl whenever be wished, as was the practice in the home. The ordinary rice bowl, which did not hold enough for a full meal, was replaced by the larger *domburi*, (*don-buri*), and throughout the nation such novel words as *ten-don* (or *ten-pura* on rice served in a *don-buri*), *gyū-don*, and *oyako-don*, came into use. Quick-lunch establishments and cheap dining-halls did not come into fashion until the middle of the Taishō period, but the stage had been set for their appearance. Ironically, the tea-shop, which had been invented only to make up for the failings of the lunch-box, eventually made it obsolete.

Full-fledged restaurants had existed in the towns prior to the Meiji era, but they tended to specialize only in fancy dishes. Even the word for restaurant, originally implied cooking in a very proper style. In the usual restaurant the client was treated as a temporary house-guest to whom a really good meal was to be served. Dining in such places was a special event, and women in full regalia waited on table and drank sake with the customers. More and more people patronized fine restaurants after the beginning of Meiji. For one thing, the limits of social life became broader, and the number of friends one might be expected to invite to a celebration increased. At the same time, tastes became more elegant, and the number of dishes multiplied. Under the circumstances, it became impossible to prepare a banquet at home. Ordinary houses in the cities had small kitchens to begin with, and anyway there were rarely enough hands to prepare the food for a large crowd of people. Consequently, there was no alternative to having one's parties in restaurants. Even people who lived in large country houses ceased to serve the home-cooked feasts required for marriages or other ceremonies and began to rely on the local restauranteur instead.

Some knowledge of Occidental cuisine spread toward the end of the Tokugawa period, and somewhat later professional Western restaurants, catering to foreigners, appeared in Yokohama and Tokyo. In July, 1873, the *Shimbun Zasshi*, No. 156, carried the following statement: " Recently Western restaurants have been flourishing in the area around the capital, and their number is increasing. While we will not argue about the relative qualities of their cooking, we will mention here one or two that deserve special praise." The names of the Seiyō-ken in Unume-chō, the Nisshin-tei in Tsukiji, and the Kaiyō-tei in Kayaba-chō were listed. In 1876 the Seiyō-ken also opened a branch in what is now Ueno Park. The Western eating establishments were patronized at first only by the stylish set or by persons who were curious to see what the strange new food tasted like, but customers became more frequent, and new houses were opened. It was commonly said that Western cooking was simple, and this idea contributed to its spread. In *Tokyo Shin-hanjō-ki*, mentioned above, there appeared the following : " The best thing about dining in Western fashion is that it is simple and easy. At a Japanese dinner, a person who does not drink sake feels at a great loss for something to do with his hands, but such is not the case at a Western meal. Here, if one wishes to drink, there is beer, or wine, or champagne, and if one does not, one is at liberty to begin eating his bread (Translator's note : Japanese do not ordinarily eat rice until after they have stopped drinking, and it is until this good day an almost universal Japanese notion that bread in the Western diet corresponds exactly to rice in the Japanese. Hence this statement.) Also, one may eat every bit of something one likes and refuse anything one does not like. Furthermore, there is none of this troublesome exchanging of wine glasses as in a Japanese dinner, and few waiters or waitresses are needed. Although people who are out to eat and not to be entertained with dancing and singing enjoy Western dinners, the influence of Western eating habits has reached few women or old people. That be as it may, however, Western cuisine is becoming more common in the city."

Chinese food did not spread until much later. The first Chinese restaurant seems to have been the Kairaku-en, which was opened in Kameshima-chō, Nihombashi, Tokyo, in 1883. Only in the middle years of the Taishō era did Chinese restaurants begin to enjoy great popularity. Noodle shops and shops serving a mixture of beans and sugar called *shiruko* were among those best loved by the ordinary people. The former were a hold-over from the Tokugawa period, but as everyone was pleased to find, during Meiji their prices dropped to a very reasonable level. *Shiruko* shops descended from Tokugawa tea houses, and they functioned also as *mochi* and dumpling shops. The merchants who sold *shiruko* frequently switched to cold drinks in the summer. In accounts of student life in the Meiji era it is stated that when students went out to eat they usually ate either *soba* or *shiruko* or hot sweet potatoes, in which last still other shops specialized.

The first modern tea (or coffee) shop is thought to have been the Kahii-kan, which was opened in April, 1888, at Kuromon-chō, Shitaya, and which prided itself on its Western manner. Places like it continually increased in number. According to a survey made at the end of 1897, there were 476 full-fledged restaurants, 4,479 food-and-drink shops, 143 Western-style tea houses, and 476 sake shops in the city of Tokyo at that time. Overwhelmingly in the majority were the miscellaneous food-and-drink shops, which aside from *soba* and *shiruko* shops included houses specializing in *tempura*, clam stew, *sukiyaki*, whalemeat, or some other particular dish. In the late Taishō era, roughly around the time of the great Tokyo earthquake of 1923, the *soba* shops were surpassed in numbers by shops specializing in Western food or in Chinese dishes, while the *shiruko* shops were to a large extent crowded out by tea and coffee houses.

Throughout the Meiji period the growth in number of restaurants and taverns was nothing short of astonishing. Whether it was the result of many new opportunities for people to go out or of the broadening of social life, this phenomenon represents a tendency that cannot be overlooked. It was indeed one of the greatest transitions in the history of Japanese eating.

3. HOUSES

a. Life Around the Hearth

If one decides that one does not like one's clothing or food, they can be changed easily, but it is not so simple to change one's place of residence, and the restraints of tradition were accordingly especially strong in the case of houses. In former times the central feature of life at home was the all-purpose family hearth, and even today this is true in the villages of the northeast and southwest, as well as in remote mountainous areas. Though in the cities the family hearth was discarded comparatively early, the family gathering around the fireplace remained until recent times one of the most prominent features of country life.

The hearth room was next to a dirt-floor section where heavy housework was done. The Chinese characters used to write the word for hearth, *irori*, have obscured its meaning, but we can see from dialectical equivalents, such as *innaka* and *ennaka*, which are compounded from the verb *iru*, "to be in," and *naka*, "enclosure," that the word signified a "central location," that is, the center of life inside the house. Over the hearth a pothook or a metal ring serving the same purpose was suspended. Since the pothook is usually employed in outlying districts, while the ring is found near the central regions, we may suppose that the former is the older. The hook was thought to be the residence of the fire god, whose presence increased the importance of the hearth. There were many religious taboos surrounding it, among them prohibitions against stirring up the ashes or spitting in the fire. Only the fire under the pot hook, purified by the god of fire, was thought good for preparing food, and at meal times the family all gathered together and shared food cooked there. The hearth fire was also important

51

as a protection against cold. On long winter nights, when the fire was left going, people took off their obis, warmed their backs and stomachs thoroughly, and then dived into their straw mats to sleep. In many places it was the custom on very cold nights to bring the sleeping mats to the side of the hearth. Furthermore, in the houses of the past the fire was the principal source of light. One of the important duties of a wife or daughter-in-law was to see to it that burning embers were buried in the fireplace each night so that the fire would not completely go out. It was not until 1882 or '83, after matches had come into common use, that the technique for keeping the fire alive ceased to be important.

Each person had a fixed place at the hearthside. The seat directly facing the dirt-floor section of the house belonged to the head of the family. In houses with the kitchen on the right side (as one faced the front of the house), the position to the master's right was the guest seat, and when there was no guest it was used by the eldest son or son-in-law. Across from the guest seat was the wife's place, called *kakaza* or *koshimoto* (or in various locales *chasenza, chaniza, tanamae,* or *tanamono*), and across from the master, next to the kitchen, was a seat called the *kijiri,* or *shimoza,* from which the fire was tended. This position was customarily left for a servant or underling, and it provided little sitting room. In houses with the kitchen on the left the positions of the guest and the wife were reversed, but the principle behind the seating arrangement was the same. While there were numerous differences in the names for the positions, the entire country was in agreement as to who sat where. The master's seat was sacrosanct. There was a saying that "only a cat or a fool would sit in the master's place," and generally this applied even when the master was absent. A daughter-in-law might well be sent back to her parents if she were careless enough to commit this crime. In a very few areas it was the practice to let an honored guest, a priest, or, on occasion, the eldest son sit in the master's seat, but as a rule the authority it represented was taken too seriously for this to occur. At meal times the master and mistress of the house remained in their positions, and merely turned to face the table, but the other persons moved to new places forming a circle between them.

When the head of the house relinquished his authority to his son, he gave over his place at the hearth as well, and similarly his wife gave her place to her daughter-in-law, along with the spatula for ladling rice, which symbolized the prerogatives for making and serving food. This custom was rigidly observed and was not quick to fall out of use.

The fire in the hearth was not merely the center of daily life but also a spiritual force that unified the family. Gradually, however, it was divided into parts. This phenomenon began with the appearance of small secondary hearths in the other rooms of the house. Since the ceilings there were low, a large fire could not be used, and in the beginning the auxiliary fires were probably no more than embers from the main hearth, but eventually people began to burn charcoal. The adoption of porcelain braziers hurried on the division of the hearth fire.

One reason for the spread of the brazier was progress in the field of ceramics, and another was simply that there was an increasingly abundant supply of charcoal. Charcoal is known to have existed in early times and it was always used to heat water in the tea ceremony, but until comparatively recent times it was not in everyday use, and indeed the techniques for manufacturing it were not widely known. By the middle of Meiji, however, lectures on how to make charcoal were being given all over the country, and these led to a general improvement in charcoal furnaces.

As the secondary fireplace or brazier took over from the hearth fire the function of protecting against cold there developed the fashion of cooking and eating in various different rooms. Also people ceased to invite guests into the hearth room. In town houses, the "long brazier"—a rectangular wooden box

houses, however, continued to be built very much according to old customs, which indeed were preserved without basic alteration through the Taishō and Shōwa eras down to the present time. Unlike most of the other changes that have taken place since the end of the Tokugawa period, the structure of houses has thus failed to reflect the social upheaval of the age.

Various limitations concerning the size and style of houses were imposed on farmers by the Tokugawa government, and these led to standardization. Also, while carpenters were available near towns and traveling carpenters sometimes visited the villages, people usually built their houses by themselves, or with the aid of the community, and as a consequence, the designs were technically limited. Moreover, in the rural districts people held conformity in high esteem, and it took quite a lot of bravery to do anything that other people did not do. This mental state on the part of country people worked as a force against making revisions in the standard plan that had come down from the Tokugawa period.

By the old arrangement, which survived through Meiji era, the interior of the house was usually divided into a dirt-floor area and a wooden-floor area comprising four rooms of equal size arranged in a square, as shown in Diagram 1.

D	B	
C	A	

Diagram 1.

Room A was usually called the *dei*, but in quite a number

This room was called the *dei* in some parts of the country, and there were areas in which the question of whether room A or room C would be used for guests depended on the status of the guest;

Room D was usually called either *nando* (store room) or simply *heya* (room), but as indicated by the fact that in many areas it is spoken of as the *nema* (sleeping room), it frequently served as the bedroom for the head of the family and his wife. The entrance to it was behind the master's place at the hearth, so that when sitting by the fire the husband at the same time was symbolically guarding the sanctity of his couch. In the bedroom rice hulls were piled to a height of two or three feet and well-dried new straw was spread over these to form a pallet. After the Restoration, however, cotton-stuffed quilts soon became common except in very remote villages. The threshold of the bedroom was raised five or six inches, so that one had to step across it to get into the room. This was a means both of hindering people who had no business there from entering and of preventing the hulls and straw from falling out of the room. As a rule this room was quite dark. This was all right as long as the pallet was of straw, but when straw was replaced by cotton bedding, which kept people warmer and absorbed perspiration, and which was usually left as was when not in use, the bedroom became a dark unsanitary place that commanded more attention from village health officials than any other part of the house.

To judge from the word *nando*, the bedroom must originally have been used as a place for storing things as well as for sleeping. It might be added that in many areas the ceding of this room to the eldest son and his wife signified the transfer of the rights of the head of the house and his wife to their heirs.

The least on which a family could make do was a hearth room and a sleeping room. If the family had many members, more sleeping rooms became necessary, and it was always desirable to have one or two rooms for entertaining guests. Furthermore, since there were occasions such as marriages, of places it was called the *omote*, or "front," and in certain areas other terms, such as *nakanoma* (middle room), *agariguchi* (entrance), and *oue* (upper section), were used. *Dei* is written with characters meaning "to come out" and "to be in," the original idea being that this was the room to which one came out to receive a guest and in which one remained to entertain him. It was in early times thought of as a very important place, but since in the usual house it was rarely used, it was eventually selected for activities in which the head of the house did not participate, such as women's sewing or children's reading, and the original use was forgotten. The decline of the *dei* may be considered to have wrought changes in the rural method of entertaining callers. Also in as much as there were many locales in which young ladies of marriageable age slept in the *dei*, the room became connected with questions of marriage and the relations between young men and women.

Room B was the basic living room of the house, to the extent that in some locations it was actually referred to with the ordinary term for house. The hearth was located here, and familiar guests were received beside it. We have already mentioned that the place at the hearth where the wife sat was called the "tea-steeping" or "tea-boiling" seat. This concept was expanded to the extent that this entire room came to be spoken of as the "tearoom." In city houses today the tearoom is the wife's room, and this fact seems to have derived from the significance of the wife's former position by the hearth.

Room C, which was called the *zashiki*, housed the family shrine and Buddhist altar. It was reserved for entertaining important guests, and was usually not in use. It had an alcove (*tokonoma*), often with shelves, and this was decorated with flowers or ornaments. This room was intended specifically for guests, and inside it the guest occupied the main position instead of taking a place subordinate to that of the master of the house. As it happened, the place in front of the alcove was considered the most important, and this remains true in the present day.

funerals, or meetings to which one was host, it was exceedingly convenient to have extra rooms as such times. Such being case, the four-room plan mentioned above frequently was expanded into the form shown in Diagram 2.

F	D	B
E	C	A

Diagram 2.

In the six-room house room E was called the parlor, or *zashiki*, and room F was usually called the inner parlor (*okuzashiki*) or the inner bedroom (*okunando*). When the function of the parlor was transferred to room E, room C came to be called the "middle room" or something on that order. As architectural techniques improved, some people were able to build even larger houses.

Two-story dwellings were forbidden to farmers in the Tokugawa period, but many farmers used the space above the ceiling for raising silkworms or for storing furniture and other things. In the Meiji era, as the restrictions on the construction of houses were abolished, two-story houses appeared here and there in villages.

The word for the parlor or guest room, *zashiki*, meant "cushion-spreading." All the rooms in the house originally had wooden floors, and the members of the family sat directly on these, but some sort of cushion was offered to guests. This was usually a straw mat, which was thin and could be folded up for storing when not in use, and from the word to fold, *tatamu*, the mat came in many places to be called a *tatami*. As time went on, it was reinforced and stiffened with straw padding and gradually converted into the *tatami* now used as flooring in Japanese houses. Around the beginning of the Meiji period, people began to consider such matting necessary for rooms other than the kitchen and hallways, though there remained many houses which stored it away when not in use. It gradually became the general practice for members of the household to sit on *tatami* all the time, and at the same time there arose the fashion of offering quilted cushions to guests. Thus the *tatami* was no longer a cushion, but the floor itself.

The convenience of translucent paper-covered sliding doors, *shōji*, was recognized long ago, but due to the high price of paper, the ordinary agricultural family was unable to use them. As time went on, however, paper was produced on a larger scale, and farmers began to teach their children to paste used paper on frames to produce a crude type of *shōji*. In pictures in children's books of the Tokugawa period one sees sliding doors covered with paper on which the Japanese syllabary is written, and indeed such doors were a usual sight in many villages until the middle of the Meiji era. Eventually, however, white paper made especially for covering doors became available to most people. Needless to say, the translucent door made interiors lighter, and this led to a number of unforeseen changes. In the first place, unpleasant features in the house that had hitherto been concealed became conspicuous. People began to sweep away dust and dirt that had not been noticed before, and to straighten up furnishings that had been scattered about at random. A love of cleanliness is often counted among the virtues of Japanese, but it is doubtful that this characteristic became prominent before the adoption of paper-covered doors. Another result of the increase in interior lighting, was that it became possible to make more partitions in the house and thus to use more of the available space. Even after the beginning of Meiji, sheet glass remained a treasured article that had to be imported, but after about 1903 it was produced in Japan, and there gradually spread the practice of using it in one panel of the sliding door, or even over the entire surface.

In the Meiji era straw, thatch, board, and tile roofs were to be seen side by side everywhere, but the last tended to replace the others. Roofs thatched with miscanthus existed from early times, but as new farming territories were developed, increasing difficulty was encountered in securing a supply of the plant, and local communities devised cooperative methods for maintaining an ample quantity and dividing it fairly. A thick miscanthus roof is good for fourteen or fifteen years, and with about ten acres in miscanthus, a farming community of fifteen houses could insure that everyone always had a satisfactory roof by building in turns. In villages where wet rice cultivation predominated, however, miscanthus was rarely obtainable, and people were forced to use barley, wheat, or rice straw, which rotted after about three years. Roofs therefore required constant replacing, and this naturally came to be an individual enterprise for each house. In order to protect the thatch, it was necessary to see that rain fell from roofs as quickly as possible, and for that reason they tended to be steep. The eaves were low and water splashed against the walls and doors so that rain blinds or auxiliary eaves were necessary. Auxiliary eaves made of wood or cedar bark are not new, but during the Meiji period they became far more common than before, and they were often furnished with bamboo gutters. After the lower part of the roof was projected in this fashion, outside hallways became possible.

Wooden roofs also date back to ancient times. In order to prevent the boards from being blown off, it was common to anchor them with stones. Such roofs were frequently to be seen in mountain or seaside villages. In towns wooden roofs were enforced not with stones but with bamboo pins or nails, and they were consequently called by such names as " hammered roofs " (*tatakiya*) or "pounded roofs (*tonton-buki*). In a book

People were still living in such buildings in certain parts of Tokyo until the end of the Meiji period. Tokyo from the outset had an area small in comparison with its population, and what with the tremendous number of new people coming in to work after the Restoration, tenements divided into nine-by-twelve-foot apartments multiplied. They usually lined side streets or alleys behind the main thoroughfares.

Such dwellings in the city were at first considered temporary lodgings, but gradually many people who lived in them lost all chance of going back whence they had come, and these houses became permanent homes. Of course, the tenants experienced many inconveniences in these cramped gerry-built barracks, but somehow they thought out ways to live together harmoniously. It was felt necessary to have a toilet in each house, but many said that they preferred the public bath to a private one. It was impossible to provide a well for each tenant, and from ten to twenty families often had to share the same one. In such cases they took turns by the month caring for the rope and bucket and cleaning the sink that stood by the well. To keep the order fixed, the names of all users were written down on a piece of wood, and when a person's month was up, he carried the bucket and this list to the next family on the list. When a new bucket was needed, the money was collected from everyone. In some places, however, it was the rule for each family to have its own bucket with its name written on it. The well-side was a community center for the housewives in the tenement, and the well-side conference was one of the sights most closely associated with tenement life.

Though a majority of city people began to think of the tenement as a permanent homestead, they nevertheless moved from one house to another with a lightheartedness hitherto unknown. After all, a tenement flat was a commodity that the tenant did not own and that he could swap for something he liked better if the occasion arose. Contrary to old customs, when there was a fire in the neighborhood, he simply gathered his possessions and his furniture together and made hasty preparations to leave. Clothes wickers, baskets, and trunks were always kept ready, and it is said that a common type of two-wheel wagon was invented expressly for fleeing from fires. When tenements burned, the only thing that bothered tenants was the danger to themselves and their personal property. They were not only virtually free of any inclination to prevent fires, but also apparently convinced that houses were things that one expected to burn from time to time. This was the psychology of the tenement shack. As a result of it, people used fire carelessly, and even considering that these huts were built of paper and wood, there was a disproportionately large number of great fires. During the Meiji period the urban firefighting services became well organized and were provided with improved equipment. The firemen of Tokyo offered a dazzling annual exhibition of their prowess each January—a custom that is still observed—but conflagrations were a specialty of the house in the city and continued to be so in the Taishō period. Appropriately, a system of fire insurance began in the Meiji period. It was strongly recommended in newspapers as early as 1872, and in 1890 the Tokyo Fire Insurance Company, the first company of its kind, was opened with the former head of the Tokyo Fire Department, Orita Shōsuke, as its president. Subsequently many similar companies were formed, but an undesirable result was that the house-owner's regard for his own property became even lighter. Furthermore, since insurance rates were high and after all were a total loss as long as the insured property remained unharmed, some people conceived of burning their own houses down, and a new form of arson came into existence.

Somewhat similar to the tenements were apartment buildings and rooming houses, which were also based on the idea that the lives of several families might be carried on under one and the same roof. Information about American apartment houses appeared in 1873, but the first such building was a five-story frame house erected in 1910 at Ikenohata in the district of Ueno. (Apartment buildings were not constructed of reinforced concrete until after the great earthquake of 1923.) With the development of such housing, we might observe, three-meals-a-day dining halls began to do a good business. Rooming houses were most frequently occupied by young men who had come to the city to study or work. The influx of students to Tokyo was greater by the year, but few schools provided dormitory facilities, and those that did by no means satisfied the demand. Boarding houses grew particularly numerous in Hongō and Kanda, the areas of Tokyo in which most schools were located. Such houses often incurred the reputation of being immoral, and in any case they do not seem to have provided good service for their tenants. Many of the latter soon found that they preferred to rent rooms in private homes, where there was some semblance of home life. Widows with no other means of support, old couples, and sometimes small businessmen invited lodgers with advertisements stressing the family atmosphere of their homes. A common sight during Meiji was that of a student loading his clothes hamper onto a delivery cart, carrying his lamp in his hand, and starting off for new lodgings.

d. Life with a Garden

In rural areas there were two meanings to the common word for garden, *niwa*. It was applied both to the dirt-floor room inside the house and to the open space in front outside. In many places various compound terms, such as " the connected garden " and " the garden with the gate," were used to distinguish the two meanings. The mortar used for pounding rice or other grains was usually kept in the inside " garden," and this was the place for work during bad weather or at night. Also it was frequently the appointed place for keeping footgear. The outside garden was used for drying grain and, on festive occasions, for various group activities. In any case in all farm house the gardens were regarded as very important, and both of them were used for work. One is prone to forget that in rural areas the house was, and is, not only a dwelling but a workshop. In the cities also many houses doubled as shops and residences, but with the general increase in the number of employees, there was a strong tendency to divide the home from the office, and this was accentuated by the erection of schools, factories, and office buildings. In town houses, the unfloored area became unnecessary, and only a small place for removing the shoes at the entrance was retained. In shops, on the other hand, there was something of a revival of the dirt-floor room in the form of a space in front furnished with table and chairs and used as both a reception room and an office. In the cities the word *niwa* ceased to indicate a place for working and came simply to mean a garden in the ordinary sense.

Although people in rural communities performed various tasks in the outer garden, they also decorated it with plants and trees, in particular a pine or an evergreen planted near the gate. This tree was thought to be a proper place for worshiping the gods on the occasions when their spirits descended from heaven, and even after such religious services were forgotten, the tree was considered to be connected with the family fortunes. If it thrived, so should they. Affection for plants is particularly evident in country villages, and it is not confined to the case of the front garden.

Many people planted copses of cedar or fur in their back yards—a relic of the old custom of placing houses with their backs to a wooded mountain, where there was sure to be a convenient supply of water. Even after wells became common the ordinary man still rejoiced at the sight of trees and the sound of water nearby. The old feeling of need unconsciously became a part of his sense of comfort. Even the inhabitants of town dwellings planted trees and dug ponds in the limited land available, though this was often minute. In the Meiji period, the price of land in cities skyrocketed, and many houses were built so close to each other that there was no space that could actually be called a garden. A number of people so detested the cramped life in such places that they developed a strong urge to move to the suburbs. The development of streetcar lines facilitated this, and land in suburban areas also began to rent at increased prices. When it became more profitable to lease the land than to plant on it, landowners in these districts left the ranks of agricultural producers and became landlords. Those who could afford to live in the suburbs were lucky. There were no gardens in tenements, and those forced by economic circumstances to live in them had to content themselves with miniature tray gardens. Still, the desire for plants was irresistible, and the technique of raising potted plants advanced so greatly that it came to be counted among the prides of Japan.

Soon parks were built, and even the unfortunate townpeople came to have public gardens. In Tokyo, Asakusa Park, which was built in 1873, was the first. Others were located in various parts of the city as time went on. The famous Hibiya Park, in the center of Tokyo, was opened in 1903. In the provincial towns the area on which the castle had stood was frequently designated as a park.

Our ideas about comfortable living have a very complicated framework, and they include many elements unconsciously inherited from the past. The desire of the Japanese for a garden is one of these, and it appears to be quite basic.

Chapter Three

TOWNS AND VILLAGES

1. THE NEIGHBORHOOD-GROUP SYSTEM

a. The Five-Man Association

IN speaking of the neighborhood-group system of about a century ago, the first thing that comes to mind is the five-man association. The origin of this group can be said to date back four hundred years to the turbulent feudal times when villages required autonomous defense units. Similar organizations were to be found in cities, which at that time were already showing a remarkable development. It is difficult to say, however, that the system of five-man groups as it existed in the Tokugawa period arose from the needs of the masses.

Though there were several types of cooperative organizations similar to this, they did not necessarily conform with the principles of the five-man association. As it appeared in the Tokugawa period, this unit was one of the means adopted by the government to secure feudalistic control. It was an imitation of the five-man and ten-man groups that Toyotomi Hideyoshi established in 1597, after he had virtually achieved the consolidation of Japan. Hideyoshi's aim was the preservation of public order. That is to say, his system was designed to prevent street murders and burglary. Groups of five, in the case of warriors, and ten, in that of townsmen or farmers, were formed, and the members were required to sign oaths not to commit crimes. Besides that, it was ordered that they accuse offenders within their own company, and, in the event that they informed

influx of outsiders to the rural areas, and a nationwide division of labor combined to destroy the need or the desire for cooperative effort in small communities. The old institutions were sometimes preserved in form, but they rarely survived in spirit. Still there was a certain *esprit de corps* among villagers that often held them together when they met in outside places. It is noteworthy for example that the young men who went to cities to work often sent gifts of sake or money to the youth associations in the villages whence they had come.

2. MOVEMENT OF FARMERS TO CITIES

a. The Smell of the Earth in the Cities

With the exception of Kyoto and Nara, Japan has no planned cities, and even the two ancient capitals refused to grow in the patterns created for them. Many towns are no more than loosely connected agglomerations of farming villages, and the great modern metropolis of Tokyo contained a fair proportion of farms until comparatively recently. One reads much of fires due to the density of the population in old Edo, but that notwithstanding, in parts of the city farmers plowed their fields just as they did in remote rural areas. The provincial castle towns were surrounded and largely supported by farm lands.

At the beginning of Meiji, therefore, much that was bucolic survived even in the most thriving urban centers. The military class had been strictly distinguished from the agricultural populace for three centuries, and in a sense towns had developed because of this fact, but even the warriors had surrounded their town houses with fields and brought underlings from their country estates to farm them. Edo tradesmen, the most citified class of all, had in many cases originally been imported from the provinces to serve the feudal lords, and after they had managed to establish separate businesses, they had

72

in turn imported more country people to work for them.

Today there are few city dwellers who have not simply accepted the role of consumer and ceased to worry about having severed their connection with the production of food. Even so, however, during the war many became enough concerned over their food supply to plant vegetables in their flower gardens, and an old link between rural and urban life was suddenly revived. Persons moving from farms to towns continued to supply their own minimum needs, and even the merchants who set up the first city shops had had a long enough background as traveling peddlers, wandering about the countryside in search of food, to make them hold tenaciously to the gardening plots adjoined to their stores. At the same time, the growth of population in the Edo period disturbed some towns to the extent that they either acted to prevent further immigration or established special areas for farming on their outskirts.

In the Meiji period it became nearly impossible in cities to maintain enough land to insure one's own food supply. At the same time, however, the development of industry and transportation relieved most urban residents of fear on this score, despite the fact that they were no longer engaged in agriculture themselves.

b. From Village to Town

Boys who went from the country to city schools and colleges in the Meiji period often considered that only they, of all their fellow villagers, had joined in the movement of the times, but they were wrong, for while the cities were shaking off their rural aspects, life in farming communities was changing at a lively pace.

For one thing, new people were constantly arriving. There had been a time when the village priest was the only outsider in most villages who could properly be called a resident. He had, of course, provided a link with the outside world, but, after all, his purpose in having left his original home and come to a new location was to avoid excessive intimacy with the laity, and, furthermore, his learning had placed something of a barrier between him and the common people. He and his wife had performed many services for their parish—they had even read and written for a good part of it—but they were for this very reason always "sir" and "madam," and their ways were in a sense quite foreign to village life.

Now new people began to arrive from without. By way of consolidating central control, the government sent new police officials, and with the development of the education system, graduates of the new normal schools came to take charge of the public schools. The latter to be sure were often second or third sons of local landlords, but sometimes they were natives of other places, and in any event they had had the experience of going to school in urban districts. Not infrequently a young mån served as a teacher in an unfamiliar district for some years and then returned to his home to become the principal of the local primary school. All these people, as well as an increasing number of doctors who had been trained in city colleges, tended to be regarded as different somehow from usual folk.

The villages that had formerly been stations along the Tokugawa-period highways were particularly quick to take on the appearance of towns. The government now required traveling officials to pay when they stopped over in such places, and this created new business, which in turn attracted younger sons from nearby farms. First, factories producing soy sauce, sake, or rapeseed oil appeared, and then gradually the industrial enterprises that characterize modern life began to take root. Tradesmen, carriers, and industrialists soon made thriving towns out of the old stations. Their efforts were of course greatly aided by expanded transportation and communication facilities.

c. From the Village to the Factory

The conspicuously low wages that have characterized modern Japanese industry result from a surplus farm population. After the beginning of the Meiji period daughters and younger sons of farmers were forced to seek work in textile factories, foundries, glass or cement works, and so on. When a new factory was set up in a provincial town, it solicited labor from nearby villages, and the metropolitan factories sent representatives to the rural districts for the same purpose. We might note incidentally that many city enterprises showed a preference for workers of one particular prefecture.

The revision of the tax system affected many landowners adversely, but often they recouped their losses by speculating on rice or simply passed on the taxes to their tenant farmers. The economic gap between landowner and tenant widened, and when the impoverished tenants heard the bright promises of the labor scouts, they did not long hesitate to send their younger brothers and offspring off to the factories. Those who went boarded the train with high hopes, but they rarely found factory life up to their expectations.

In those days the laborer had no contract with the management. He might be forced to work at any time of the day or night, and he had to manage to live on a pittance. The average worker wanted nothing so much as to pack his bags and go back home, and in the early years of the period the resulting labor turnover was exceedingly high, especially in the textile mills. Those who forced themselves to put up with working conditions sooner or later lost their health and returned to their homes to spread the tuberculosis virus. Even if they managed to get out of the factory while they were still healthy enough to wield a spade, however, they were likely to find that there was no land in which to sink it. Consequently, more and more stayed in the towns. In this connection, we cannot of course overlook that despite gruelling working conditions, many who had had a taste of city life found it difficult to go back to the farm and take up where they had left off.

The textile companies who employed mostly women seem to have had to compete to secure an adequate labor supply. Wily farmers sometimes made contracts for their daughters with labor recruiters from two or three different companies in order to collect the money that was given upon the signing of the agreement, and it is said that the factories thus defrauded had little recourse. In some cases the recruiter, having discovered that a girl had made an arrangement with another company as well as his own, either carried her away virtually by force or used sweet blandishments to coax her into coming to his company. Under the circumstances, once the girls had started working, the company kept a close watch on them, even when they were off duty, for fear that they would run away. Wages were low everywhere, but since the girls were governed by a complicated system of efficiency merits and demerits, they rarely complained even when they were exploited and deceived.

The women textile workers were crowded into dormitories, to which they were unaccustomed, and there they were so jealously supervised that they had no chance to organize themselves into a self-respecting social group. Some reacted to these conditions by becoming wanton and offending against what are called public morals.

As a rule, even when the girls returned home to their parents they became the targets of much criticism. Actually they had by no means grown accustomed to luxury in the cities, as the country people often said, but they had indeed often grown so unaccustomed to the rhythm of village life that they found it difficult to readjust. Too, they had often missed out on much of the training in house work that a young woman was expected to have received, and it was consequently difficult to find husbands for them.

d. New Employment

Not all the people who left the farm and came to the cities went to work in factories. During the depression of 1883 and 1884 quite a number of them became ricksha pullers on the streets of Tokyo, and in the various urban slums there were numerous coolies of other sorts as well as peddlers of various types who had formerly worked on the road. Shabby rooming houses served as the first foothold for countless poor boys who came to the cities with no definite jobs, but anxious to try their luck.

In the Meiji cities small businessmen and even salaried workers frequently contrived to have a maid, and country girls were often hired into such positions. Actually their families often regarded this as an opportunity for them to obtain the necessary training to become proper housewives, and it would be a mistake to consider that the motive for hiring their daughters out was purely economic. During the first half of the Meiji period so many girls came to the city to work as maids for two or three years that special employment agencies for them appeared. These enterprises were often guilty of various kinds of malpractice. Laws governing them were instituted in 1903, but the truly modern employment agency did not develop until somewhat later. The first concern of the sort was established in 1906 by the Salvation Army, and five years later government-operated employment bureaus were opened in Tokyo and other urban centers.

During the latter half of the Meiji period, the practice of selling sons and daughters into service became increasingly common. In all fairness we should say that the concept of selling was not usually as rigid as it is today, and the person sold was not necessarily bound into slavery for life. In the case of young men, it was generally expected that the buyer would treat them more or less as adopted sons, and after a length of time set them up in independent households of their own. Still in the modern period the tendency was for persons hired in this fashion to become permanent underlings, and even when a shopkeeper established an apprentice in a separate store the latter was in effect a branch of the former employer's business.

When employers hired young men or women from the country they ordinarily chose them from among the residents of their native villages, and similarily when country people sought employment in the cities they applied to former residents of their communities. As a consequence, even in the large cities there remained old-fashioned feelings of village solidarity.

3. THE LOSS OF COMMUNITY PROPERTY

During the Tokugawa period, mountainous areas and forest lands were to a large extent considered to be the common property of nearby villages, which relied on them for lumber, fuel, and fertilizer (*i. e.* leaves and grass that were allowed to rot and later used as compost). How old the concept of community ownership was, it is difficult to say, but even when such property was nominally under the control of a feudal lord it was actually used by the farm communities. In the beginning of the Meiji period the new government revised the land tax and provided that such land would remain the property of the traditional owners, but would be subject to tax. In actual fact, the government attempted to annex as much of these lands as it could, and the courts were often inclined to disregard the claims that villages put forward. At the same time, a number of villagers either transferred their property to the government or registered it in the names of leading villagers in order to avoid taxes. Still, in many places the rural population continued to hold the privilege of using this property, and the same applied to publicly owned forest land that the government had inherited from the Tokugawa shogunate.

There is no denying, however, that as the Meiji period advanced, agricultural communities were to a greater and greater degree deprived of these lands. In 1889, when the new system of local administration was instituted, and the old villages combined into larger units, such property came under the ownership of the new townships, or was taken over by a few of the wealthier members of the community, or was divided among the people who had formerly used it. Furthermore, in 1909 the Ministries of Agriculture and Trade and the Home Ministry increased their efforts to bring this land under the control of the new townships, and much more of it was released by the old communities at this time. This governmental move was joined with an attempt to unify the former village shrines, and as a result of this combined attack, much of the spirit that had given the old villages their identity was lost.

After the Meiji period, a number of lawsuits concerning the privilege of cutting grass or trees on the former communal property arose, and in general it appears that when such lands were put under the control of the new administrative units they tended to be exploited for the benefit of a few influential persons. In times of economic difficulty ordinary people frequently raised a cry for the return of the property to the village farmer.

Aside from forest lands, many villages had maintained gardens or fields of miscanthus (for thatching roofs) in common. These were originally worked by the community but in many cases they were gradually relegated to tenant farmers. As a rule they were inferior lands, and when the new tax system was enforced they were often abandoned.

Broadly speaking, the loss of common property contributed to the spread of commercial economy in rural areas. Farmers were no longer able to go into the woods at will and secure lumber or fertilizer, and it became necessary for them to rely on merchants for these supplies. The loss was a great one.

4. THE DISINTEGRATION OF THE CLAN

Since the Tokugawa period there has been a proverb, known in even the remotest mountain hamlets, to the effect that a family remains neither wealthy nor poor for more than three generations. As a matter of fact, Tokugawa society contained many families who were able to maintain their wealth longer than three generations, but there was certainly no guarantee that a similar length of time would see a poor family flourish and grow rich. It was not the sort of social structure in which a person could get ahead through work and perseverance alone. Chances were better in the Meiji period, but at first families who had been well off in the Tokugawa period were comparatively successful in retaining their economic superiority. When the land tax was revised in the early part of the period, farmers who had belonged to the highest bracket during the Tokugawa became landowners, and this rendered the social structure of farming communities virtually inflexible. Those who had had good family status for the past centuries retained it, and family status, rather than personal qualifications, was what people in rural communities valued. For a family to enjoy high rank did not necessarily involve being rich, but as a rule the oldest and most respected families were also the ones with property. It was only at the end of the Tokugawa period that the oldest families ceased in some instances to be better off than newcomers. A gazetteer describing the manners and customs in the province of Mino during the early Meiji period pointed out that even when lower-class families prospered and built new houses, they were not allowed to use tile roofs, auxiliary eaves, or many of the other architectual devices that marked the better buildings of the age, while persons who had been in the upper classes, but had lost their money and their educational prerogatives, still lorded it over the rest. Even the village officials, this source averred, favored houses of good rank, by which is meant the village leaders of the past, over the common people.

In places where the better-off farmers had formed guilds to take charge of the local shrine, there was a clear distinction between old and new families at the religious festivals. To be sure, new families did in many instances gain entrance into such organizations or form similar ones of their own, but they did not succeed in replacing the old members, even when the latter had become impoverished. The fee or stock shares required to enter these guilds were usually quite high, and only families who had acquired a fair amount of property were able to buy their way into them.

The old families were as a rule descended from rich people, or the retainers of rich people, of the fifteenth and sixteenth centuries. In the Tokugawa period such families not only became local officials or heads of neighborhoods, but also were employed as forest inspectors, artillery inspectors, leaders of guilds of masons or of *tatami* makers, managers of dyeing establishments, or owners of houses where daimyo stopped when traveling.

During the early half of the Meiji period a strong pioneer spirit was abroad in the country, and many of the older families dreamed of establishing successful new businesses. They were encouraged of course by the general atmosphere of freedom resulting from the removal of Tokugawa restrictions on work. Those first seized with the fever of enterprise were the old houses who knew something of letters and the ways of the outside world, but despite their enthusiasm, they so often failed that their lack of business sense became proverbial.

They may have been the most logical people in the rural areas to succeed, but by modern standards they had little capital and less experience.

Most of the old rural families who went into business either opened mining concerns or tried their hands at manufacturing textiles, sake, tea, or other specialties of particular areas. Some, however, gambled on the stock market, where they often lost everything they had, not only because of their inability to understand the machinations of capitalistic society, but also because the local banks were unsound. Actually, even the richest of the country people had few assets other than their traditional prestige and a limited amount of property accumulated over a long period of time. Their failure in business is hardly surprising.

After the Meiji period the influx of foreign commodities to a large extent destroyed the various types of home manufacture that had existed. Indigo was replaced by German chemical dyes, and the importation of cane sugar from the tropical regions put an end to Japanese sugar production. The industrial revolution, spreading from Europe to Japan, choked off village manufacture, and reduced the old families, who had been in charge of it, to poverty. The old isolated villages were now being invaded by economic forces of the whole nation and the rest of the world. A number of old houses had been engaged in the manufacture of sake, but around the middle of the Meiji period, the government prohibited home manufacture of alcoholic beverages and gave permission to only a limited number of people to produce them. Due to rises in market prices, the manufacture of certain special products exhibited a tendency toward centralized management, but this was usually counteracted by sudden drops in prices. Attracted by the high price of hemp, many farmers put all the land they could into growing it, but the demand for hemp soon switched largely to cotton, and hemp farmers lost heavily. Farmers engaged in sericulture were particularly affected by international economic conditions.

In a number of districts, most notably Kōchi Prefecture, the old houses threw themselves into politics and spent much more than they could afford trying to appear modern and affluent. Not a few borrowed their way into bankruptcy attempting to become members of the prefectural council. The speed with which the scions of ancient houses exhausted the inheritance that their parents and grandparents had sweated to amass was almost unbelievable. In the southern part of Chiba Peninsula people invented a proverb that said "the parents wear cheap straw sandals, the sons wear fine straw sandals, the grandsons wear the finest of all straw sandals, the great grandsons go barefoot."

The atmosphere of city life began to invade the rural districts. The first to be attacked were the sons of old families. One heard more and more talk of degenerate sons who squandered their inheritance on wine, women, and gambling. Dissipation, however, was by no means the only reason for the financial disaster that struck down the old houses. It was simply the factor that most offended the traditional morals of villagers and consequently the one they noticed first. The leaders of the nation were strongly prone to make city ways the standard for everything, and people who had formerly made what they needed themselves began to long for fine urban products. Neither influential villagers nor rural educators helped to correct the excessive yearning for urban culture. Not enough thought was given to the improvement of farm labor methods or to creating a new form of culture suitable to farming areas. The sons of average farmers gasped in admiration of the fine new symbols of city life to be found in the houses of the leading members of the community and admired these people even more than they had before, without stopping to notice that this new life had no roots in rural soil. After the Sino-Japanese War country families adopted city ways on an even greater scale, and for this reason there is no need to point to dissipated heirs to explain their frequent loss of ability to maintain their former position. The old families were the quickest to adopt the new culture, but it turned on them and brought about their downfall.

It is important to observe that the heads of established families ceased to control the labor forces that they had maintained in the Tokugawa period. One reason for their ability to remain strong until now had been their practice of using younger sons and daughters virtually as slaves, and this ceased in the modern era to be possible. Such families usually had a good deal of land, and although they bequeathed bits and pieces of it to descendants other than the true heir, the latter retained the lion's share, while the others remained more or less dependent on him and consequently obliged to contribute to his welfare. Now, however, they were free to choose new work, of which there was an abundance, and to live where they wished. Few of them felt inclined to continue on as underlings, and many of them actually ceased to cooperate in any way with the main branch of their family. A few patriarchs in remote villages managed to resist the tide, but in the communities near the cities the head of the tribe lost all control over his former minions.

As old families declined, a number of parvenus, in particular a class who accumulated a large amount of land through usury, appeared. The transfer of land to such persons had begun in the middle of the Tokugawa period and was mentioned, disapprovingly of course, by a number of Confucian writers engaged in efforts to improve the deteriorating agricultural policy of the government. Pawn shops and moneylenders operated even in small villages, and some of them came from the class of old families spoken of above. In the early Meiji period many of these borrowed money on their land and invested it in commercial or industrial enterprises on which they hoped to get rich quickly, but more often than not they failed. During the first decade of the era, business was good and the new investors, flushed with profits, learned to buy extravagantly and live high. In 1881, however, a sudden depression threw them into complete consternation. For the most part, their creditors were financiers living in the cities, and these suddenly found themselves to have become absentee landlords. In the villages a leading part in finance was taking by the middle-class landowners, to whom small farmers, having no recourse to city bankers, went for loans. Having received such land, the creditors borrowed money on it from the banks and large landowners and used it as capital. When panic struck, the large financial organizations collected the land, and the middle-class landlords gained control over the tenant farmers through the strength that their ill-gained capital brought them. Among others who profited in the villages were people who managed to buy up the former community property that had to be converted into personal property at the beginning of the Meiji period. Many of these started successful charcoal businesses, and some of them at least began selling lumber.

Quite a few people who did not make out well in the cities invaded the villages as merchants. Being fairly wise in the ways of world, they were frequently able to profit considerably at the expense of country people. Often they set up shops and, having accumulated a certain amount of money, became moneylenders as well. The new-rich families in the farming communities were regarded by the typical farmer as outsiders and were often unable to enter into community life. Too, when a small landowner managed to raise himself a little in the world, he often found that his neighbors were both critical and envious of him. The villagers were particularly shocked to see new people entering their community and making an outstanding success. By way of resistance, the older members of the community excluded the newcomers from festivals or made them make absurdly large contributions in order to join in. The young men's associations, for their part, occasionally applied sanctions to the children of the new families or even attacked them physically, in the name of keeping order among the youth of the community, but actually out of spite. Still, the trends of the time were in favor of the newcomers, and the older villagers proved to be no match for them.

5. ARTISANS BECOME SEDENTARY

a. Itinerant Artisans

There have always been persons in Japan whose principal occupation has been handicrafts, but in antiquity they only rarely manufactured their products with a view to supplying them to the general public. Rather they were usually attached to some government office. For a certain fixed period each year it would be their duty to work for the court, to whom they presented their handiwork, and the rest of the time they were generally engaged in agriculture. In old Kyoto there appear, to have existed almost professional handicraft workers, but the appearance of large numbers of artisans working to private order is a somewhat later phenomenon. These artisans were of two kinds, those who went out on jobs and those who worked at home, but most of them went about wherever work was to be found, receiving as wages the materials with which they worked plus a sum of money. In the towns those who worked at home usually were paid a price for finished work. Artisan was hardly to be distinguished from merchant—a man sold what he made. In the later metropolitan centers were found not only the artisans working for the various shogunate officials, but also those operating back-street shops and catering to the general public. But it was rather the itinerant with whom the people in the villages were most familiar.

It was not easy for a specialized craftsman to stay in one small village and still make a living ; hence the story of how the artisans gradually became sedentary is interwoven with the growth of the large metropolitan centers, but in the Meiji period there were still many, many itinerant artisans in the villages. Metalworkers became sedentary comparatively quickly, but even here there are cases on record of celebrated metalcasters who after establishing quite extensive permanent shops, continued to spend half the year on the road. Stone masons also settled down comparatively early, but it required a long time before they became completely assimilated to the population among which they settled. Woodworkers continued their itinerant work longer than most others, but even they began to settle down during the Meiji period. There is also the case of a famous metalcaster who, unable to modernize, became a plasterer and settled down to work in an area far from his home.

Carpenters and the like, were especially needed for the construction of temples and shrines, so much so that they worshiped the Buddhist pioneer Shōtoku Taishi as their patron saint, and they naturally gravitated toward the cities and other developing areas where such construction might be expected to take place. Actually, however, their real focus was about the mountains which supplied them their lumber. Carpenters often hailed from villages which in the past had paid their annual taxes in lumber. The villagers continued to produce the materials, while the carpenters, based as it were on their efforts, went out on their itinerant labors.

There were also itinerant thatchers, as for example in the Kantō area, who made their journeys in the winter repairing roofs. People came to depend upon them for such tasks. The makers of stone fences originally centered about the Ōmi area, but gradually moved to and settled in areas more convenient for the transportation of stone.

The initial step in this gathering of the itinerant artisans into the large cities seems to have taken place, at the earliest, at about the time of the building of the feudal castle towns. As these people came to the towns they appear to have gathered into particular districts, and to have got along with temporary lodgings for long periods of time, until finally they were able to set themselves up independently. Meanwhile, in those villages which had grown to a considerable size, carpenters and plasterers were beginning to settle down, but in general these two occupations continued to have extremely large numbers of itinerant artisans.

For the villagers, the visits of the traveling artisans were rare opportunities on which they might hear the gossip of the outside world. Gradually the visits grew more and more infrequent, but as this was happening, knowledge of the outside world was beginning to reach the villages through other media, especially the printed page, and the villagers' world-view and sense of values were also changing.

B. Artisans in the Towns

In order to obtain the materials needed for their trades and to insure the marketability of their output, artisans found it necessary to league up with merchants. This was another force tending to draw them toward the towns, but as they did this, they more and more found themselves coming into conflict with the modern industries then rapidly developing there, and the area of their operation was year after year reduced.

According to Yokoyama Gen'nosuke's *The Lower Classes in Japanese Society*, by the end of the nineteenth century, there were already in the Tokyo area more than a thousand households of carpenters, plasterers, coopers, wood-turners, and weavers. Of these, forty per cent of the coopers and seventy or eighty per cent of the wood-turners and weavers were located in outlying, non-urban portions of the area. In addition, there were over 500 households classified as stone masons, floormat makers, blacksmiths, tailors, foot-mitten makers, dyers, joiners, paper makers, timber suppliers, etc. Of this list, of course, almost all the timber suppliers were located outside the urban area proper. Furthermore, there were more than 300 households of roofers, gardeners, metalcasters, paper-lantern makers, shoemakers, *geta* makers, paper hangers, and tinplate workers, while bag makers, wood-turners, writing-brush makers, laundry men, printers, and umbrella men accounted for more than 200 additional households. In addition, there were certain others connected with comparatively new enterprises.

In the first half of the Meiji period hatters, knitters, glass makers and soap makers appeared here and there, and while their activities were on a small scale, their technical skill seems to have been fairly advanced. According to the *Tokyo Nichinichi Newspaper* for May 22, 1892, a total of nine Europeans were being employed at salaries ranging from $100 to $200 per month, including a master glass maker and two helpers, a master knitter, a master weaver, and a master dyer.

Carpenters, plasterers, stone masons and rooftile workers, who went from place to place plying their trades remained somewhat special, but in a certain sense those artisans who worked at home, such as *geta* makers, clog-thong makers, bag makers, and workers in inlaid lacquer ware, were at the same time merchants. The artisan who went out to do his work had, instead of customers, permanent patrons, and his business depended upon his relation with them. Artisans working at home in cities like Tokyo were not without regular customers who might just as well be called patrons, but at least in principle their customers were drawn from the larger world of general consumers. A relationship comparable to that between the other kind of artisan and his patron arose between them and the commission agent or wholesale dealer through whom they worked.

These differences showed themselves in the everyday life of both kinds of artisans. The one who went out on his jobs was a cocky, spunky type. The one who worked at home developed the elegant, refined, even precious airs of the merchant class of the time. The former took care that money never burned a hole in his pocket—with him it was " easy come, easy go." As one result, his home was virtually ruled by his wife, the celebrated Meiji type of the " lady of the house " (*okami-san*).

But as an increasingly modern economy developed, this type

of artisan found himself in trouble. More and more his functions and his patron-relationships, at so-many *sen* a day, began to be encroached upon by contractors, and with these changes his temper also altered. Much the same was the development in the case of the other artisans, who found themselves coming more and more under the control of capitalistic commission agents. The relationship between the latter on the one hand, and the producers and owners of goods, the middle-men, and the retail merchants on the other, was of a thoroughly feudal master-servant type, and the agents' financial power assured their unquestioned preeminence among the merchants. They also exercised much the same power among the urban artisans. From the Meiji Restoration on, anyone with sufficient capital was free to begin operations as a commission agent, so of course their numbers increased greatly. As a result the position of the middle-man in the center of the artisan hierarchy became insecure, and the artisans came to be directly controlled by the commission agents.

It was difficult enough for the artisans to produce really fine products for the market, but it was even more difficult for them to satisfy the ever-increasing clamor of the commission agents for larger and larger production. Itinerant artisans such as dyers, for example, had been in possession of certain carefully guarded trade secrets. They produced a highly individualized product and aimed at catching the fancy of the masses. But all this was quite impossible for the sedentary dyers in the cities, who had all they could do to meet the production demands of the commission agents and as a result finally ended up turning out their products in a completely mechanical fashion. Unfortunately, it was not the commission agents but rather the artisans who acquired the bad reputation of being cunning and underhanded. Not only this, but the commission agents were accustomed to resort to anything short of sheer physical violence when it came to milking the artisans for profits. By 1900 the labor problem was being generally discussed, and the artisans who were being oppressed by such commission agents as these began to show spirit and to form unions. One such was the Tokyo Japanese and Western-style Dyers' and Leather Workers' Union.

The commission agents were especially hard-hearted in their treatment of artisans from outcast groups, such as leather workers. Actually the general public, although it took a prejudiced view of these groups, did not feel their "outcast" position very deeply. Their reaction was rather one of fear, and a feeling that associating with these persons was to be avoided by all means, but they did not in general go as far as the government administrators did when they specifically assigned them to a segregated area of social activity. The role of the commission agents as a neo-feudal force is undeniable. Even as society progressed on the road toward a capitalistic system, the commission agents continued to grow fat upon the merciless exploitation of the cheap labor of these unfortunates. One result was that in the process their discriminatory social position as virtual outcasts became more and more evident.

Actually, there was even a certain element of fear and awe in the way the general public viewed the itinerant artisan. There were from time to time cases of families who in order that their children might become adept in trade secrets, patronized certain itinerant artisans regularly. The relationship between the artisan and his patron was a fairly intimate one. As the urban centers became more and more modern, this relationship tended to change, and the patron became more and more a master, the artisan more and more a servant. The patron would on certain occasions call together the artisans he employed and entertain them, and the artisans for their part would present the patron with gifts of dried salmon and bonito. In established homes in the towns there was a tendency to develop a strong feeling for regular "family" artisans, and once this relationship was established it was no simple matter to change and start to patronize some other artisan. Families would even present their artisan with short loose work jackets, prominently inscribed on the back with the patron's name or crest, or some other distinctive mark, all the more clearly to show their mutual relationship. This was the *shirushi-banten*, or "marked jacket."

In this period, however, when the contractor was developing the scope of his activities, especially in engineering and construction work, the relationship outlined above tended more and more to break down, and in time many artisans began to wear *shirushi-banten* which they had received from contractors. These contractors had themselves generally been artisans originally, sometimes carpenters, or stone masons, or the like. As the occasion demanded they would, in order to complete some fairly major undertaking, arrange for the services and assistance of their plasterers, for instance, or roofers. In an increasingly bureaucratic society there came to be more and more calls for major construction projects, and the custom arose of demanding the payment of a guaranty by the contractor before the work was begun. This meant that contracting was impossible without a certain amount of capital and led to the appearance of persons who specialized in contracting alone. The artisan, a master carpenter, perhaps with a long tradition behind him, extremely conscious of the traditional aspects of his craft, and extremely anxious to hand them on down, found himself confronted with a contractor as "boss," who shared none of his feelings. Naturally he lost his pride in his own skill and the ability that had long characterized the Japanese artisan.

At one time there were various factors tending toward a feeling of group participation on the part of the artisans. Take for example the case of the carpenters. As mentioned above, they honored the Buddhist pioneer Shōtoku Taishi as their protecting deity, and this devotion, with its annual observances, especially in the New Year season, was an important unifying force among them. As a result they tended to respect each other's rights and hesitated to infringe upon one another's patronage. As the social structure continued to change radically, their devotion to Shōtoku Taishi lost all real meaning, and the way was left open for the fiercest kind of competitive practices. Competition is of the essence in a capitalistic society, and from its progress among the artisans we can judge how far on the road toward capitalism their society had come. In the case of the various producers' unions mentioned above, they existed, it is true, in name, but they lacked the spirit necessary to organize and actually contend with the capitalists and the contractors.

Of course, as long as there were artisans at all, the apprentice-master relationship continued to survive to some extent, and the technical tradition continued to be handed down, but the period of apprenticeship was no longer seven or eight years, but generally only up to the time the boy became eligible for military service, which meant in most cases no more than three or four years. Furthermore, it became more common for an apprentice to continue living in his own home, going each day to his master's. Needless to say, in such a case the relationship between master and apprentice bore but little resemblance to what it had been under the older system.

Formerly it had been customary for the apprentice after completing his initiation into the trade to continue to serve his master for from six months to a year, as a kind of repayment. Not only was this almost never done how, but many apprentices were too much concerned with their own independence, and strove to limit their relationship to their masters only to the period when they were actually receiving training. The world of the old itinerant artisans was closed to such persons; and as one result they remained much less men of the world.

An experiment was attempted in 1885 at establishing an Artisans' Company in Kyoto, and there were other cases in which two or three great merchants contributed capital and established artisan management enterprises. Actually what made such establishments possible was the precarious situation in which the artisans found themselves now that their old ties had been severed.

9. THE NEW CULTURE IN THE TOWNS AND THE OLD EVILS

a. Cultural Enlightenment at Nihombashi

The importation of Western civilization was spoken of in the Meiji period as a "cultural awakening," and the words became as much a slogan of the times as democracy is today, but the enlightenment was confined largely to cities. It spread in waves to the countryside, but the waves were not so violent as those that reached Tokyo and Yokohama from foreign shores.

Unlike the metropolitan area around Kyoto and Osaka, Tokyo and Yokohama had nothing that could be called a traditional way of life. Yokohama of course was but a hamlet until the Meiji period, and even Tokyo, although it had been a large city since its establishment nearly three centuries before, was essentially a cultural hodge-podge. The most powerful members of its populace, the daimyō and samurai, regarded it as a temporary residence, since they customarily stayed there only in the years when they were required to do so by the shogunate, and while there was certain unique atmosphere in the downtown area, revealed in the wood-block prints of the age it was essentially little more than a collective *joie de vivre* exhibited by customers in places of entertainment.

The shogun's capital was an ideal place for introducing Western culture. At the beginning of Meiji, the people of the city were crying for reform. The change from Edo to Tokyo had not merely been a change in name. It had meant the departure of many members of the military class and unemployment for their servants and underlings. The great merchants who had depended on these people were threatened. For a time, indeed, the whole city was thrown into confusion, and thieves and prowlers roamed the streets at night. The samurai who were left were sometimes so poverty-stricken that their children opened

94

tea-houses in their front yards or set up shops where they sold the family possessions.

The new government planned to make Tokyo a half-agricultural, half-commercial city, and in an anachronistic move it urged the cultivation of mulberries and tea on the land surrounding the mansions of the daimyos. Townspeople promptly composed sarcastic songs about this back-to-nature movement, and in fact it soon came to failure. After two or three rather aimless years, however, business began to thrive again. The market at Tsukiji grew lively, steamships clustered in the harbors, and rickshas clanged noisily through the streets—the enlightenment was on.

The first persons to take up Western styles in clothing and deportment were members of the military class, but other members of the same class offered considerable resistance to Westernization. These latter were particularly disturbed over the abolition of their practice of carrying swords as a mark of their rank. This step was discussed for a number of years before the government finally decided upon it in 1875, and even after it was taken, many proud samurai continued to object. According to one newspaper of the era, some of the more stubborn old-timers felt so lost without their weapons that they began to carry wooden replicas. The *Tokyo Nichinichi Newspaper* had the following to say about dress in Akita Prefecture :

The only persons at annual ceremonies who wear proper Western dress are officials. The military class still wear the garment inherited from their ancestors, with its wide hemp epaulettes and two swords hanging from the waist.... They put their hands inside their kimonos, throw back their shoulders, and swagger in the most offensive manner.

The abolition of the ancient marks of the samurai was actually the cause of much of the political opposition to the new government. The leaders of the enlightenment themselves came from the samurai class, but they paid absolutely no heed to the objections raised by their more conservative brothers. Instead they simply complimented themselves smugly on their role as leaders of the new awakening. In October, 1872, the *Nichiyō Newspaper* carried the following statement :

Nowadays when officials are dispatched to Iruma Prefecture and walk in the streets of the city of Kawagoe, all the people stare at them just as the people of Tokyo stared at foreigners ten years ago. We record this with amusement on the supposition that it will make a good story when the enlightenment has reached the people of Kawagoe.

The enlightenment, however, was not to become nationwide for many, many years to come.

When the government replaced the lunar calendar with the solar, one part of Hōjō Prefecture rose in revolt. Still, Fukuzawa Yukichi stated flatly that people who opposed the new calendar were ignorant fools, while those who favored it were intelligent. The self-contentment implied in this judgment was typical of the new leaders, but their notion that they could all of a sudden bring Western culture into a country as diverse and complicated as Japan reveals a very superficial conception of culture.

b. Criticism of the Enlightenment

The revolt against the new calendar was an exceptionally strong reaction, but there were other people who objected to the fact that the enlightenment was centered around Tokyo exclusively and to some extent around the upper-class members of the bureaucracy. Many felt that the government was completely ignoring rural areas. The following appeared in the first issue of a journal called *Minkan Zasshi*, (*The People's Magazine*) :

The national fiscal policy provides money for the salaries of foreigners and officials, for stone buildings to house the various bureaus, and for school buildings for prospective officials. The purpose seems to be to take the fruits of rural labor to make flowers for Tokyo. Steel bridges glisten in the capital, and horse-drawn carriages run on the streets, but in the country the wooden bridges are so rotten that one cannot cross them. The cherry blossoms bloom in Kyōbashi, but weeds grow in the country fields. Billows of smoke such as rise from city stores do not rise from the farmer's furnace. The greatest need for the whole nation is for national expenditures to be reduced and local expenditures increased. We must cease making Tokyo richer and concentrate on the rural districts.

A similar statement appeared in the *Yūbin Hōchi Newspaper*:

All of the nation's taxes are submitted to the Minister of Finance, and the income of the nobility also pours into the capital. A hundred times as much gold and rice circulate in Tokyo as in the feudal days. Consequently, the city has railways, steam engines, fine stone buildings, military ministries, gaslights, and bridges. Construction expenses for one day are astounding. Cannot something be done to cause riches to flow into the outlying provinces?

Others lamented that the enlightenment was all a matter of techniques and forms with too little emphasis on the rationalization of principles and social education, and indeed, the Meiji version of European culture was in many ways artificial and unrealistic. It was a luxury of the cities and had no real basis in Japanese life. For this reason it had the unfortunate effect of creating various barriers between the urban and rural populace and between the upper and lower classes. A new intelligensia with a veneer of Western culture were accepted as leaders, and lead they did—toward the misfortunes that Japan has suffered in the past two or three decades.

One group of arch conservatives put up a very emotional resistance to the enlightenment. Typical of them was Sata Kaiseki, who preached that the oil lamp was destroying the nation. He said : " Culture and enlightenment do not belong to the West alone. The West has its culture and its enlightenment, but Japan also has hers." This is perhaps true enough, but Sata went on to attack all imports from the West, scholarly as well as material, and to castigate the Japanese who were proudly using them. Kaiseki is said to have authored a program for an imaginary wrestling match among idiots, which listed as two of the leading contenders " the Japanese who prefers bread to rice " and " the man who uses imported oil instead of native vegetable or fish oil." The other names on the program were similar. Few paid much attention to such diatribes or to extremist arguments against foreign trade, but they were welcome among a number of poverty-stricken ex-samurai who lacked the ability to succeed in the new age.

Leagues were formed in some places to boycott foreign products. In 1879, according to the *Asahi Newspaper*, the people of the village of Amikake, Sarashina County, Nagano Prefecture, for example, agreed not to use oil lamps, hats, or Western umbrellas, and even to sell the chairs they had bought for the village assembly hall to the neighboring community. In 1882 the residents of the Kanazawa district, Ishikawa Prefecture, formed a patriotic society which decided to boycott all foreign goods. In Masuda Hongō, in the province of Iwami, patriots not only rejected foreign goods, but formed a society that forbade its members from supporting any other religions than Shintoism or Buddhism. The area of Nagahama in Shiga Prefecture agreed to expel any person in the community who used foreign goods.

In brief the second decade of the Meiji era was a period of chauvinism in the rural areas, and the new culture did not penetrate into these regions until later.

7. SOCIAL CONSCIOUSNESS AND ETHICS

a. New Social Organizations

In ancient Japan individual households were joined together in large clans, but as the latter deteriorated, small separate families sought security in cooperative groups based on territorial proximity or occasionally on community of interest. As a rule, the neighborhood group was the basic social organization, and this was the case even with associations of a more or less religious nature, such as those formed for the purpose of financing pilgrimages to the shrine at Ise.

One vast change that took place in Meiji society was that social organization became centered not around particular areas but around particular types of work. By work is meant not only labor, but something on the order of " life work "—the role that individuals play in society, whether it be that of a worker in the ordinary sense or that of the politician, the artist, or the champion of some principle. When people gained the right to live where they wished and choose their own their profession, they were thrown into contact with many new people, and they were naturally inclined to form social attachments with those who shared the same work or the same ideas. Equality for the four classes into which the nation had been divided (samurai, farmer, artisan, merchant) was a slogan among Meiji political leaders, but individual equality had little real meaning. The society of the previous age may be classified as feudal, but it differed markedly from medieval European feudalism in that it had no religion like Christianity that might have cultivated the ability of individuals to be free and independent. Even when the feudal system was officially abolished, therefore, people lacked the self-reliance needed for living a completely independent life. Consequently, there was a strong tendency for individuals to rely on strength in numbers.

At the same time government officials and other leaders usually posed needless interference in direct proportion to the freshness of the many new associations. The people seem to have had the instincts and experience needed to run their organizations autonomously, and had they been allowed to do so, they might have accomplished much, but the leaders of the time refused them sufficient leeway. These leaders for their part were mostly members of the old warrior class, and while there had previously existed certain factions among them, they had little experience with social organizations, and they lacked understanding of the cooperative societies which the ordinary people sought to form. The result of their restraining influence was that the new societies did not encourage free and active participation on the part of individual, but rather instilled in him a tendency to rely on others in the group to do everything.

Still the number of small organizations was an outstanding feature of the era. During the popular rights movement, landlords in the cities and villages began to take a strong interest in politics, and this resulted in the formation of many small political societies. Other associations were formed to boycott imported goods, while on the other hand still others centered around the imported Christian faith. In the villages new youth organizations were formed to take the place of the traditional ones. During the latter half of Meiji, when interest in labor problems increased, a number of rather fly-by-night labor organizations appeared. The farmers in various districts organized discussion groups for the purpose of improving farm methods, and later a number of national agricultural societies were formed. Coordination among them was poor, and around the time of the second National Industrial Exhibit in 1881, several of them met in Tokyo and formed the Japanese Agricultural Society (*Dainihon Nōkai*). This, unfortunately, tended to be dominated by scholars instead of the farmers themselves. A number of other societies of the same nature were subsequently formed, and in

1889 a law governing their organization and functions was enacted, but the societies were little more than loosely connected assemblages of farmers with diverging interests, and they passed easily into the control of landowners. Accordingly, farmers in various districts reverted to smaller local organizations.

Trade guilds might be considered to have begun with the founding of an organization called the Hōtokusha in the late Tokugawa period, but the first modern organizations of this sort were founded in around 1878 or 1880. Among the earliest examples were two formed by the farmers of Gumma Prefecture who were engaged in producing raw silk. In 1883 a guild of tea merchants was founded in Shizuoka. All of these were designed to improve and control exports. In the Meiji twenties credit associations were formed by producers, and after the Sino-Japanese War there appeared consumers' unions. In 1900 a law regulating industrial guilds was promulgated. It is important to note, however, that these various unions did not fulfill the important function of giving aid to impoverished laborers. They were not a natural outgrowth of the traditional cooperative spirit that had formerly prevailed in farming communities. They had little sense of independence, and they tended to be run for the benefit solely of the representatives or officers who controlled them.

One important type of union had been the mutual financial groups maintained by the members of farming communities. In the new era the concept of getting together and raising a fund to help a neighbor in need was largely lost, and these organizations came to constitute little more than a means of facilitating loans. They were often operated by professionals.

b. Concepts of Society

Despite the large number of organizations or unions formed then, there were few that avoided domination by a special class of leaders. The associations could possibly have operated to train people as good citizens, and their members might well have been expected to take an interest in an increasing member of social subjects, but their hierarchical structure prevented this. The people as a whole had no feeling of intimacy or familiarity with the new associations.

Actually, most individuals still felt closest to their family, their neighborhood, and their village, and consciousness of unity with the local community and of isolation from other places remained strong. The persons who came from other villages to become policemen or teachers were regarded as foreign, and few villagers could become thoroughly frank with them. The same was even more true of people who moved in from the cities, and as the gap between urban and rural culture widened, the rural inhabitants began to assume a prejudiced outlook toward all outsiders, with which was compounded a feeling of inferiority.

The villages were organized into larger administrative districts; the traditional common property of the neighborhood passed into private hands; the local shrines were unified into larger units; and people ceased to some degree to be oriented around their little neighborhood groups. But still there remained a strong feeling of obligation to them. Society in a larger sense was regarded as a rather unfortunate growth, and the villager entered it with caution and often misgivings.

In the various social organizations there was a tendency for people to form cliques with their relatives or others from the same community, and the same held true in political parties. Young men coming to work in Tokyo went for aid to seniors from their native villages. In companies, official bureaus, and even in schools there were tight organizations of persons born in the same village. In the last instance, the tendency was strengthened by the fact that the former provincial rulers sometimes financed local foundations to sponsor the education of children from their districts. In Tokyo, boys from the same rural vicinity often collected in the same dormitory, and occasionally one found two separate buildings for towns removed from each other by only a small distance. Lingering ties with the village birthplace contributed a rather unique feature to life in the new metropolis.

Chapter Four

THE FAMILY

1. THE WEAKENING OF CLAN CONSCIOUSNESS

a. Cooperation within the Clan

ONE of the important differences between the villages and cities during the Meiji period was that in the former large clans functioned as such, while in the latter the single family was the social unit. The urban family was often friendly with its cadet branches or in-laws, but there was little cooperation in vital matters.

In ancient times the clan connection was firm, and the classic pattern was for a family to secure its position through cooperation with other families of the same blood strain. Since the development of Japanese social life was sluggish, this remained the rule for many centuries. Nevertheless there were changes from time to time and in varying localities, and the general effect was to reduce the significance of the clan to individual members. Presumably villages were first organized by single clan groups, but by the Meiji period, there were almost no villages that centered around a single family; nearly all communities were composed of several familial groups, and even if there were only one clan in name, by this time it was a complicated organization comprising not only a main family and its branches, but also the families of servants or employees not necessarily related by blood.

In eastern Japan the aggregate of persons in the same lineage is frequently referred to with the word *maki*, but this term must originally have indicated a living tribal group. The reason for the change in meaning was that the mutual connection between family branches weakened to the extent that nothing like the original *maki* could actually be assembled. In some places the word is now used to refer merely to all the people in a community who have the same name. Thus, Ōkawa-*maki* would mean everyone in the village named Ōkawa, a group having no practical significance or function.

On the other hand, in other territories the *maki* is a group composed of a main family, its blood relations, the families employed by it, and all their relations, while in still other places *maki* refers to a group who work together at the same task. This suggests that whereas a *maki* comprising a family and its branches once worked as a single unit, the strong feeling of mutual dependence weakened to the extent that outsiders were taken into the labor organization.

During the modern period it became relatively simple to secure labor from outside the family. Various types of work were performed in cooperation with neighbors, and at times help was enlisted from laborers in nearby communities. There was no longer any necessity for the clan to rely on its own strength alone, and for this reason the *maki* lost its sense of unity. The head house, which had formerly held absolute authority, ceased to be able to exercise control over branch groups, and clan gatherings were confined to occasions such as an unusually large rice transplanting or the construction of a building. A great show of clan solidarity was often made at such times to help the main branch keep face, but even this came to be considered more troublesome to its beneficiaries than it was worth, since it involved their financing the conclave. Some of them began to refuse the obligation, and eventually great family gatherings occurred only when religious services to the family ancestors or ceremonies commemorating the death of some member made them necessary. In places where there was a tutelary deity to bind clans together, celebrations dedicated to that being tended to preserve something of the clan spirit, but after the last years of the Meiji period, when the movement to consolidate shrines took on force, obscure clan gods were largely forgotten.

b. Relatives and Persons of the Same Surname

The word *shinrui*, or "relatives," has become quite vague, but it is clear that among persons classed as *shinrui* there was in the past considerable exchange of labor. In the Kantō area and in what is now Nagano Prefecture *shinrui* were frequently called *yuishu*. This was generally pronounced *yuisho*, which now ordinarily means "lineage," and this is often considered to be its original meaning, but in the past it really indicated the group (*shu*) who belonged to a cooperative labor organization or *yui*. In the Tōhoku area, *shinrui* were known by the name *edoshi* or *edosu*, in which terms *e* is a shortened form of *yui*, and *doshi* and *dosu*, forms of the ordinary word *dōshi*, which means a comrade or fellow. Consequently, it appears that *shinrui* really indicated those who worked in the same cooperative organization. Whereas *maki* did not include in-laws connected through women, *shinrui* did, although it should be noted that in the case of a wife's relatives, the connection became more distant and had less practical meaning from one generation to the next—there were such saying as that "the in-laws on the mother's side split off after one generation."

Unlike townspeople, the inhabitants of farming villages set great store by common ancestral names or surnames. In 1870 all commoners were permitted to take surnames (*myōji*) and two years later it was forbidden to change them. Many people chose the ancestral name of an influential person in their district, and this led to problems in many communities. The popular judgment eventually came to be that the same surname should be taken only by persons united by blood or persons deriving their livelihood from the same plot of ground. In the towns the taking of surnames by commoners was entirely new, but in the villages there had frequently existed for some time a local appellation for separate houses or for the houses in a cooperative association or guild, and the adoption of a surname did not seem so novel. The word for the surname group, *myō*, meant the same as *maki* in some locations. There was a tutelary deity who was worshiped by all the members of the *myō*, and the mountain sacred to this god was called *myō-zan*. Annual gatherings of the families in the group were known as *myō-kō*, and a *myō-shin*, or "parent of the *myo*," presided on such occasions. The same person ordinarily took care of the shrine dedicated to the deity. The colloquial name for this group was the *myō-ji*, which has gradually come to be the ordinary term for "surname."

In earlier times *myō*, which literally means "young rice plants," was also customarily applied to a particular area under cultivation, and later to the families working such land collectively. In the middle ages the head of this group seems to have been called *myō-shu*, and in some villages the ancestral fields, which were under no circumstances to be abandoned, were called *myō-den*, a word used even in the Meiji era. In brief the tendency was for all persons working the same plot of land to take the same name. In some areas, for instance, the *maki* was spoken of as *jirui*, or roughly, "those of the same land," and in Yamanashi Prefecture those with the same surname were referred to with one of several terms meaning "common property," while in parts of Nagano Prefecture they were called the "land group." In certain areas the term for branch houses appears to have meant "land held in common," and in the northeast these were spoken of as *azechi* or *ajichi*, from *azeuchi*, meaning "within the boundaries of a field" and therefore indicating specifically the persons who worked on the same land. However, while these various words for clan relationships originally connoted cooperative work groups, people later lost the collective view of the land that had held such organizations together, and eventually the early meanings were forgotten.

Originally when a member of a family moved into a separate residence, he took a new name. Thus, even ancient court nobles of the same ancestral name took new appellations when they lived separately. To be sure, when first sons of nobles moved to far away places, they took the names of their original families with them, and members of the warrior class tended strongly to do the same, but more distant branches of the family adopted new names as they saw fit. In periods when there was a need for the clan to join forces to face a crisis, there was actually some advantage in giving the same name to all branches, but pride usually prevented old clans from spreading their names and the authority that went with them all over the countryside. In the Tokugawa period the shoguns, trying to strike a happy medium, gave a variety of new names to their close relatives, but called all of their distant connections by the name Matsudaira. As all this indicates, the concept of family names was so confused when the Meiji government permitted everyone to have a surname that there was no rhyme nor reason to the names that were subsequently adopted.

In some areas people had nothing that resembled a surname, and there was considerable confusion when the time came to select one. A family that had no special genealogical connections as a rule took the name, or a revised form of the name, of some family that had patronized it. In extreme cases people requested temples or official bureaus to give them names. Curiously, however, no particularly startling new names were thought up. Most often the selection reflected social relationships in the locality involved.

Branch families or servants and farmers under the direct control of a head family usually took its name. As the Meiji period advanced, however, the historically servile classes became more independent and conscious of their rights, and many of them came to dislike having their masters' surnames, but by then it had become illegal to change names, and their requests for special permission to do so were not readily granted. Consequently there was considerable discontent on this score. The various incidents that arose in connection with such matters illustrate the decline in group consciousness on the part of branch houses and former retainers.

2. THE DECLINE OF FAMILY OCCUPATIONS

a. The Freedom to Choose One's Work

The loss of a common faith was no doubt one of the large reasons for the weakening of the clan group, but it was not nearly so important as the fact that families ceased to hold land in common and work it cooperatively. This latter development was spurred on by the recognition of the individual's right to choose his own work. Obviously, no matter how intimate the members of a family were, if they all had different work, they soon had less occasion than otherwise to act as a group. Actually, getting new work usually meant leaving the village and taking up a new life in the city. Thus even the intimacy that arose from physical proximity was destroyed.

It required great determination to leave the land on which one's ancestors had always lived and move to a new location. Those who did so were fired with hope for an easier and happier life than they had had in the country. Unfortunately, they rarely had the training needed by anyone going to an entirely new place to live. The education that had been offered in rural areas up until this time was extremely narrow, and it provided no hints as to how one might adjust oneself to a society of unfamiliar people. In fact, it produced people to whom " society " was no more than their own village. They were oriented only to that, and it was tremendously difficult for them to accustom themselves to an urban milieu.

At the same time a young man with enough ambition to go

to the city was usually by no means the village idiot, and too he was not living in this modern age of over-populated cities. He had a relatively good chance of finding suitable work and considerable hope for rapid success. On the other hand, for that very reason many young men of the period failed to exercise proper care in choosing their work and ended up with jobs suited neither to their nature nor to their upbringing. In the city, a country boy might become a hired man in a shop, an apprentice to a tradesman, an office boy, or a factory worker, but he could be sure that in any occupation he would have to work long and hard for small pay. Boys other than those employed in factory work frequently managed after a time to set up shops of their own near their former employers and in turn called new helpers from the country. One consequence of this was that today in many urban sections merchants and tradespeople from one particular rural district dominate.

Thanks to the rise of modern industry, those who went to work in factories or mines were particularly numerous. Under the cruel working conditions of the time, they soon became seasoned workers with superior technical ability, but there were few who could stand up under the strain permanently. As a rule, such laborers were transients, as were a number of young people who went into house service for a set period of time. No matter how long they stayed in the city, they would eventually return to their villages. While away, they figured in the finances of their family, but were unable to participate in its work. In the event that their people were farmers, this caused much difficulty, because there arose the uneconomical situation of families with plenty of children of their own having to hire outsiders to do the farm work. Many country people were very disturbed about the possible affect of current trends on the future of agriculture.

b. The Deterioration of the Family

It became difficult for the family to maintain the character of a single work group. Instead of producing together, they simply consumed together, and as a result the bonds between them tended to weaken and break. People had to think consciously about the ethics of family relationships to keep them from falling into disuse. The rules taught in Meiji period ethics courses for conduct within the family would have been entirely superfluous in the previous age, before the family ceased to be a work unit.

Members of the landowning classes began to give their children and younger brothers a higher education in order that they might seek prosperity on their own. Even small landowners and owner-cultivators frequently sent younger sons to normal schools and had them become teachers. Many farmers also began to relegate all farm and house work to hired help instead of dirtying their own hands with it. Thus in numbers of villages there came into existence a class of families who were ostensibly farmers but who actually were not. These people did not always live sumptuously, but as long as they did not undertake risky new enterprises, they were secure. Some of them by virtue of their property and education became postmasters or doctors, and in such cases, we might note, they often built houses that differed architecturally from the ordinary farm dwelling.

As time went on, there were more and more persons in the villages who had no actual connection with the land. As a rule, they were small shopkeepers or persons who had returned from working in the cities. Many villages became saturated and were unable to re-absorb those who had left with the intention of returning. In particular, there was a tendency to avoid receiving youths who had become tradesmen back into the fold. Under the circumstances, it would seem as though these persons might have settled down to city life and attempted to take an active role in the improvement of their new environment, but comparatively few did. Most of the ones who had planned from the first to return were slow to take root in the city. They tended to rely in the final analysis on their village group.

Actually those who did not quite succeed in the cities usually did more for their native villages than those who did, no doubt because of the half-conscious notion that they would some day go back to the old home town to live. One often heard that a group of city dwellers from such-and-such a rural community had made a contribution to their old grammar school or paid for having the village shrine repaired. Furthermore, it was such persons who were most willing to help newcomers from the country. Among them, the managers of shops were most numerous, those who had made names for themselves as military men or scholars not usually having much interest in such matters. There were so many public bath operators who took in young people from their home towns and put them to work scrubbing the customers' backs or tending fires that villagers sometimes complained of losing their farm hands to the bathhouses of Tokyo and Osaka.

Many, having had their hopes shattered in the city, were forced to return and live on the good will of their fellow villagers. At first, these persons, far from being welcomed back, were objects of scorn, particularly if their parents had already died. Country people, however, usually ended by arranging for them to make some kind of living. On the other hand, villagers took an attitude of resistance toward those who had made their mark and then returned to live in their old home. It was usually complained surreptitiously that for people who were well off, they were remarkably stingy.

During the Meiji period, villages came to include a number of different elements, and this was usually the case with individual families as well. Brothers went their separate ways, and consequently thought differently about things in general.

Young men who had come to the city and accumulated a certain amount of culture suffered deeply from family conflicts, particularly when the time came for them to choose wives. Frequently they clashed directly with their people in the country, but it was not such a simple matter to leave one's home for good and take up residence in the city with a bride of one's own choosing, for that involved the establishment of a new tradition that would give meaning and security to urban life. During this age the philosophy of success haunted everyone, and of course, the persons that a young man wanted most to dazzle with his achievements were the people of his home town. Even if he lived in the city he could not forget about the country, because something called the "honor of his family" was always tugging at him. This was especially true of youths from poor but respectable samurai families, who felt it their duty to their ancestors at least not to be beaten. Many of these boys actually bore terrible hardships to bring glory to their family names, and though some of them regarded this as unjust to themselves, they usually preferred it to making a head-on resistance against the tribe. In Shimazaki Tōson's novel *The Family*, there was talk of breaking up the old-style family group, but in fact there was little that could be done about the existing situation, and such suggestions were purely academic.

3. PARENTS AND CHILDREN

a. The Words *Oya* and *Ko*

Nowadays the words *oya* and *ko* mean "parent" and "child" in the strict sense, but in the past they did not always denote a direct familial connection. *Ko* was used in farming and fishing villages to mean an individual person, and particularly one who was able to work. It signified something on the order of "hand" as in the English expressions "farm hand" and "boat hand." Similarly *oya* had a number of meanings other than that of father or mother. It was often used, for instance, of persons who gave their names to children or sponsored them in coming-of-age ceremonies, not only because the position of such persons was analogous to that of the parent, but also because there were lingering traces of an ancient social organization, transcending matters of birth, in which the *oya* was the head of a work unit and the *ko* its members.

Accordingly, there are many examples in which *oya* and *ko* were used in referring to relatives or *shinrui*, who, as has been pointed out, constituted a labor unit. Specifically, the leader of this group was the *oya*, and all other persons *ko*. This relation was more important in historical times than that established by birth, and a number of special terms were invented for the latter. In old documents, for instance, we find such words as "parent by birth" (*umi-no-oya*), and "children by birth" (*umi-no-ko*), which sound anomalous today. As the clan ceased to work as a unit, the old meanings of *oya* and *ko* were lost, but extra-familial connections of the same sort were quite frequently established. Individuals who felt insecure when deprived of clan protection sought new foster parents, and those in a position to become foster parents sought protégés to strengthen the ranks of their families. The tendency toward forming such relationships was still pronounced in the Meiji period. In many instances the actual parent attempted to find for his child a second father who was better able to guarantee the child's future. Nor was the foster relation exclusive. People took new "parents" throughout their lives—even landlords were known by that name.

The question of choosing a foster parent, now ordinarily referred to as an *oya-bun* or *oya-kata*, was solved in various ways according to the locality. In some places it was customary to choose the scion of a well-known house, while in others people called upon uncles from one side of the family or the other. With the passage of time, requests by the weaker party tended to become the more frequent, but many men of high standing were by no means averse to accepting a large number of protégés. During the modern period their economic motives, that is to say, the desire to secure a steady labor force other than their own children, virtually disappeared, but often they continued to feel a need for underlings to enhance their fame, to comfort them in their old age, or merely to crowd their funeral procession. Men with political ambitions often maintained such protégés to facilitate vote-getting.

The relationships between oya-kata and ko-kata, as the foster child is called, often pyramided. In one village near the Sea of Japan a certain oya-kata who had a number of ko-kata was himself a ko-kata of a wine merchant in a neighboring town. When the latter was busy, the smaller oya-kata sent his underlings to help. A story in Ibaraki Prefecture has it that when a certain man brought up in a farming communtiy visited an influential person in a nearby town, the latter immediately recognized him as a foster grandson.

One unusual type of foster relationship was formed when a soothsayer or priest was asked to guard over the fortunes of a newborn child, as was often the case. The connection was life-long, and the child not only visited his spiritual protector on annual holidays, but also invited him to be present on important occasions, such as the opening of a business enterprise. In many places when a child was born in a year that was considered unlucky to the parent, the latter would ostensibly abandon the infant at a crossroad and have him picked up and returned by another person, who thereupon became a foster parent to the child. Parents who had little luck in bringing up children frequently asked someone else to take charge of a newborn child, and this custom exists in southern Kyūshū today.

Whether the request for a foster parent was directed at obtaining spiritual or economic protection for a youth, the practice indicates that even in modern society it was difficult for a Japanese to be an independent individual. Such being the case, the adoption of the electoral system, based on modern Western individualism, brought on a number of evils. The tendency among voters was to reflect the views of those on whom they depended. Political parties spoke in terms of "solid constituencies," which were in essence an insult to the voters, and took full advantage of their influence over their *ko-kata* to secure elective offices. Foster relationships were such a strong institution in provincial areas that it was possible for a candidate for the Diet to predict just how many votes he would gather in each in district, whether he knew the minor ramifications of his organization or not. This situation prevailed even after the election law was expanded to include all adult males.

b. Distribution of Labor by *Oya-kata*

Although labor organization based on the relationship between *oya-kata* and *ko-kata* largely disintegrated in the Tokugawa period, it survived into the modern age among certain kinds of laborers. It was especially pronounced in the case of stevedores and dock workers, and any effort to establish progressive non-hierarchical unions among them ended only in a loss of efficiency. The men themselves avoided personal responsibility. They apparently liked the freedom from worry that came from entrusting their lives to someone else. Workers displaying this attitude were almost always men who had left their homes to find jobs. Away from their families they inclined to be entirely dependent on a protector, who might be thought of as a work-parent (a word meaning something of this sort, *shoku-oya*, was used among the coal miners in the northeast). As a rule, the latter was originally a person of some means who assisted newcomers to his community until they had gotten on their feet, but in the usual instance his status soon became that of a boss pure and simple, who decided which persons could be taken into the union of workers and what function each was to perform.

In the early Meiji, many types of city workers—among them barbers, dyers, noodle makers, restauranteurs, proprietors of *sushi* or *tempura* shops, butchers, bakers, bathhouse proprietors, drayers, male and female entertainers, and fishmongers—found it impossible to obtain work without the protection of a boss, and with the appearance of more modern trades, new bosses appeared to control them. Out of this institution grew offices that acted as modern employment agents.

The boss was in some cases called *heya* (room) and the word is still used in Tokyo in the very special society of *sumō* wrestlers. The organizations of bosses who controlled many gangs of carpenters were known as *ōbeya*, or large *heya*.

Thus, the earlier paternal system, in which groups of laborers were headed by foremen who actually directed work, was replaced by a new system in which a boss distributed the labor. As the society grew more modern, however, enterprises based on free labor sprang up, and the boss system weakened. The bosses saw to it that their men were provided with clothing and shelter, but they took a fairly large cut out of labor fees, and although this seemed natural to them, many workers of the new age determined to shake off the old bonds and throw themselves into the free market. In short, new types of labor rapidly led to a new system of labor distribution. The methods for making labor contracts were revised, and a standard wage system was established. Bosses lost their *raison d'être*, and only a few continued to maintain their power. These operated mostly in the fields of construction and mining, and their unscrupulous conduct became notorious.

4. FAMILY SUCCESSION

a. The Meaning of Family Succession

The person who succeeds to the position of a house is

usually called the *atotsugi* (the one who continues) or *atotori* (the one who takes charge afterward). The term *ōyakego* is also used on rare occasions, but *ōyake* is a term signifying the control of an entire clan, and *ōyakego* properly indicates only the person who is heir to the head of such a group. In the Meiji era the heir rarely assumed control of anything more than one small household.

Many terms connected with succession contain the element *yo*. For example, the head of the house is called *yonushi* (master of the *yo*), whereas the elder son is called *wakayo* (young *yo*), and branch families are called *yo-wakare* (divisions of the *yo*.) *Yo* ordinarily means "generation," but in the past it was also connected with the economic affairs of a family. Specifically, it seems to have indicated the yield from farming. When the crop was abundant, for instance, it was often said that the *yo* was good.

The people of the Meiji period considered the head of a house to be the person who held the family seal, and a man who had ceased to be a youth, but had not yet come into his inheritance was described as *imban-motazu* (not holding the seal). When the family affairs were actually handed over to him, which was usually in the first month of his predecessor's sixtieth year, the seal was imprinted on a folding fan, and the latter presented to him in a formal ceremony. It is important to observe, however, that in the past the heir did not gain exclusive rights, but divided them with his wife. In many instances, when the son received the seal, his wife was given the family rice ladle, which symbolized her share of authority. Just as her husband now took the seat at the hearth reserved for the master of the house, she took that reserved for the mistress. There were words such as *baoji* (old woman and old man) and *ojimba* (old man and old woman) that referred not to two individuals but to the pair as joint heads of the family. In many places the term *enushi* which means, component by component, "head of the house," was applied to wives.

This was not the case in the warrior class, where the Confucian principle of primogeniture was strictly observed. When the Meiji civil code was established, therefore, the question of joint or single succession rights arose. Ume Kenjirō, among others, urged that popular customs be followed, stressing that this would give the law greater force. The majority of the legal committee charged with writing the law, however, agreed with Hozumi Yatsuka that "the customs of farmers are not to be made general customs—instead we must go by the practice of samurai and nobleman." Hozumi even went so far as to argue that the customs of ordinary people were not really customs at all. In the end instead of adopting the usage of the people, the committee gave absolute rights to the first son, specifying that they included control over "the family genealogical record, the burial ground, and the implements used in ceremonies."

Nevertheless, the civil law was not completely binding in actual practice, and custom remained important. In the places where the latter changed, the revision came not as a result of the new law, but from changes in social conditions. The wife in a farming family played a large role in production, and her position commanded respect. On the other hand, in the households of modern laborers and salaried men in the cities, the wife was often reduced to the position of cook or kitchen-hand, and her authority accordingly decreased. She came to occupy a position similar to that of wives in the military class of earlier times.

Each Japanese clan carried on religious ceremonies as a group, and the worship of ancestors tended to strengthen family ties. Even after clans were atomized and the worship of the tutelary deity came to be regarded most lightly, clan action in this respect remained more common than in economic matters. The right of conducting ceremonies belonged to the head of the chief family in the clan. There were no special ceremonies for succession to this right since it was not passed from one person to another but remained a prerogative of the head of a particular family. Apart from clan deities, there were household gods such as the god of the furnace, who watched over individual families. The worship of these, along with offerings to the Buddha, came within the province of the mistress of the house, and for that reason she was in some places called the " stewardess of the furnace," (*kamado taifu*). Again there was no special ceremony for the inheritance of this ritual prerogative.

b. The Meaning of Adoption

In examining the population registries of remote islands, one often comes upon the term *yōshi*, or " adopted son," and in many instances it appears that the *yōshi* was adopted into a family already having a son. Nowadays it is generally assumed that adoption exists for the purpose of securing an heir when there is no true one, but in earlier times this was not the case. As the organization of the clan grew lax, the heads of houses not only established foster relationships, but also actually adopted young men to increase their labor force. In 1878 a compilation entitled *Zen Kokumin-ji Kanrei Ruiji* (*Customs of People throughout the Nation*) carried the following statement concerning Keijō County in the province of Echigo (Niigata Prefecture) : " The word *yōshi* is not used. Whether an adopted boy is the bridegroom of a daughter or not, he is referred to as the *muko* (a term which ordinarily means ' bridegroom '). He may or may not succeed to the family capital. At times he is simply used as a servant in the house into which he is adopted." The method of questioning on which this book was based was faulty, and it is not a completely reliable guide to contemporary customs, but at least it appears from this that in the area in question young men were adopted specifically to work. Adoptions of this sort were common in the military class from medieval times, and there are many proofs that old military families consciously resorted to this method to ward off any decline in their strength.

In some places it was the practice for people to entrust weak children to families who were noted for their ability to bring up youngsters. This was true in the southern part of Kyūshū. In Kagoshima Prefecture, for instance, it was generally held that salt merchants were the most successful people in bringing up strong children, and the most frequent cases of adoption were those in which salt merchants became the new parents.

All this points up the fact that in former times arrangements for adoption were entered into fairly lightly. There were many cases in which the son or daughter of a poor family was taken in by a more fortunate one to look after children. These full-time "baby-sitters" were taught the profession of their adopted house, and when they grew up they established branch houses under its name. This type of adoption was actually more common in the country than the type directed at obtaining an heir.

In warrior families of the middle ages an adopted son was sometimes selected as heir when the true heir was too young to assume control, but in large well-organized clans this rarely occurred, since there was always a broad field of candidates for the position of intermediate heir. By "intermediate heir" we mean a person who acted on behalf of the true heir until the latter came of age. Frequently this guardian was a younger brother of the former master. In Sado and other places, when the successor reached the age of twenty-six the intermediate heir ceased to function. As a rule he and his wife were allowed a *shō* of rice each day, together with the privilege of farming any plot of ground they wished, but their children rarely succeeded as heads of the clan.

It seems to have been an unwritten rule that in order to be head of a house a man had to be married. Accordingly if an heir died before succeeding, a bride was chosen for his son, who then became the successor. The practice of making the husband of a daughter the adopted heir is really based on the same idea. When the true heir was young, but had a much older sister, the bridegroom of the latter was sometimes adopted as intermediate heir, ceding his position when the true successor came of age.

5. HOUSEHOLD ECONOMY

a. Attachment to Money

It is said that in the third decade of the Meiji period a foreign teacher in a Tokyo middle school aroused considerable excitement and scorn among his pupils by asserting that money was the most important thing of all. The students understood that money was important, but they considered it immoral to say so. In those days, even more than now, this was the general view. People in Tokyo seem to have maintained a special aloofness toward money, probably because in old Edo, despite the fact that society had been predominantly mercantile, government regulations had made it difficult to reinvest money accumulated. The tendency had been for those who had it to use it freely on the pleasures thought becoming to men of the world, and those who saved had been spoken of as idiots. The Edo feeling about money remained strong in the Meiji period, and even spread to rural areas to some extent.

At the same time there was widespread envy and hatred of rich people who as usurers oppressed the ordinary people, and they were frequently criticized as skinflints or misers. The poor for their part considered lack of money a virtue.

In the Edo area a person was expected to spend according to his means. Those who spent less were called stingy, and those who spent more were thought lacking in a proper sense of their status. As a rule the amount of money a man spent on marriages, funerals, or festivals was judged by rigid standards. Face, which ought to have had nothing to do with economic life, was in fact a governing factor therein. In small villages standards were even stricter than in towns. Even if a man in a rural community lost his money, he could not move to a smaller house or sell his property without creating a furore. He had instead to spend as much on social functions as before and try to conceal the fact that it was difficult. Old families had to keep up appearances until they absolutely collapsed, and this necessity made it even more difficult for them to recoup after a loss. Some moved from villages to towns for no other purpose than to escape their traditional obligations.

b. The Will to Save

In the days when Japanese society was centered around the production of rice and was forced to meet its own economic needs, the storing of surplus products was regarded as vital. In addition to laying away supplies for non-productive seasons of the year, it was important to store provisions against disasters such as famines, floods, or tidal waves, which might come at any time. Even after the beginning of the Meiji period, many farmers still felt the need for saving, and most villagers tried to purchase consumer goods as sparingly as possible. Actually, after 1881, farmers fell on extremely hard times, and it was out of the question for them to make unnecessary new purchases. Even those who had grudgingly sold their products to buy fertilizer lost their ability to do so. After 1890, however, the difficulties that had resulted from the depression more or less disappeared, and as a result of the increase in national demand, there was a stronger tendency toward the commercialization of agricultural products. Farmers were to a greater extent than before drawn into the commercial economy, and as a result their goods began to fluctuate in value with the market. Although for a time their situation looked brighter, in fact few of them managed to increase their income materially or to save much.

c. Difficult Times in Farm Economy

In Yoshida Shōzaburō's *Kinji Fukeiki Genin oyobi Kyūsai-saku* (*The Growth of Recent Hard Times and an Economic Policy*), there appeared the following statement:

In recent years because of the extreme poverty in rural areas, good simple people who up to now would not eat until their taxes were paid are having their property confiscated for a paltry sum. They are reduced to eating bran, millet, and barley mixed with vegetables, and in many cases the situation is so dire that the home has split up, and its members are starving. Those who live in the country see this all about them. At the moment the number of vacant houses for rent is increasing, and more and more persons are absconding from their communities. At the same time there are many who beg for government relief. All of this results from the current depression.

Officials of the central government made an investigation of the panic in agricultural communities and in 1885 issued a report entitled *Kyūmin Jikkyō Hōkokusho* (*Report on Conditions among Poverty-Stricken People*), which included many accounts of cruel hardship. In the northeast region of Aomori, crop failure was particularly serious, and farmers were eating biscuits made of ground unhulled buckwheat, while in some places the diet was fried unhulled fodder. Even this food was used up by April or May, and seventy or eighty per cent of the country people were living virtually like animals. It was pitiful beyond words, said this account, to see farmers gathered around a tiny fire to ward off the bitter cold and sighing about miserable conditions. There were similar reports about Akita Prefecture, while in Ishikawa Prefecture the situation was rendered more serious by a money panic that affected samurai as well as merchants, farmers, and tradespeople of the middle or higher classes. The more charitable of the richer houses were constantly busy doling out money and providing rice gruel for the unfortunate.

In Fukui Prefecture, fishing communities were suffering from poor catches, but at the same time the market price of fish was low. Many families were reduced to extreme poverty. For lack of quilts they slept on straw mats. They could not afford their own cooking utensils, and so when one family finished preparing its food, it passed the community boiler on to the next house. The following was written about prefectures west of Osaka : " Poor people who have exhausted their supply of rice or barley beg thin gruel from rich farmers and merchants to keep alive. Those who succeed in doing so are fortunate, for many manage to keep body and soul together only by eating grass, fungi, and seaweed. In the poorest territories even the edible grasses have almost disappeared."

The above conditions represent exceedingly hard times, and there may be some exaggeration in the reports, but farmers were besieged with the fear that at any time they might be reduced to such circumstances. Even in the latter half of the Meiji period, disaster visited area after area, and living conditions were often as bad as those described above. Nor was any outstanding relief policy forthcoming. The main help came from public-spirited rich farmers, who, basing themselves on actual experience in farm communities, provided guidance in farm management in the various districts. For example, they urged people to save the burnt rice in the bottom of the boiler, which if dried and put away would make better eating in hard times than the starch from bracken. This sort of information exerted considerable influence on the economic outlook of farm people.

The idea spread that in times of trouble those who had goods should give them to help the poor, and rich farmers saved particularly for this purpose. At the same time, relief from old and well-to-do houses came to be expected. The old families who were respected and spoken of as leaders all had the experience of providing for the needy at one time or another.

Chapter Five

TRAVEL

1. INDIVIDUAL AND GROUP TRAVEL

a. Travel in Groups

IN the past, people more often traveled in parties than alone, and as in Europe their journeys commonly had a religious purpose. Even in the Heian period so many groups went to pay reverence at the three shrines of Kumano that the pilgrims were likened to ants. In the middle ages religious pilgrimages became more popular, and as the hermit priests associated with that form of Buddhism known as *shugendō* gained in favor, groups of people going to their mountain temples and hermitages became a common sight. Until the late middle ages or early Tokugawa period most of the travelers were members of the upper classes, but gradually this ceased to be the case. Farmers in small communities began to organize mutual funds to sponsor pilgrimages to the shrine of the sun goddess at Ise, which replaced Kumano as the Mecca for pilgrims. During this epoch the traditional histories of many shrines and temples were written down and put into circulation, with the result that the scope of pilgrimages was broadened. Various religious centers became noted for specific benefits to be obtained by visiting them, and in the Tokugawa period there developed the practice of going around to a number of different places instead of limiting the goal to one shrine or temple. Extended excursions were made to the thirty-three famous temples of the western region or the eighty-eight sacred places of Shikoku. One gets the feeling that there was a genuine desire on the part of people who had been worshiping at one small local shrine to strengthen their faith by paying respect to the gods of other areas. At the same time, however, there was a tendency for the religious aspect of the journey to become less and less important. Travelers often made detours in order to see the sights of Kyoto or the ancient province of Yamato, and some went as far afield as Kotohira or Miyajima, both famous for their scenery.

In the Chiba Peninsula and other locales it was the custom for great crowds to make pilgrimages each year. When the white leggings and tinkling bells of the travelers appeared in a village everyone dropped everything and busied himself welcoming them. It was thought that a family would receive a blessing by providing free lodging for the pilgrims, and a good deal of trouble was expended in entertaining them. In return the travelers sang or danced for the hosts, and there was much fun for all concerned.

Among the pilgrims, young men and women of marriageable age, particularly the latter, predominated. The trips were in a way part of the social education that a young woman received before becoming a wife. As the religious meaning was lost, the pilgrimages became nothing more than trips in the ordinary sense. The coming of the railroad in the Meiji period made group travel of this sort even more fashionable. Inside the train the travelers, occasionally glancing suspiciously at lone passengers, had parties and carried on more boisterously than they would have ever dared at home. Being in a group, of course, gave them confidence.

Mutual funds organized during the Tokugawa period to finance trips to shrines deserve special attention, since they were an important social institution. There were Ise funds (*Ise-kō*; see Chapter 12) all over the country, and other less ambitious cooperatives in many local regions. As a rule, everyone contributed a certain amount, and those who were to go were chosen by lot. In former times every family in the locality

may well have joined in, but gradually the group came to include only a number of friends. Since each person contributed money, the organizations often had the same character as groups that banded together for purely economic purposes. One feature that most of the journeys had in common was that the shrine to be visited was that of a deity whose function was to insure a good crop or in some other way to aid farmers.

It was generally felt that when people separated themselves from the community and went off on a trip they would likely become lonely and weak. Consequently, when travelers returned it was the custom for those left behind to gather at the edge of the village and hold a feast to welcome them back to the fold. This remained true in the Meiji era, and even today little hills outside some farming communities are designated as places for such parties. While the pilgrims were away, other customs were observed in their homes. For instance, in the central part of Nagano, when a person went on a pilgrimage to Ise, his family placed a small straw effigy of him by the side of the well and bathed it each morning in order to purify his soul and protect him from harm. In many areas places were set daily at the dinner table for the absent members of the family. A trace of the feast held to welcome pilgrims back is found in the modern custom of gathering to meet children when they return from the trip they customarily take at the end of their primary schooling. In modern times, however, the welcome consists of little more than a few words of greeting. Indeed, nowadays journeys are regarded with such delight that it is difficult to imagine how seriously they were taken by people in the past.

Pilgrimages to distant shrines tended to weaken or alter the cults of local tutelary deities. People began to believe that it was better to worship a well-known deity than an obscure provincial one, and some local shrines were actually renamed for more famous deities in other parts of the country.

In the Meiji period many villagers considered that modern

transpoi ʻation facilities were for the use of city people only and continued to make their trips on foot or by boat. As a result they observed sights along the way more closely than present-day travelers, and what they saw increased their knowledge of the world and of the their fellow creatures more than the average trip today would.

b. Private Travel

So long as travel was accompanied by insecurity and difficulty, few ventured out on journeys alone. During the Tokugawa period, however, road conditions improved, and simultaneously quite a number of persons were relieved of the necessity of working at home to the extent they were free to go on leisurely trips about country. In some cases the travelers were men of lettes who wrote journals describing in some detail conditions among the people in the places they visited. A few even noticed local variations in customs and engaged in a sort of comparative research thereupon.

Ancient population records mention people who absconded from their homes, and a number of these must have become vagabonds wandering from place to place to seek food. We might note in this connection that the ordinary word for food, *tabe-mono*, seems to be related to the old imperative *tabe* which meant " give me," and the word for travel, *tabi*, may also have some connection. People did not always become mendicants because they were poor. Some, indeed, found begging a fairly remunerative profession. There is a saying to the effect that if one begs a living for three days, one can never forget the pleasure of a beggar's life, and we hear of mendicants who spoke of feeling better after going home for a bath and a change of clothing. Some were reputed to have had large sums of money and numerous underlings, with whose aid they monopolized certain areas.

In the Meiji period the beggars' ranks were swelled by

displaced farm personnel, who often banded together in groups of five or ten and went to the cities. In 1890 a beggar in Tokyo could go to around three hundred houses in an eight-hour day, and as a rule one house in ten would contribute one mill, so that the income for the day was three *sen*. Some mendicants established strongholds in parks and compelled passing trades-people to give them money, while others raided fields. There was an increasing number of temporary beggars, including many farmers reduced to such circumstances by a drop in the price of silk. The yield from begging was greater in rural areas than in the cities, and Yonezawa and Izu were said to be beggars' paradises. In certain places in the latter district it is said that a hundred came to each house in a year, extracting several yen in all.

During the Meiji era there was still a class of beggars called *hoito* who received money for casting lucky spells on the houses they visited. They were considered to be low-class prophets, in a sense. The word *hoito* is a corruption of *hogito*, from *hogi*, " blessing," and *to*, " man." Such people frequently showed up on New Year's Day or some other felicitous occasion. They usually circulated around in rural areas, but similar types were to be found on the streets of Tokyo.

Until recent times there were merchants who traveled alone from place to place distributing their wares. More often than not they had so little capital that they were forced to live from hand to mouth, and it paid them to be sufficiently good at talking to please the villagers with whom they dealt. In the process of carrying on their business, they passed on much information about other regions. They were considered liars, but actually there was little need for them to falsify.

One group of merchants, known as " the sages of Kōya," were in fact poor priests who went about with baskets of odds and ends which they sold for their sustenance. They were particularly famous for their laziness. Clothing merchants were similarly called " sages," though in this case the use of the word seems somewhat farfetched. Actually it was originally applied to religious devotees who went about begging for food and later broadened to include merchants. Many of the " sages," especially the priests, pronounced blessings on the houses of their customers, and some of them encouraged religious faith. Even when this was not the case, they acted as bearers of outside culture. In the province of Shinano, for instance, the merchant who sold sickles always held a meeting with the villagers on one evening of his visit and sang ballads or played *go* with them. In slightly more modern times merchants carried phonographs along and played new songs to attract customers. Village families gave these salesmen lodging, and in most places each merchant stayed at the same house on each trip. In brief, these travelers, in addition to bringing their merchandise, brought whatever else they thought the villagers would like, and this of course made them popular. Nowadays, unfortunately, they more often than not pay little attention to the customers' wishes and instead rely on high-preasure salesmanship.

Certain villagers in the mountainous central region made a business of coming to the coast to obtain fish, rice, and salt. They carried their goods in baskets tied with ropes and suspended from short clubs that resembled baseball bats. Some of them lugged as much as one hundred and seventy-five pounds at a time. In return for the salt and fish, they received a variety of inland products, notably hemp cloth.

Other lone travelers were ox or horse drivers who sold nothing and were entirely dependent on drayage fees. With the development of wholesale merchandising, these men were forced to hire themselves out to large dealers and live on what the latter chose to give them for their work. As trade routes expanded, it became impossible for one carrier to supply a given locality, and corriers began to be employed in groups. Water transport was carried on by boatmen who also worked on the orders of shippers, but who were allowed to do a little private trading on the side. Since the wholesaler or shipper could not actually oversee the final sales of his goods, the carriers, especially the boatmen, were given a degree of freedom in fixing the prices. Eventually, however, there appeared small local dealers who took charge of these transactions, and the drayman's role became less important. At the same time he gradually lost the privilege of taking along merchandise of his own.

In Japan, lack of territory and density of population prevented the development of caravans like those that moved across the Asiatic continent. In modern times even breeders of cattle ceased to lead their horses and oxen to markets, and wayside areas that had once been used for sleeping the animals en route almost disappeared.

In the Meiji era, the post stations that had been used by the Tokugawa government along the main highways fell into the hands of wholesale merchants, and fewer villagers were employed in the trade or loading operations that went on in them. This, of course, meant fewer jobs available to the young people in farming families. Vegetables were still carried from suburban communities into the cities, but otherwise merchants from the towns took charge of village trade. As a result, the inhabitants of rural areas lost an important contact with the outside world.

Among the old-style merchants there were those who with large sacks or buckets went from village to village buying up odds and ends. They usually had little money, and they were not respected by the villagers, but by the same token, since the customers paid little heed to the prices offered, the profit was considerable. The increased cultivation of silkworms after the middle of the Meiji period brought to the villages a series of merchants clad in tight-fitting white pants, who came with scales and writing equipment to buy up cocoons. These were in reality the former house-to-house buyers in a new role and costume.

After the bicycle was adopted, more merchants came to the villages, but comparatively few villagers took advantage of the new vehicle to commute to the towns. During the third decade of Meiji, there developed local organizations on the order of trade unions which attempted to reduce the number of merchants coming in from without, and this in turn separated Japanese villages even more completely from the outside world. The culture of the interior owed much to wandering traders, and the absorption of their enterprises by the cities, though perhaps necessary for national economic development, was certainly a loss from the point of view of social education in rural areas.

Aside from Buddhist missionaries, the first outsiders to enter farming villages were probably roving craftsmen, mostly blacksmiths and coopers. They were as a rule looked down upon by the farmers, but since they could do something that others could not, they were granted a certain type of respect. Among the folk tales in a number of villages today there are some that appear to have originated among these artisans, and they may therefore be regarded alongside the merchants as purveyors of culture. With the increase in village population during Meiji, however, most of them settled down in one place.

On the whole, during the Meiji period fewer outsiders came to villages than before, but certain localities which advertised especially for the purpose succeeded in attracting travelers. Around a number of famous scenic attractions and ancient remains there arose sightseeing communities linked by modern transportation facilities to the urban centers. Their success was often due more to propaganda than to actual superiority over other places, but another contributing factor was the promotion of hero-worship in history classes, which brought flocks of visitors to see the places where great statesmen or warriors had lived and performed their feats. Sightseeing trips became common, and enterprising persons began to make a business of them. This, of course, increased popular interest. In the Meiji thirties there appeared for the first time a guide to railroad and steamship travel. A new species of traveler also appeared. Clad in regular clothing, instead of the straw sandals, leggings, and tucked-up skirt of the past, he made no complaints as long as he got to his destination and back. Unlike his ancestors, he paid little or no attention to sights or local customs along the way.

2. SHORTENED DISTANCES

a. Roads and Bridges

During the Tokugawa period the roads on which the feudal lords journeyed to and from the shogun's court were comparatively good, and there were inns along the way. It was possible, therefore, to travel along certain routes with complete safety except possibly in one or two spots. (Even the foreigners who traveled along the eastern coast route at the end of Tokugawa period pronounced it an excellent road.) Nevertheless, there were very few villages and almost no vehicles, so that progress was slow. Aside from the main highways, moreover, roads were miserable, and lodging facilities so poor that one often had to resign oneself to sleeping in the open.

At the beginning of Meiji, when it rained in Tokyo the streets were like paddy fields. The government soon undertook to improve them, but at first all that could be done was usually to gravel them. In 1883 a mortar pavement was begun on the street in front of Babasaki-mon in central Tokyo, and the project was completed in the following year. Somewhat later the same street was repaved with concrete, but hard roads were not common in the city for many more years. As a rule the early streets were all lined with trees on both sides, but around 1871 or 1872 these began to give way to telegraph poles. Shortly afterward, however, there arose a movement to protect them, and the government not only adopted a policy to this end, but even planted new trees along some roads that had not hitherto had them. The impetus probably did not come from the government itself but from warnings from foreign advisers.

One of the changes that most impressed travelers in the new

age was the disappearance of government barriers along the highways. As a matter of fact, these blockades had already lost most of their real meaning by 1864, when the Tokugawa government undertook to quell the Chōshū rebellion. In 1867 there was an attempt to restore them and increase the government's powers of inspection, but in the first month of 1869 they were abolished altogether, and in the seventh month of 1871 the chancellery declared that passports from the various local administrations were no longer necessary for temporary residence or travel. This step brought complete freedom of travel.

In the Tokugawa period there were ferries on many of the great rivers lying across the chief highways, and in 1871 ferry service was even begun at the wide crossing of the Ōi River on the Eastern Coast Route, a famous ford since early times. In many places, however, bridges took the place of ferries. The most famous was a wooden one over the Rokugō River near Tokyo, built by farmers of Yawatazuka Village in Ebara County, who had been granted special permission to carry out the project. The government permitted the builders to charge a toll equal to the old ferry fare—three-tenths of a *sen* for a ricksha, and 6.25 *sen* for a horse and wagon—for the first fifty-two months to cover costs. This project was undertaken in about 1874, but by that time there were already steel bridges in some places. The first was constructed in 1869 in Nagasaki under the supervision of one Motogi Shōzō, and in the same year the Yoshida Bridge at Isezaki-chō in Yokohama was reconstructed of steel. At first the toll for crossing this latter structure was one *sen* for a horse and wagon and one-half for a ricksha. It is said that when a horse came onto the bridge a wicket was lowered while the driver and the bridgekeeper haggled about the price. The first steel bridge in Tokyo was constructed at Shimbashi in 1871. Between that time and some five years later similar structures were set up in several other places, but ferry boats continued to operate, and their captains, understandably annoyed

about the bridges, belabored the government with attempts to
the halt the construction of them. During the Tokugawa period
there was at the center of most bridges a little guardhouse and
a sentry who usually sold paper or odds and ends, kept a
watch on passers-by, and restrained persons attempting to
commit suicide by throwing themselves into the river. Around
1877 the watchmen were replaced by policemen, and only shortly
later boat patrols were introduced on the Sumida River in
Tokyo.

b. The Ricksha

One of the few inventions that Japan has given to the world
is the ricksha, said to have been perfected in 1870 by a man
named Izumi Yosuke and a few of his friends. Actually there
is no definite proof that Izumi Yosuke invented the machine,
and it is perhaps safer to assume that a number of people
devised it at around the same time. Its ancestry probably goes
back to certain hand-drawn vehicles of the middle ages, but its
immediate forerunner must have been the horse and wagon used
by foreigners in Yokohama. This supposition is corroborated
by the fact the earliest rickshas were wider than they were
long and had flat bottoms like those of wagons. When Izumi
Yosuke asked for permission to use the vehicle, he described
it to the Tokyo Metropolitan Government as follows:

It is a little seat in the Western style, mounted on
wheels so that it can be pulled about. It does not shake
as much as the usual cart, and it is easy to turn round.
It will not hinder other traffic, and since it can be pulled
by one person, it is very cheap.

The vehicle was an immediate success. By 1872 or '73 it
was to be seen in any town in the country, and it was soon
afterward exported to China. The following extravagant praise
was made by a Japanese:

We are happy beyond words that this invention of one

of our compatriots has spread to other parts of the world. In the fields of Musashino, where the miscanthus blossoms once billowed in the wind, a great imperial city has been built. Sea has been pushed back by land, and streets extend further each day and month. Our country has become a busy place to which even foreigners have come to reside. All this is due to the development of this vehicle.

In the modern view, to substitute a man for a horse could hardly be considered great progress, but in those times pull-horses were very expensive, whereas people were if anything too numerous. At first, the fare was a tenth of a silver tael per person per *ri* (=2.4 miles), and it was better to give a tip. People regarded the pullers very much as they had palanquin bearers of former times, and as a matter of fact most of them were just that. It may be noted, however, that among them there were members of the warrior class who had been reduced to menial labor. As time went on, various regulations were published for the control of pullers. They could not operate without displaying their numbers on their vehicles, their lanterns, and the back or collars of their jackets. The price was fixed, and it was forbidden to demand extra money for food and drink, or to go at full speed when old people, women, or children were in the streets. When two rickshas met, they were ordered to pass to the left.

At the very beginning of Meiji, people on the streets had been urged by the government to keep to the left. While the rule was not actually fixed in the case of pedestrians, it was often restated with reference to horse-drawn vehicles. Around 1874 it became the general practice for vehicles to take the middle of the road and pedestrians the edges, and in some places the lanes were separated by trees. Then, in 1906 the police ordered pedestrians to walk on the left, whether there was a sidewalk or not. The same command contained other general traffic regulations. It was forbidden, for instance, to allow children under four years of age to walk the streets alone. Fathers and elder brothers were exhorted to take care of the young. It was prohibited to walk on streetcar tracks or lanes intended for vehicles except to cross, and the public was asked to use extreme caution in jumping on or off trolleys. There were special rules for army personnel. When soldiers met an ordinary vehicle they were to go to the left like civilians, but when they met other soldiers, cannon wagons, or supply wagons, they were to go to the right. Actually, the latter seems to have been more in accordance with the ancient Japanese practice.

After the Restoration there was a great deal of traffic between Tokyo and Yokohama, and, alongside horse-drawn carriages and small steamships, there appeared on this route large rickshas capable of carrying several passengers. Those seating more than two usually had four wheels, and the seats were placed on the sides so that the riders faced each others. The passenger compartments had cloth roofs and curtains in the back and front. As a rule, one man pulled, and another pushed from behind. The going was very slow. In 1879 rickshas seating four or more persons were placed in operation in Aichi Prefecture, but since men and women rode together in them, they were criticized as bad for public morals.

At first there were colorful pictures on the backs of rickshas, painted with imported paints and looking rather like varicolored kites. The decorations were deemed too showy by many, however, and they were later replaced by plain colors or simple crests. On the handles of the carts there were little bells that tinkled gaily when the vehicle was in motion, and the puller often added his loud cries to the general din of the streets. In the beginning the wheels were of iron, but later they were covered with rubber, and eventually air tires were adopted. The vehicle was hardly ideal for distant hauls, but prior to the coming of the railroad, one saw it even on the little paths leading through rice fields deep in the country.

There were pullers who could travel from eighty to one hundred kilometers a day. At times, in order to increase their efficiency, the pullers worked in relay, or extra hands were added. In any event, the passenger reached his destination faster than he would have in one of the ancient palanquins. Presently, however, there appeared horse-drawn buses, and in some places railroads, and the ricksha was soon confined to the cities and the areas around railroad stations.

In 1872 there were around 56, 000 rickshas in Tokyo, 16, 412 in Osaka, and 612 in Kyoto, while in 1883 there were 166, 659 throughout the country.

When the vehicle first appeared in Tokyo, the drivers would gather in groups of three or four to wait for customers and, in good Japanese fashion, raise a flag bearing words that begged pardon for their existence. Their lanterns carried a similar inscription, and when they moved along the streets they often screamed apologies to the people they passed. Their manner was rather grand, but it evidently failed to impress. Customers were so rare that the price was outlandish. A person going only a few kilometers had almost to pay the puller's wage for the day. For a time the pullers were the butt of many jokes by palanquin bearers, but as streets improved, there were more and more passengers, the price came down, and eventually the ricksha business flourished to the point indicated by the figures given above.

The life of the ricksha man was not easy. There was a song which went roughly: " I pull this cart because I have no money and not enough brains. I don't hate anyone, and there is no reason for me to resent my lot." If the puller did not step lively, he was apt to go without customers, and as more and more people depended on this means of transportation, the competition became fierce. The most envied puller was he who was in the regular employ of a kind master. Such fortunate ones received in 1901 from five to seven or eight yen per month in addition to their food. Some of them were even given a little house next to the garage for the ricksha. It had long been the custom for rich men to take along flunkies to carry extra footgear or attend upon them in other ways. Now these hired men took on the task of pulling the ricksha.

Among the ordinary pullers working on the street, some were connected with large garages and others were independent. The former always carried on the backs of their vehicles flags which bore the marks of their garages, together with the number and position of the ricksha therein, so that persons who forgot something when leaving the vehicle could easily trace it. The independent pullers were frequently called "obscure drivers." The rivalry between them and the organized pullers might well have involved the same sort of violent conduct that had prevailed among palanquin bearers, but it was effectively prevented by strict official regulation of prices. In the end customers were attracted to particular pullers not because they would give lower rates, but because they looked stronger or because their vehicles were better.

There were many improvements in the vehicles themselves. They were equipped with hoods that could be lowered when it rained so that the customer could remove his raincoat and ride in comfort. Also window grills were added to protect the passenger from the sun or conceal his identity. Vehicles of many various types were tried, including the ones mentioned above that allowed two or more passengers to ride together. Although these latter were devised as a means to accommodate customers, they soon lost their charm, since after all they were very slow. Furthermore, not many pullers felt strong enough to take them on.

In order for a ricksha coolie to obtain a place to wait for customers, he had to join an organization known as a *ban*, which consisted of a group who worked out of a particular stopping place. There were such gangs at various places throughout Tokyo, always bearing the name of the locality where they worked. In order to enter one of them, the puller had to the contribute a bottle of sake and ten *sen* as an entrance fee and then ten *sen* per month afterward. The money was theoretically used to help members of the group who were prevented by illness from working, the *ban* being, in effect, a sort of labor union organized by the drivers themselves, but though at first funds may have been spent for the purpose stated, as time went on it more often went to buy food and drink for the healthy members.

Unaffiliated pullers were the more numerous. They led a very poor life, and while they occasionally belong to a *ban*, more often they simply roamed the streets looking for customers. Even in the evening when the gaslights began to shine the wheels of their cabs could still be heard. Few of them owned their own vehicles. Most of them rented one for a sum known as the " price of tea," or *chadai*, and the poorest of them even rented the jackets and breeches that they wore. In 1897 the daily *chadai* was ten *sen* for the best rickshas, eight for the middle class, and six for the cheapest. At this time the average income of pullers was about fifteen *sen* per day. As a rule the return was best in January, April, May, and December, and worst in February and October. In 1893 the daily income for pullers in Osaka was only about eighteen *sen*, and the wear and tear on the vehicle amounted to two or three *sen* each day. As a matter of fact the rickshas in Osaka were smaller and older than those in Tokyo, and the Osaka coolies looked weak and bedraggled. A person had to be in serious need to hire them.

c. Horse-drawn Buses

The Japanese first recognized the value of the horse and buggy when foreigners introduced it at the end of the Tokugawa period, and in the early Meiji period this useful vehicle was often to be seen on the road between Yokohama and Edo. Eventually a group of Japanese opened a horsecar service between

Yokohama and Hakone, charging one silver tael for a two-horse, and one-half tael for a one-horse, vehicle. Later the service was expanded. Just after the Meiji Restoration there were apparently even two-story buses, but in 1874 these were outlawed as unsafe. Even in the heyday of the ricksha, travelers on the Tokyo-Yokohama route preferred the buses, since they charged only 75 *sen* for the trip, which was much less than a ricksha would have been. A two-horse vehicle usually seated seven or eight.

Passengers in no special hurry rode on steamboats, which were even cheaper than the horsecar, but merchants from going from Tokyo to Yokohama were often so pressed for time that they hired special carriages at higher rates. In Tokyo there were commercial stables that kept sixteen or seventeen horses each and had branches in Yokohama. In spite of temporary prosperity, however, when the railroad was opened over this route, the horse-and-carriage business collapsed. The same was true of the Tokyo-Yokohama steamship lines, except that the latter continued to be used for transporting luggage.

At about this time the Bureau of Transportation and Communication, in order to facilitate interchange between Tokyo and Takasaki, engaged the services of the Postal Horse and Carriage Company, which subsequently carried passengers and ordinary cargo as well as the mail. The development of the textile factories in Tomioka owes much to the opening of this route. The fare for one person from Tokyo to Takasaki was 2. 75 taels. Passenger buses were put on the line between Tokyo and Utsunomiya in 1879, and in general the horsecar was an important means of interurban transportation in the Kantō region until the spread of interurban railroads. Even afterward, it was adopted for intraurban transportation. In 1872 horse-pulled buses began operating between Shimbashi and Asakusa, charging one *sen* per horse. Drivers sounded bugles to attract customers. Later buses were placed on the road between Shinagawa and Shimbashi. In 1877 the line from

Asakusa to Shimbashi is said to have taken in 100 yen per day rain or shine. Horsedrawn buses, however, were doomed by the opening of the Tokyo electric railroad in 1899.

Another famous sight of Meiji-period Tokyo was the horse-drawn streetcar. A petition to operate such vehicles was submitted a few years after the Restoration, but refused because of the crowded condition of the streets. In 1876, however, the lanes for pedestrians and horses on the road between Shimbashi and Manseibashi were separated, and in 1880 permission to operate rail cars along this route was granted. Operation began in 1882, with six cars running between Shimbashi and Nihombashi. At the very beginning there sometimes arose occasions on which an outbound car met squarely with an inbound car on the single track, and a good deal of time was wasted while the horses were switched to the opposite ends and both cars pulled away. The word *shashō*, which is now used to mean " conductor," was first used of the conductor on the horse-drawn streetcar.

d. Railroads

Of the new transportation facilities, the one that most impressed people with the shortening of distances and had the greatest influence on Japanese life and society was the railway. Aside from astounding travelers with the new ease of traveling, it called forth people who had never even wanted to go anywhere and carried them off to great distances. One train passenger might think to himself how difficult his journey would have been if he had walked, but more often than not the person beside him would be thinking that if it were not for the train, he would never have come at all.

A very small number of Japanese knew about railways from books and pictures even before the Meiji period, but there was virtually no one who thought they could be laid in Japan. In the early years of Meiji, foreigners suggested building them,

but the work was too difficult for the government in its finan
cially weak state. For a time there was a plan to set up an
experimental line on the route between Osaka and Kyoto, but
as it turned out the first line was constructed between Tokyo
and Yokohama. At the outset the project caused a considerable
uproar. It had to be financed by a loan of one million pounds
from England, and many people considered that to borrow this
money was simply a way of selling the country to a foreign
nation. Others feared that to build railroads would only add
to the convenience with which a foreign power might invade
Japan, and still others, while recognizing the need for trains,
thought that the time was not yet ripe. Even after construction
was begun, there was heated opposition, and a group within
the army actually tried to prevent the necessary surveying of
land. Thanks to the efforts of statesmen like Ōkuma Shigenobu
and Itō Hirobumi, however, the object was eventually accomplished. In May, 1872, the line between Yokohama and Shinagawa was opened, and in August of the same year, service was
extended from Shinagawa to Shimbashi. As a rule there were
three trains going each way in the morning and three in the
afternoon. An Osaka-Kyoto line was begun in 1876 and opened
in the following year, since which time railroads have virtually
covered the country.

Accordingly to the November, 1872, edition of the *Tokyo
Nichinichi Newspaper*, if one wanted to go from Yokohama to
Tokyo to see a play at the Morita theater, one wired for
reservations at eight in the morning, got on the train a few
minutes later, and arrived at about nine, the journey having
consumed a little less time than coming from Kanda, which
was much nearer. Also, the paper said, the speed with which
the evening train returned to Yokohama was thoroughly marvelous. In June, 1873, the *Shimbun Zasshi* recorded that one
lady in Yokohama put her children to bed, went to a pawn
shop in Tokyo, transacted her business, and returned home all
in the space of two hours. The children slept through it all.

More and more people expressed their amazement at the speed of the so-called land steamers, although by present-day standards they did not go very fast. A story that illustrates the feelings of the day appeared in the *Tokyo Nichinichi Newspaper* for February 28, 1873. It seems that a man and his wife boarded the five o'clock train at Shimbashi Station, but in the rush lost their two-year-old child. They were frantic, but the train was by this time flying "like a bird." The instant it arrived at Shinagawa the man jumped off and told his story to the official in charge. The latter wired to Shimbashi, where a search producted the missing infant. Immediately a reply came to Shinagawa, and the father and mother, dancing for joy, got off and waited for a gentleman from Shizuoka Prefecture to deliver their offspring. It was, the paper said, as though the dead had returned. In a trice the government and its marvelous enlightenment had brought the lost child back to safety. The account overflowed with eulogies on the shrinking of distances that had resulted in this happy ending.

After the railroads opened, people crowded into Tokyo to see its famous sights and festivities. Often the travelers were less pleased than the couple who recovered their child. According to the *Tokyo Eiri Newspaper* in 1881, the annual festival at a famous temple in the district of Ikegami was such a hit that trains plied between Shimbashi and the station nearest Ikegami until 2 : 30 in the morning. A group of three passengers, foreseeing that the third-class car would be jammed, decided to spend the extra fare for second-class passage, but in the general confusion an overflow from the third-class section crowded in on them, and they were sorely angry. They screamed at the conductor all the way to their destination, but it did no good.

In 1874 the number of passengers between Shimbashi and Yokohama was 1, 438, 417, and the fares collected totaled ¥ 441, 000. 657. By 1875 the figures rose to 1, 732, 613 passengers, while the fares fell to ¥ 393, 749. 025, of which ¥ 1, 244. 35

was taken from people who went farther than their original ticket called for. The passengers of those days liked to enjoy themselves on the trains, and there was considerable noise and bustle in the cars. Sometimes dignified gentlemen arose to make political speeches and, when the train officials attempted to stop them, refused to yield on the grounds that freedom of speech was their privilege so long as they were not infringing upon the assembly laws. There was, of course, a good deal of miscellaneous talk among passengers, and some of it was entertaining or interesting enough to find its way into magazines and newspapers.

On the Tokyo-Yokohama line there were at first no toilet facilities, and those who could not wait until they arrived at a station were forced to relieve themselves out the window, but in 1873 a fine of ¥ 10 was enacted to prevent this. There are a number of ribald stories concerning infringements of this rule, such as, for instance, one about determining the fine for merely breaking wind (¥ 5), but as train lines were extended, it became necessary to install lavatories, and in 1889 they were provided in third-class cars on the Tōkaidō Line. At first they were in the middle of the car and had entrances on either side. Unfortunately, most of the passengers thought it wrong to use the toilet while the train was in progress, and when it came to a station there was always a mad rush, with the result that the tracks in the stations were filthy beyond description. People were therefore requested specifically to use the toilet only when the train was moving, and if possible at places remote from houses and villages. At first passengers in the first and second class cars were given hot-water bottles in the winter, but only at night. In 1903 steam heating was installed. The development that called forth the most approval of all was the opening in 1889 of the line from Shimbashi to Kōbe. The trip took about 12 hours, and people often marveled that one could look at the flowers by the Sumida River in the morning and those at Arashiyama, outside Kyoto, in the evening. With the extension of railway lines, there arose the problem of eating along the way. Around 1905, an organization called the Union of Lunch-box Salesmen on the Tōkaidō Line gained the privilege of running a dining room on the train. They soon were able to advertise that they served a full meal of soup, vegetables, rice, and pickles for only 20 *sen*. On New Year's Eve the dining cars on express trains made very special arrangements to serve the customary New Year's breakfast for the price mentioned.

There were many persons who used the trains to commute over short distances. Travelers from Shinagawa to Yokohama became so familiar with each other that they organized a commuters' club, and similar groups soon appeared in other locales. They often had parties or picnics together.

e. Bicycles and Automobiles

The bicycle, although less conspicuous than the railway, produced as many changes in national life, if not more. It was not entirely new, of course. Pictures of it had come to Japan during the Tokugawa period, and primitive wooden models had been constructed, but they had been used only for amusement. In contemporary wood-block prints, one occasionally sees a three-wheel vehicle for one person, which was propelled by means of stick. In 1876 a house called the Yamamoto near Ueno Park in Tokyo allowed customers to take a short ride on a machine of this sort for 1. 5 *sen*, and in 1879 a shop renting regular bicycles at two *sen* for ten minutes was opened in Akihabara. Apprentices off duty and other passers-by vied for the privilege of borrowing the vehicles, and the proprietor made a cosiderable profit. Somewhat later people were organizing bicycle clubs that rather resembled modern golfing societies. Students in school, it is said, neglected their studies to ride on bicycles, and in some places the vehicles were banned as pernicious. The serious-minded were especially concerned over young women students who took riding. No doubt the sight two or three young things flying by on two-wheelers, the long sleeves of their kimonos trailing in the wind, must have caused many an old-timer to lift his eyes to heaven in despair.

Still, in 1904 the sports society of Japan Women's University incorporated a riding section, and there were twelve or thirteen girls at that college who rode, along with seven or eight at the College of Music and a like number at the Toranomon Women's Seminary. Actually the bicycle riders were mostly people of the leisured class, but presently they were joined by officials and others who found the vehicle useful in their work. At that point it began to be manufactured in Japan. In the beginning parts were made by individual producers and sent to a factory for assembly, but gradually manufacturers undertook to make the whole vehicle. Also there appeared even in rural areas shops specializing in repair or exchange of bicycles. As a result of efforts on the part of merchants, bicycle races or conventions were held in various places, and they invariably attracted numbers of sightseers.

Shopkeepers in towns began insisting that their apprentices learn to ride, but then had to devise ways of preventing the young men from loitering when they went off on long errands. Thanks to the new vehicle, the length of a day's journey was double what it had been, and one result was that people could work at greater distances from their homes. On the other hand, whereas there had formerly been inns or resting places at easy walking intervals along the highways, many of these were forced out of business. Doctors and midwives were quick to employ the bicycle, but it was not accepted by farmers until much later. After all, the latter lived near their daily work, and even if they did occasionally go to some other place, the roads on which they traveled would often have been impassable by wheel. Furthermore, farm implements and products were usually too bulky for such small vehicles. Still, farmers in suburban areas, who had begun to feel the need for going to town for purposes other than farming, began buying them, and after the introduction of bicycle railers, they came to be widely regarded as a necessity.

As one looks backs on Meiji manners and customs, one feels that the age was still a little early for the automobile, but in the latter years of the era it was imported. The first horseless carriage is said to have been brought from France in 1904 by a baron of the Mitsui family. Noblemen and rich people thereafter began to whiz about in cars and to consider it part of their education to learn to drive. By 1909 several women in high society were numbered among the "automobile ladies." Sumako, the wife of Ōhashi Shintarō flew about the town in a car covered with purple tenting, while Hideko, the spouse of Tamaki Suzutarō, was reputed to have been the champion of them all. She even participated in long-distance races. In a word, the automobile of this age was a toy of the bourgeoisie. It belonged to a different world from that of ordinary people.

3. TRAVEL BY WATER AND THE DEVELOPMENT OF HOTELS

a. The Decline of Water Transportation

When trains began to climb every day into the steep mountain recesses of the Japanese interior, river transport became virtually obsolete. Japanese rivers, which were for the most part rocky mountain streams with perilous rapids, were largely unsuited to navigation anyway, but before the Meiji period river traffic had prospered considerably. Boatmen had manipulated through the mountain gorges with amazing skill, and the relatively broad rivers of the coastal plains had been regarded as far more convenient than roads. Shipping along the Tone, the Sumida, and other rivers near Edo had been very active, and sightseeing by boat had been a popular pastime. Rice and other products gathered into Edo had frequently been delivered to outlying castle towns by river transport, and warehouses along the river banks had made a great profit handling cargo.

The steamship, which was imported before the locomotive, added zest to river traffic, but there were relatively few rivers where it could be used. In Tokyo, the steamer transport system on the Sumida and Edo Rivers was maintained until a comparatively late date, and the passenger ships on the Sumida were for a long time popular among city dwellers, but by and large the railroad took all the passengers away.

Before the Meiji period, sea routes were also an important link between different parts of the country. Shipping in the Sea of Japan was far more profitable than along the Pacific coast, and marine trade between the northern region and the Osaka or Edo districts followed this route. Even today in small northern villages on the Sea of Japan one finds faint traces of the prosperity that existed when the ships were running in nearby waters. In places like Sakata and Mikuni, which were famous as ports, people still remember the day when many ships lay in the harbor, and there are countless small coastal towns that once echoed the songs of sailors on shore for a good time.

The distance between ports lengthened, partially because ships improved to the extent that they no longer had to stop at the small ports, but mostly because the cargoes once carried by ships were now transported by rail. Even passengers disappeared. Until 1887 all passenger movement between Osaka and Tokyo depended on steamship, and short-distance travel in the west provided a livelihood for a great number of small ports along the Inland Sea. As movement became more rapid, however, many of these were virtually taken off the map. A number of industries that had shown signs of developing in coastal towns petered out, and the separation between the people of these communities and society in general became more pronounced. In the Japan Sea area, however, the steamship drew the cold northern region into national life, since the new ships were able to navigate all year, whereas sailing vessels had usually been forced to cease operation during the winter.

But by and large people and cargos ceased to travel on the waterways. River boats continued to transport rock and sand on the rivers of Tokyo, and people connected with this business sometimes lived in house boats. The authorities attempted to eliminate these latter, but though orders to abandon them were issued, other quarters could not always be provided, and they continued to exist.

b. Steamships

The first regular steamer transport was established between Edo and Yokohama by an American firm, but its ships had a number of accidents, and after a time it went out of business. In 1867 a group of wholesalers in Edo put a small steamship into operation on the same line, and afterward a number of similar companies were established. All of them were virtually ruined by the opening of the railroad between Shimbashi and Yokohama. More important was the regular passenger service begun in 1872 between Edo and Osaka by a company called the *Yūbin Jōkisen Kaisha*. This concern was an outgrowth of one that had handled mail in the Edo period and furnishes an interesting example of adaptation of old enterprises to new needs.

After about 1869 the government, in an effort to stimulate marine transport, encouraged companies to buy or make Western-style ships. In 1875, for example, the Mitsubishi Company was given a great sum of money and ordered to establish a school for the training of crewmen. In the same year the government turned over thirteen of its own steamships to the same company along with a yearly subsidy. As time went on, a number of other transport companies began to compete with Mitsubishi, and in 1885 several of them merged with it to form the famous *Nippon Yūsen Kaisha* (NYK). In western Japan, the development of steamships and port facilities was proceeding at a rapid pace, and by this time two-wheel steamers were running on the lines connecting Kompira, Shimonoseki, Nakata, Nagasaki, and the other harbors of that region.

All these lines provided eating facilities on the ships and bragged about their food in their advertising. As for prices, in 1875 it took only one and a half yen to go from Tokyo to Kōbe, and for as little as ten yen one could set out from the capital, take a jaunt around the Kyoto region and return with presents for the whole family. The steamship companies tried to impress people with the low cost of such trips in comparison with the high prices of the times.

Communication with Europe was at first monopolized by English and French ships, but in 1896 a ship belonging to NYK crossed the Pacific to Seattle, and once this feat had been accomplished, Japanese ships began to appear in other foreign ports. In the Meiji thirties lines were extended to London, Melbourne, San Francisco, South America, and other parts of the world.

When the Japanese travelers of the late Tokugawa and early Meiji periods had gone to America and Europe, their leave-taking had been as though they were going to their death. Only an intense desire for knowledge about foreign countries persuaded them to take the risk. Now, however, travel abroad meant membership in the new intelligentsia, and in the society of the times, which was thoroughly devoted to the philosophy of success, many people began to consider the journey to America or Europe a fine way to get ahead. Occasionally there was even talk of men who married for money so as to be able to make such a trip. The word for foreign travel was so popular that country people pretentiously used it to refer to trips to Tokyo and Osaka. There is a certain similarity incidentally between scornful words used by city people to refer to sightseers from the country and the expressions of criticism uttered by those who came back from overseas journeys about their less privileged countrymen. There developed a breed of snobs who laced their conversation with expressions like "while I was over there" or "back in England." This was one of the sad results that occurred when people who had had little chance to learn about their own country went off to study in another. It is no exaggeration to say that the faulty knowledge of both Japan and the West acquired by many contemporary travelers was a cause of mistaken Japanese policies in more recent decades.

The overseas activities of the late middle ages and early Tokugawa period are ample proof of a Japanese bent for expansion into foreign areas. Now that the country was open to intercourse with other nations, many who formerly would have been satisfied to live in these little islands began to yearn for the chance to go elsewhere. Aside from intellectuals who went abroad to learn Western ways, there were many less ambitious, but perhaps more practical, persons who set out to see the world as merchant sailors.

c. The Development of Inns and Hotels

Cultural changes in the Meiji period altered the nature of travel, and transportation facilities improved miraculously, but interchange of knowledge among various rural areas was in many ways made even more inconvenient. The simplification of hotel service in these years offers an illustration. The business of providing lodgings for travelers was perhaps essentially the same before and after the Restoration, but the attitude of the innkeeper and that of the traveler changed completely. In former times their relationship followed one of three general patterns. First there was the case in which a landlord rented part of his own house to a traveler of higher station and adopted a subservient attitude toward him. This was the pattern when daimyos or noblemen stopped on their way to and from Edo, and it was preserved for a time even after the Restoration when government officials went on trips. There was no fixed price in this instance.

but it was customary for the traveler to leave a tip. Even after this kind of lodging was put on a regular commercial basis, it was felt necessary to add a tip of sorts. A second type of hostelry was that in which a number of people working for a particular business stayed at an inn on a more or less permanent basis. The owner of the house thought of his travelers as temporary members of his family. This was especially frequent in ports where brokers or wholesalers took into their houses the crew members of ships that called periodically. In the harbors on the Japan Sea many such hotels were known by the name of the town from which its guests came. The Wakasa-ya, for instance, was the name of a broker's establishment which took in people from boats hailing from Wakasa, and even after the owner's brokerage went out of business, his inn continued to be known by the same name. There are many similar examples. A special related type of lodging was the house of prostitution, which was in effect an inn for the women to live in between the appearance of boats. With the decline in numbers of regular ships, such places began to cater simply to ordinary customers. The third type of lodging was that provided by village families for pilgrims or priests who were passing through. In this case the houseowner actually attempted to attract these nonpaying guests for the spiritual good he might derive.

As a rule, in the Tokugawa period the innkeeper felt obliged to provide the visitor with shelter and protection, but not necessarily with superior entertainment. In houses where there were many servants, traveling pilgrims warmed themselves by the same fire and ate the same food as these underlings. In any case, however, the connection between the innkeeper and the guest was relatively close, and the latter had a chance in his lodgings to drink his fill of local color, while the innkeeper for his part was able to gain considerable knowledge of the outside world. The mutual exchange of ideas was even greater because the concept of taking money in return for lodgings was vague, if not absent. In the recent period, it has become difficult for an innkeeper to expect any form of profit from the traveler other than the monetary compensation, and the ordinary person cannot set out on a journey without first accumulating money for lodgings.

In the Tokugawa period the shogunate maintained postal stations at the principal stopping places all over the country, and people and horses were provided at a fixed price for travelers who wished to employ them. Persons moving about in the service of the shogunate could usually engage these men and beasts for nothing, and this gave rise to considerable objection in station towns, who felt the practice unfair. The Meiji government continued to use the stations for a time, but was careful to provide subsidies for the communities that operated them. Government personnel were prevented from using facilities free of charge or for nominal fees, and instead ordered to pay according to the local market. Innkeepers for their part were requested to post price lists. According to rules for a station in Kyoto in 1868, when an official wished to use men and horses he had to apply in advance to the local authorities, who would then see that he received services in his proper turn. The station was forbidden to provide lodgings or palanquins. The usual rate for transportation was 639 cash for a coolie, 1278 for a regular horse, and 832 for a light horse. Still it was felt that this price was too cheap and constituted a burden on the people, and in a proclamation of 1872, the post stations along the eastern coast route were finally abolished. Officials on journeys were ordered to pay a suitable sum for transport or lodgings and to avoid troubling people in the former station towns, who by the way were relieved of all corvée duty after August 30th of that year. Henceforward it became the rule for public and private travelers alike to pay the same price for lodgings, and this was made an official regulation in 1877.

By 1880 there had arisen a number of cases of reprehensible conduct on the part of innkeepers vying among themselves for customers, and control measures were being discussed. At the time people coming from the country to the city usually had to rely on employment agents to find work for them, and a number of these latter made shady deals with unscrupulous innkeepers. Innocent bumpkins were sent to hotels where after two or three days they were charged a tremendous amount for board, relieved of all their money, and thrown out, the agent splitting the take with the hotel operator. In other cases innkeepers employed touts on the bridges across the Sumida River, who, when they spotted a fellow in straw sandals and leggings coming into the city, not only tried to drag him into a hotel, but offered to take him around to see the sights of the famous Yoshiwara district. In addition, there sprang up a number of flophouses that were adopted by hoodlums as hideouts. To avert this evil the police in 1883 instituted a system of travel passports and ordered hotels not to accept customers who had none. At the same time a number of supplementary measures were attempted in an effort to control innkeepers.

A contemporary issue of the *Tokyo Nichinichi Newspaper* commented on the great fashion for hotels, but in reality most of them were like the countless crowded rooming houses that have appeared since World War II. The hotel of that time was a foothold or perhaps even a permanent residence for young hopefuls coming to the city. In 1883, in the police district of Hisamatsu-chō, which comprised 48 blocks, there were 225 hotels, housing 36,950 persons per month. If we assume that the rate for one day was approximately 30 *sen*, the monthly intake would have been 11,815 yen.

4. TRAVEL AND THE STANDARDIZATION OF CULTURE

a. Travelers to Villages

The loss of local variation due to the development of modern transportation and communication was an exceedingly important phenomenon. In earlier times whatever the way of life or the cultural level, the people of each village had had a general feeling of belonging—of being a part of things. When the government set up new transportation facilities, however, villages too remote to profit from them began to feel left out. They made strenuous attempts to secure roads or railroads and keep up with city fashions, but they were not always successful, and to make matters worse, the traveling traders who had hitherto brought information from without became fewer and farther between. Country towns unable to enter the new transportation network tended to become desolate places, or at least to consider themselves so.

At the same time, however, more and more villagers began to go outside their home towns to see the world for themselves. Whereas before they had managed somehow to accommodate themselves to conditions around them, they now looked more and more to the cities for their standards and to deplore the less advanced civilization of the provinces. School education promoted the urge toward duplication, while newspapers and magazines, all of which were written from the standpoint of the city, tended to make country people even more discontent with their condition. A more important factor perhaps was the adoption of universal military training, which in effect meant that boys from even the most out-of-the-way villages had to live for a time in an urban district. When these lads went back to their homes, they attempted to carry with them something of the new culture they had seen.

In general, during the Meiji period the Japanese for the first time began to think of themselves as a single people. Rural life became difficult to maintain by the ancient method of cooperation among a few villages. Villages began to form economic ties with nearby cities and even with the distant metropolises. Simultaneously, country people began to be conscious from day to day of what was going on in other places.

Together with the spread of transportation facilities, there were rapid developments in communication. Until now the most distressing element about travel was uneasiness about the family back at home, but now it became possible to keep in touch at all times. The simplest way to communicate was to send a postcard, and the Japanese took to postcards with a vengeance. At the beginning of the Meiji period the number sent annually was much smaller than the number of letters, as was the case in the West, but by 1907 they were twice as numerous. In foreign countries postcards are as a rule used only for announcements of various kinds, but the Japanese began using them for all sorts of communications. In particular, after about 1887 they began to employ them for the important New Year's greeting, and thereafter the New Year's card became an annual ritual. In the cities some people even dropped the age-old custom of making New Year's calls as a result.

Picture postcards came a little later. At first they were used primarily to spread information about Japan to foreign countries, but during the Russo-Japanese War, the Ministry of Communication published a great quantity of them as memorial pictures for people to send to the boys overseas. Aside from adding to the general excitement of the war, this action popularized the picture postcard once and for all. It was no time before the famous tourist resorts and historical sites began printing them, and travelers not only wrote home on them, but even took them back as presents. Country people were especially fond of them, and the colorful pictures of famous places no doubt increased the general yearning in rural areas for information about the outside world. In the cities, the picture postcard store replaced the little shops that had sold wood-block prints during the Edo period.

With the installation of telephone wires, the rural population was beside itself with gratitude to the urban centers for the new culture they had created. Even islands off the coast were brought into the central cultural sphere by this device. People in such remote places were amazed and thrilled to find that "you could sit right here and hear them talking on the mainland," and often, it is said, the sound coming through the receiver was drowned out by hurrahs and banzais.

All in all, as modern means of transportation and communication replaced the ancient roads, little communities that had been left to themselves out in the sticks, began to pray for the day when the new culture would descend upon them, their hopes being greater in proportion to the distance that separated them from the center of things. Those persons who actually brought elements of the new civilization to them were accorded unquestioning reverence. At the same time the admirable spirit of independence that had formerly existed tended strongly to give way to reliance upon urban arbiters of culture.

Chapter Six

MARRIAGE

1. CONSENT OF THE BRIDE

a. Various Types of Marriage

During the Meiji period marriage customs varied considerably, but four general classification were discernable.

The oldest type of marriage was one often observed in other cultures. The man first began to pay suit to the woman and then, if accepted, to sleep with her at her house. After the families of the two agreed to a formal marriage, the bridegroom took a quantity of sake to the bride's family and drank it with them. Subsequently, he continued to spend his nights at the bride's house for a time before taking her to his own home. In many cases the word signifying the interval when the bridegroom was commuting to his wife's home meant literally "working for the parents-in-law," and in general there was a strong feeling that he owed a certain amount of labor in exchange for his bride. This was particularly true in the northeast area where the requirements were so specific that young men were spoken of as "three-year bridegrooms," or "five-year bridegrooms." The drinking of sake by the husband and his parents-in-law constituted the marriage ceremony. In the northern part of Iwate Prefecture this was actually called the "confirmation sake," and after it had been drunk the bridegroom was committed to sleeping at the bride's house for one or two years before taking her home. In Amami-Ōshima there was a similar ceremony, but in this case the bridegroom stayed in the bride's house for four or five years. The transfer of the bride to her new home, then, came at various times in different localities, but the ancient practice seems to have been for her not to go until her husband became the head of his family.

The second type of marriage was similar to the first, except that the ceremony was held in the house of the bridegroom. In this case also the selection of a mate was left to the young people, and when they had decided whom they preferred, the man began to stay at his girl's house overnight. Subsequently, his family formally proposed marriage, and if it was agreed to, the young woman visited her husband's house and confronted her new parents. This visit was called *ashiire*, or " putting the foot in." Sometimes the bride visited her new home alone, but more frequently her mother went along with her, and at times a person who had acted as go-between went too. On the island of Ōshima, off the coast of the Izu Peninsula, the mother greeted the husband's family with the following words : " I hear that you are going to make my daughter a member of this family. Please take care of her." The new mother-in-law then offered tea, but as a rule the bride's mother said that she has just had some at home and left without drinking. On this occasion, the bride always drew some water from the well and filled the water barrel at her husband's house. After this confrontation, the bride returned to her father's house and continued to work there, going to lend a hand at the bride-groom's house only at busy times. The groom spent his nights by his bride's side, and frequently had his evening meals at her house. After a number of years, she moved to his home, but there were various conditions that had to be satisfied before this took place, and in some instances it did not occur until the couple had two or three children. To judge from documents and surveys of Hachijō-jima, another island off Izu Peninsula, the *ashiire* marriage prevailed from at least as early as the middle Tokugawa period until very recently. As a rule, in the

Izu islands the bride did not move to her husband's house until she became mistress thereof. In areas where young women worked as divers and were therefore valued for their income, the *ashiire* marriage was dominant until some time during the Meiji period.

The third form of marriage, in which the bride went from the beginning to live at her husband's home, was first practiced by the warrior class, but it later spread among the common people, and in the latter part of Tokugawa period, it largely replaced the types mentioned above. In a book entitled *Nihon Konrei-ki* ("A Record of Japanese Marriage Practices," first part published in July, 1894, and second part in May, 1896), which covered many areas, it is clear that by the middle Meiji nearly the whole country observed marriage forms that came under this head. The formal wedding ceremony used today was common, and the part played by the go-between was more important than previously.

During the Meiji period there appeared a fourth type of marriage, in which the marriage celebration was as a rule held cooperatively by both the families concerned, and the couple subsequently set up a new and independent household. This type developed first in urban society, and it has gradually gained in favor, but is still relatively rare.

We might note that among the various forms of marriage practiced during the Meiji period, the type in which the husband lived at the bride's house for a time and that in which the bride performed the *ashiire* ceremony were usually confined to a single village. The type in which the bride went immediately to her husband's house to live might also be a village affair, of course, but as a rule it involved her moving to a different locale, as did the last type. Throughout the era one of the most pronounced trends was the disappearance of marriage forms involving the consent of the bride. The union between man and wife came most often to be arranged by their parents.

b. The Disappearance of Yobai

Yobai is the noun form of the verb *yobau*, which means "to call continuously." In ancient times it was written with a number of different Chinese characters, but in any case it meant for a suitor to go at night to sleep at the house of his prospective bride. This was the proper method of securing a girl's consent in the days when marriages involved the young man's working for his bride's family for a time. Even in the Meiji period, the *yobai* practice still existed, and the men often went so far as to carry his bedding along with him. He made no sexual approach, however, until after the young woman, having convinced herself of his fidelity, gave her consent.

In one fishing community in Wajima, Ishikawa Prefecture, for a young man and woman to fall in love and decide to marry was called making a *michi-yakusoku*, or "street promise," and, as the name indicates, this matter was left largely to the boy and girl themselves. When the promise was recognized by both families, the young man went to sleep with his bride. The entrance that he used was called the *yobai* door.

There are a number of localities in which *yobai* referred simply to social calls by groups of young men at the house of a young woman. As a rule, two or three boys at a time would drop in and sit on the porch or, in winter, by the hearth and talk with the girl. It is said that the parents of girls did their best to see that boys came in large numbers and stayed for a long time. In the mountain villages in the eastern parts of Tosa province this was called simply "going to see the girls" (*nēsan-mi*). If the girl was pretty, it was said, one had to go early in order to get a seat. The families of such fortunate daughters considered this a great honor. This type of *yobai* allowed both parties to select a fitting mate while associating with other members of their own age group.

In Tsushima, Nagasaki Prefecture, throughout the Meiji period and for some time afterward, the most gala event in a girl's life was the blackening of her teeth at the age of thirteen. This was the occasion for a large celebration. The girls with their freshly stained teeth invited each other to call and held parties at each other's houses. Young men were invited, and everyone played games. After this year, it was the young lady's privilege to associate freely with boys. There were many other areas where a girl who had passed the age of puberty was tacitly allowed to become familiar with men.

It should be stressed that according to the ancient custom of *yobai*, a suitor did not ordinarily go to a woman's house at night without her permission. The young man used one of a number of methods to show his intentions. As a rule, he secured the intercession of a friend, but often he instead made a pair of straw sandals or a basket and rope for the girl, and in many areas he merely gave her a hand cloth. The acceptance of this present was left to the woman's own judgment. To take it meant to agree to his proposal, and after she had accepted he was free to go to her at night. These simple presents were in effect tokens of a marriage agreement, and in the event that the young man ceased to come around afterward, they were held as proof that he had broken his promise. In districts such as Hachijō-jima, where dormitories for young people remained an institution in the Meiji period, *yobai* consisted of going to sleep in the girl's dormitory. In other areas the parents often encouraged *yobai* by letting an eligible daughter sleep in some such accessible place as the kitchen, the hall by the doorway, or a little house outside.

The *yobai* custom provided considerable freedom of association to young people, but though a small number of them may have abused the privilege, as a rule the severe limitations imposed by the constant surveillance of other young people prevented them from becoming very disorderly. Ordinarily, to be allowed to " become intimate with men " meant in effect to become familiar with one man, and the young lady who associated

with a number of boys was bitterly criticized. The local organizations of young people acted as a force that prevented love
from becoming libertinism (the influence of these organizations
in this respect is discussed at greater length Chapter 9 and 10).
In the Meiji period and afterward, however, a number of mis-
guided educators, feeling that the customary courtship practices
were immoral, or perhaps unaware of the restrictions imposed
by the group, saw fit to teach that by ancient and proper
Japanese custom marriages were decided by parents, and that
love is not a prerequisite to marriage, but something that comes
afterward.

As the type of marriage in which the bride moves immediately
to her husband's home became dominant, the practice of *yobai*
came more and more to be considered wicked. Simultaneously,
the control exercised by young people's associations grew weaker,
and in fact *yobai* degenerated to the extent that it was little
better than rape. In many areas, the term was given a folk-
etymology that meant literally "night-crawling" and implied
extreme promiscuity.

2. THE SPREAD OF LONG-DISTANCE MARRIAGES

It was not until the Meiji period that marriages between
people from different communities became common. Thitherto
people were bound to the land, and few of them ever had a
chance to leave the villages in which they were born. Also,
there were few visitors from without, and the ones who came
were workmen, wandering tradesmen, or priests. As a result,
people rarely chose mates from other villages. Still, there has
always been a strong tendency for people to marry others of
equal status and means, and even in the days when most
marriages were confined to a single village, large landowners
sometimes had to go outside their own communities to arrange
suitable marriages for their offspring. The same had always
been true of the military class, and when this group became

dominant, marriages between persons of different areas tended to become more common. The most pronounced feature of such unions was that there was as a rule no courtship. The bride was simply brought to live in her husband's home on the day of the wedding. In the Meiji period this type of marriage virtually replaced all others.

Aside from the influence of the upper classes, one reason for seeking brides in different villages was simply a need for female workers. There are numerous areas in which the word for receiving a new bride means literally to take in a worker, and in Kyushu there are many signs that a marriage agreement was considered virtually the same as a contract for the exchange of labor. Still another reason for the spread of this kind of marriage was the increased social interchange between rural villages and the outside world. In the Meiji period improved facilities for travel broke down the isolating barriers that had formerly confined marriages to the village. It ceased to be unusual to go away to work in towns and cities, and as a result young men and women gained a broader scope for social activities. Furthermore, whereas marriage between persons in different feudal domains as well as between members of different social classes had actually been forbidden in many districts during the Tokugawa period, after the Restoration all these restrictions were removed.

Simultaneously, the local associations of young people, which had previously exercised considerable control over the marriage system and had usually insisted on intra-community marriages, declined in strength. Large farmers often kept their daughters out of the girls' groups, and the groups were greatly weakened by this boycott, particularly since it was carried out by the leading members of the community. In many places the young women gradually disbanded or at least ceased to sleep together in separate dormitories. The young men's groups continued to exist, but ceased to function as they had in the past, and the girls' dormitory disappeared very rapidly after the beginning of

Meiji. Still, as late as 1890 local youth groups put up considerable resistance to the importation of brides from different communities. Often they employed annoying tactics, such as throwing mud or rocks at the house of the newlyweds or persistently arriving uninvited as supper guests. In order to avoid being victimized, those about to marry persons from other communities began to send presents in advance to the local youth and to try in various ways to secure the assistance of the ring leaders. Much of the mischief of the young people's associations is preserved in form today, but it amounts to no more than the American custom of tying tin cans to the automobile in which newlyweds are about to go off on their honeymoon. The placating of the villages youth was often the function of the go-between who arranged the marriage, and the part the latter played in this respect added much to his general importance.

Often the young men were asked to take charge of entertaining guests at the wedding feast, it being virtually certain that after they had begun drinking and singing songs, the various barriers between them and the outsiders would disappear. The modern expansion of the wedding party is, incidentally, largely due to this sort of thing.

Marriages between persons from different districts usually proceeded in the following way. A go-between arranged a meeting of the principals, which was also attended by the parents. At the second stage, there was an exchange of gifts between two families. The marriage contract having been sealed in this way, it remained only for the wedding ceremony to be held and the bride to be taken to her new husband's home. The main feature of this type of marriage was that the families were usually able to push the wishes of the principals into the background. Young women and men were simply forced to accept mates they did not know and then try to learn to love them. In general, of course, the personality adjustments had to be made by the bride. There was an increasing number of young wives who hated their parents for marrying them to men they could not stand, and who cried themselves to sleep nightly over their misfortune.

In mentioning the difficulties experienced by young women under this system of marriages, we cannot omit that of having to live under the jealous eye of a mother-in-law. In the older types of marriage, which retained the various traditional forms of courtship, a bride was not usually brought to her husband's house until her mother-in-law had died, become sick, or in some other way reached a stage at which it was necessary for her to relinquish her duties as mistress of the house. In some places, when the first son took a bride, his parents went to live in retirement at a separate dwelling, accompanied by their younger children, and even when this was not the case, it was felt that in principle there should not be two mistresses in the same household. It is not known exactly what gave rise to this attitude, but it seems to have been one of the basic ideas in the old family system, and certainly after mothers-in-law and brides began to live together, much of the harmony of family life disappeared. Some city couples skirted the difficulty by living apart from either the bride's or the groom's parents, but throughout the Meiji period and down to the present time the problem of the mother-in-law has continued to be serious. We might note incidentally that it underlay a Meiji tendency toward choosing younger brides. Prospective mothers-in-law generally felt that they could discipline a new daughter-in-law more effectively if they got her when she was young.

3. GO-BETWEENS

a. Pre-Modern Go-Betweens

In ancient times, when marriages were confined within limited areas, young men and women were to a large extent free to choose mates for themselves, and as a rule all the parents had to do was agree. On the other hand, the youth associations exercised a good deal of influence. When two young persons began to form a deep affection for each other, it was always possible for their companions either to encourage them along or to break them apart with criticism or ridicule. Thus in a sense the youth associations controlled the selection of mates by their members. In places where the groups slept in separate dormitories, the adults who had charge of these buildings were in effect delegated by parents to take charge of match-making. They were, therefore, go-betweens of a sort. As a rule, they were much older than the inhabitants of the dormitory, but prone to give the latter a good deal of liberty in ordinary situations and to intervene only when necessary. Still, it often became necessary for them to take a hand in the thorny problem of relations between the sexes. When associations of young people and dormitory superintendents ceased to play a part in the marriage system, other go-betweens had to take their place.

The young people's groups of the past often came into conflict with the family system, and this was particularly true in matters relating to marriage. Families frequently attempted to secure their own position by making profitable marriages, regardless of what the youth in the community thought. On the other hand, when the young people did not approve of a marriage, they usually tried to stop it, and they rarely approved when the will of one of their members was ignored by his or her family. It might be noted that the supervisors of the dormitories often sided with their charges. The clashes that arose may be understood as symptomatic of the transition that took the control of the marriage system away from the young people's groups and gave it to the family.

As the youth groups grew weaker they tended to become irresponsible, and parents felt even less inclined to trust their judgment in matters pertaining to matrimony. Herein lay the main reason for the appearance of the modern go-between, who acts on behalf of the parents alone.

b. Various Types of Go-betweens

There are many different kinds of go-betweens. No doubt if one studied them in great detail one would find a logical historical trend, but in the Meiji period old and new types existed simultaneously.

In central Nagano, somewhat west of Tokyo, it is the practice to invite to weddings not only the go-between who has acted for the groom's family, but also another person more closely connected with the bride. In many other areas, the custom in the past was actually to employ two go-betweens, one for each family involved, the purpose obviously being to insure that no one's rights would be ignored. The practice very probably goes back to the time when the supervisors of the men's and women's dormitories made arrangements for marriages.

In the case of the long-distance marriage much was expected of the go-between, and his task was not one to be taken up by anyone who disliked hard work. Aside from the travel involved, he frequently had to employ considerable diplomacy. When marriage became first and foremost an arrangement between family and family, the problem of ironing out differences grew greater than ever. Usually whenever one side became particularly anxious to get on with the wedding, the other became reluctant. If the go-between managed in the face of the various difficulties to arrange for the marriage, he won the admiration of all about him. In the Gotō Archipelago, Nagasaki Prefecture, go-betweens are spoken of as "seven-and-a-halfers," by which it is meant that they must resign themselves to seven and a half voyages to the mainland or another island and back before a marriage can finally be arranged. Also in many areas, there is a proverb roughly to the effect that the go-between has to do everything but stand on his head to accomplish his purpose. When the go-between also had to placate outsiders who objected to a long-distance marriage, his lot was particularly unenviable.

In the northeast regions, as well as in at least one section of Nagano, the go-between was commonly referred to with the same word as the deity of marriage, and in this case he seems to have conducted the marriage arrangements from start to finish. In Aomori, Iwate, and central Fukushima, however, there was a type of go-between called by one of a variety of terms meaning "guide," who appears to have had no other function than that of directing the wedding ceremony itself. These sections incidentally seem to have been the location in which the very formal Ogasawara ceremony, which is standard today, originated, and no doubt the rigid etiquette involved in this ritual required the assistance of experts. We should note, however, that in the background, there was evidently a more important go-between who carried on the pre-marriage negotiations.

In any event, the custom of using two go-betweens developed. When, for instance, the person who actually did the leg work required to make the match was regarded as unsuitable in rank or situation to take charge of the ceremony itself, a person of greater parts was asked to perform this task. The former was spoken of with words that stressed his role as preparer, while the latter was called by such terms as the "wine-cup go-between," or the "reception-room go-between." In cities it was a popular practice in the Meiji period to put the name of an affluent gentleman on the invitation cards and have him greet the guests at the wedding party, but only after all preparations had been made by some less important person. The go-between whom one met at a wedding party, then, had no real function —he was rather like the treasured lacquer ware hauled out for such occasions, but never used otherwise. There are stories that revolve about the formal go-between's forgetting the names of the bride and groom, and in fact the newlyweds in many cases never saw this person again after the wedding. People in rural areas mimed the city folk by asking an *oya-kata* or some other person of wealth or influence to serve as go-between at the marriage ceremony, but in this case the new couple virtually became in-laws of their patron and continued to associate with him through the years thereafter.

Originally go-betweens aimed not at remuneration, but simply at assisting the two houses to maintain their lineage or at securing the happiness of the married couple. As a rule, however, when the family had requested a person to perform this difficult task, they rewarded him handsomely on its successful completion. According to strict etiquette, the family of the groom presented a fixed present of food and wine to the go-between as soon as the marriage ceremony was finished, but in actual practice most people added a certain amount of money. In many areas, the go-between was required by custom not to keep the payment all to himself, but to use part of it to give a party for the new couple and other persons concerned.

In modern times not a few go-betweens perform their function for the sole purpose of making money. According to a newspaper of 1881, a professional marriage bureau was opened in Kyoto in that year. This seems to have been the first business concern of this sort, but the new age was marked by the appearance of many more in the cities.

c. The Interview between the Bride and Groom and the Exchange of Presents

The main function of the go-between before the marriage was to arrange an interview between the prospective bride and groom and to carry out an exchange of gifts between their families.

In the old village marriages the young men and women were always together anyway, and there was no need for an interview. This formal meeting must therefore have begun in connection with long-distance marriages. The go-between was invariably present on this occasion. In rural areas, after the general arrangements had been completed, the go-between accompanied the bridegroom to the house of the bride. If the young man liked the girl, he drank some of the hot water being prepared for tea and in some cases made the final arrangements then and there. In many districts he customarily left behind a fan or something of the sort when he took his leave. It might be noted that in some areas the interview was referred to by a word that meant " seeing the wife " (okata-mi), the implication being that the selection had already been made before the interview. Even the ordinary word for the interview miai, originally meant " meeting the bride " (me-ai) and apparently signified the principal ceremony in the marriage. In the Meiji period, people in the cities began sending photographs before the interview took place, and this practice presently spread to the country. City people also began holding the interview in parks, theaters, or restaurants.

When the interview had ended and both parties had made up their minds, the go-between, acting on the part of the groom, sent a present of wine or tea to the bride's family. The gift was known by such names as "hand-clasping wine" (tejime-no-sake), or "hardening wine" (katame-zake). Once it had been accepted the engagement could not be broken except under very special circumstances. The word yuinō, which today signifies these presents, originally meant simply the token of a bond, and it referred specifically to the food and wine on which the families feasted to celebrate their alliance. The early custom was, as remarked above, for the groom himself to take a present of sake to the bride's parents, but the go-between began to assume an important role in this ceremony. On the appointed day, he led the groom to the bride's home, where the latter gave his gift. As time went on, clothing and other articles, including money, were substituted for the wine. In many areas it was customary for the bride's family to return half of the gift.

To summarize, in village marriages, the marriage contract was settled with one gift of sake from the groom, but in long-distance marriages two separate ceremonies were held. The first was not necessarily binding, but the second was. At the beginning of the Meiji period there were still many places where the bride first applied tooth stain on the day when the groom formally presented his gift. Also there were areas in which it was a custom when a parent of the groom died after the presenting of the gift, but before the transfer of the bride, for the latter to take her place in the funeral procession as a wife. In Kyushu the presentation of the gift was customarily held the day before the bride went to her husband's home, but in most other places the day for the latter event was not even decided until the groom brought his present, and a certain amount of time passed before the bride actually moved.

4. THE CEREMONY AND THE RECEPTION

a. The Marriage Ceremony

The wedding ceremony included many small rites. In this section we shall confine ourselves to those performed on the day when the bride went to her husband's home, focusing our attention on the type of marriage in which she did this from the beginning.

(1) *The greeting of the bride.* On the day of wedding, the custom in many areas was for the bridegroom to visit the parents of the bride, this call being known by such names as "a look at the bridegroom" (*muko-ichigen*). As a rule the go-between and possibly several of the bridegroom's relatives accompanied him. At the bride's house there was a feast, and the groom drank sake with the bride's parents in token of their union. Often other relatives of the bride participated. Afterward the bridegroom either took the bride to his house or returned alone leaving the go-between to bring her after she had completed her preparations. The visit by the bridegroom was a relic of the earlier type of marriage in which the bride-

groom lived with the parents of the bride for a time before taking her to his home. It symbolized the acceptance by the bride's family of the groom as a son, and his acceptance of them as parents.

Originally the exchange or drinks was so important that the bridegroom himself had to be present, but now the greeting of the bride has come to be performed by a proxy. The change appears to have been the result of a general desire on the part of bridegrooms to avoid the ceremony, which they found troublesome and embarrassing. There were several intermediate stages. For instance, in some places the groom would put on his wedding clothes and go out of his house in time to meet the bridal party on the street, and then they would all go to worship at the local temple. In other cases the bridegroom would pay his respects to the bride's parents during the interval when the go-between was leading the bride to her new home. Nowadays the whole affair is left up to the go-between.

In many places the bridegroom was acccompanied by one or more men of the same age, and the bride was similarly attended by bridesmaids. In either case the attendants were chosen from among the young unmarried people in the community, and in some localities it was considered wise to choose persons who were not quite as good looking as the principals, but the custom was not simply a means of making the latter appear to advantage. It was practiced mostly in places where young people's associations were strong, and we may therefore suppose that it represented a lingering assertion of their right to control marriages. Although this prerogative was gradually being removed from them, they apparently insisted on having at least a few representatives present at weddings. In certain districts the bridesmaids, who sometimes numbered ten or more, all wore ceremonial clothing, and in western Japan at least they often sang songs and contributed much to the gaiety of the occasion.

(2) *The departure of the bride.* Frequently the family of

the bride had a large farewell party on the day before the wedding, and in many places this was the occasion on which the bride first blackened her teeth, but often she did not do this until after going to live with her husband. As we have remarked before, the blackening of the teeth was originally associated with puberty rites. Gradually it was put off until the time of marriage, and after the Meiji period it ceased to be a custom at all.

When the bride was finally on the point of leaving her house, she bowed before the miniature Buddhist altar and had a farewell cup of sake with her family. Sometimes they all had a light meal together.

When the bride departed, a fire was built at the gate and the teacup she had last used was thrown on the ground and broken. The fire was evidently intended to symbolize the cutting off of the road that might lead her back home. A similar ritual was performed at funerals after the coffin had been taken away from the house, so as to prevent the spirit of the dead from returning. Frequently, the bride's family comforted themselves after her departure with more eating and drinking, and this practice too was similar to one of the funeral customs.

(3) *The delivery of the bride.* The place for handing the bride over to the groom varied. It appears that the ancient practice was for the parents to deliver her personally when the bridegroom called at their house, but as go-betweens became more active, they began to take charge of this function.

Often the bridal party did not proceed directly to the groom's house, but stopped at another on the way whither the groom came to receive his wife. In such instances the "middle house," as this was called, was often that of an *oya-kata*. When a bride came from a different village, it was necessary in any event for her to obtain support from the local *oya-kata*, and therefore the latter's residence was a logical place for her to confront her new husband. In many communities, however, the house of the go-between was chosen. Apparently this custom was intended to provide the bride from another district with a chance to get settled in the new community, but as time went on this meaning was lost, and the middle house became simply a place to rest or straighten up clothing after the bridal trip. In any case, it was considered that the bride's family was responsible for her until she reached the middle house, and the groom thereafter. In some districts the handing over of the bride was further complicated by the presence of an additional go-between.

(4) *The bride's trousseau.* When a girl married someone in her own community, she usually took only a small number of personal belongings, and often she left even these in her parents' house for a long time after going to live with her husband. In the case of long-distance marriages, however, the trousseau was relatively large and required a good deal of attention. Parents tried to provide their daughters with as much as possible, and there was talk in many villages of men who were ruined financially by having too many daughters. Sometimes the bride's property was delivered to her new home by her family. Otherwise it was transported to the border of the groom's village, where his messengers received it with appropriate ceremony. In certain villages the trousseau was sent one day before the wedding, while in others it was not delivered for one month afterward. In a few districts, it was sent at the same time as the bride, but by a different road. As a general rule, however, it was carried by the vanguard of the bridal procession, and the bearers sang songs and swaggered energetically to make the most of the occasion.

(5) *The bridal procession.* The bustle and clamor of the luggage carriers seems to have been part of a scheme to give the bride a rousing introduction to society. She herself rode in a ricksha if she lived in the city, but if she were a country lass, she had to content herself with a sedan chair or more often a horse. In any case, her vehicle or steed was bedecked with pretty flowers and other ornaments. The wife of the go-

between, also on horseback, preceded the bride, while the others walked.

(6) *The entry of the bride.* The bride usually arrived at her new home in the evening, and this was considered proper form, but the only reason seems to be that there were a number of ceremonies that had to be performed at her house during the day. In the cities, the bride usually simply walked into the main room of the groom's house together with the guests, but in the country the occasion was accompanied by much ado. All over the country, she was required to enter alone through a separate door, ordinarily that leading to the kitchen, and having entered she was usually given a wine cup from which she took a drink of water. Often she was required to pass over a small fire by the gate. In various places, there was a curious custom of giving her a whack on the posterior with a bundle of straw, and in others her head was covered with a kettle lid when she entered the kitchen. In the latter case the person doing the honors usually chanted something to the effect that he had been asked to do it by the god of fire. In other instances the bride walked around the hearth fire three times before being led into the interior of the house. All of this seems rather too much commotion just to welcome a new feminine member into the tribe, and one wonders if these symbolic acts were not a holdover from the time when the rights of the family head were passed on to the son upon the arrival of the latter's wife. The fact that most of the various performances were related to water, fire, or the oven tends to confirm this assumption.

(7) *The bridal cup.* In city marriages of the so-called Ogasawara style, the principal feature of the wedding was a ceremony in which the bride and groom each took three sips of sake from each of a set of three sake cups. The ceremony was rather stiff and showed the influence of the warrior class, by whom it was first used. In the country, there was no wedding cup, and in most places even the word for it, *meoto*

sakazuki, was unknown. Very often, in fact, the bridegroom in rural areas was required to be absent when the bride entered the house, and if there was any drinking, it was done by the bride and her mother-in-law. After all, the ancient village marriage agreement was sealed with sake long before the bride moved to the groom's house, and no one felt it necessary to repeat the performance later. Even the spread of long-distance marriages failed to alter this feeling, but we should note that during the Meiji period many villagers began to imitate the urban practice in order to be elegant. As one might expect, the exchange of drinks between parents and sons-in-law grew correspondingly less common.

b. The Reception

The wedding reception was actually a part of the marriage ceremony, but it had a rather special significance. To be a success the marriage itself required the approval not only of the principals and their families but also of the community around them. The reception, then, was a sort of publicity act designed to gain this approval. In the broader sense it included a number of steps that the bride took to insure her acceptance into her new village. When she arrived, for instance, she usually visited her new neighbors, as well as the friends of her husband's family, and distributed gifts from her native town. Often this visit took place on the day after her official entry into her new house, and as a rule she was accompanied by her mother-in-law. The gifts might be hand towels, tea, or boxes of rice cooked with red beans—a dish used only on festive occasions. In Shikoku and the areas around Kyoto the young lady usually presented a gift of tobacco, and in many other places she took dolls or rice crackers (*sembei*) for the village children. The reception proper consisted of a feast to which the neighbors, and often the village as a whole, came. In areas where the young people's groups retained considerable say-so in matrimonial matters, they were given special attention. Sometimes, instead of inviting them, the new couple called on them with gifts of sake, and as we have mentioned before, in a number of districts the youth did not wait for an invitation, but simply came and stayed until they had been properly wined and dined.

In the cities, houses were generally too small for people to invite a great crowd of guests, and the reception was often held in a restaurant. It became a fashion to invite the relatives and friends of both bride and groom at once. As time went on, families began to take a back seat, and the feast was directed primarily at entertaining friends and acquaintances who could be of assistance in business or society. People invited as many friends as possible, even if this meant curtailing the quantity of food and drink. The feeling that feasting together created invisible bonds remained strong, even if the fare was simple. In the country, however, there was a tendency to go all out. Often the feast went on for days with the guests in attendance changing several times. The expense was terrific, but apparently no one felt as though the party was really a success unless it was fairly costly. Unfortunately, all this expenditure of cash frequently became a meaningless point of etiquette.

5. DIVORCE

By tradition, in every district of the country a man could make a formal written declaration against his wife and return her to her family. A go-between was required as a witness, but the wife had no recourse. The return of her population registration or her personal belongings to her former home constituted a final separation. It is very clear from dialectic terms concerning divorce that the woman's position was exceedingly weak, and this is what we would expect in a society centered around the family patriarch. Still it is clear that in the earlier years of Meiji, before the majority of the people could read and write, written declarations could not have been the sole means of separating. In fact, historical evidence suggests that they were largely confined to the upper classes, and one suspects that they originated within the warrior class itself.

Among the common folk the rights of the patriarch were not absolute, and there were fairer means of divorce. In the northern parts of Iwate Prefecture, for example, whereas the real marriage began with the exchange of drinks by the bridegroom and his parents-in-law, either the bridegroom or bride could effect a separation by presenting the other with a casket of sake and letting him or her know that the marriage was off. This example is perhaps a little extreme, since the form of marriage in the area in question involved a long trial period, but in general the woman appears to have had more rights in marriages of the pre-modern era. After all, in the earlier types of marriage the selection of a mate was more or less made by the young people themselves, and it is only logical that the question of divorce should be similarly handled.

With the spread of long-distance marriages it became the practice for the bride's personal property to be sent to the groom's house along with her, but in earlier times she had frequently left most of it behind for a good long time, sometimes as much as ten years. Furthermore she had often visited her family, and in various other ways indicated her continued dependence on them. This was no more nor less than a tacit assertion of the right to divorce her husband, at least during a given interval after the marriage.

There are no complete statistics on divorces in the Meiji period, but it appears that most of them occurred in the first few years after marriage. No doubt young brides suddenly uprooted and carried off to live in a new place with a new and possibly severe mother-in-law found this the most difficult period of married life.

Chapter Seven

FUNERALS

1. CHANGING CONCEPTS OF DEATH

SINCE ancient times Japanese have regarded death as not only sad, but unclean, and this rather inconsistent attitude is strongly reflected in funeral customs. Simultaneously with an urge to express love and respect for the deceased, one can recognize not only a desire to avoid being soiled by contact with the corpse, but also a distinct fear of the departed spirit.

It is clear from historical sources that in ancient Japan when a person died, those closely connected with him retired to a separate mourning house, ordinarily constructed especially for the purpose, and remained there for a certain length of time. This practice had more or less been abandoned by the Meiji period, but it was still observed in various remote locations. On Ōshima, for example, the children of a deceased person built a small funeral hut in which they lived without working for fifty days after the death. During this period they used the white cloth in which the casket had been wrapped for sashes. Similar customs prevailed in the islands of Niijima and Miyakejima, as well as in the mountain villages of the Tamba area. They have also been reported in Tsushima, Kumano, Amami-Ōshima, the Yaeyama Archipelago, and at least one section of Ise. In Kyūshū and other areas it was common for people to erect a miniature house over a dead person's grave, and this must surely have been a remnant of the earlier custom.

Most people broke their fast by eating fish. Others ate rice cakes of the type served during the festive New Year season. With the changing times, it became ever more difficult to observe long periods of mourning, and the fast came to be broken on the twenty-first day, the seventh day, the third day, or in some cases the day of the funeral. To give an example, in Hata County of Kōchi Prefecture mourning lasted at least three days and at most seven. Farmers and merchants usually closed their doors for three days, after which they held a feast for friends and neighbors. The name for this meal, incidentally, was *arabiake*, which might be roughly translated "the beginning of the free use of fire." In other words, the mourning having ended, it was all right for outsiders to eat food cooked over the fire used by the bereaved.

Today when Japanese send presents of food other than meat or fish, it is the standard practice to attach to the package a red and white strip of paper called a *noshi*. Originally this appears to have been a piece of abalone, or in some places the tail of a fish, the purpose being to inform the receiver that the sender was not under the food restrictions involved in mourning, or, in other words, that he was not contaminated by death. Feelings about fire and food taboos were strong enough in the past to require this reassurance, although today the significance has been forgotten.

There appears to have been a general belief that the contamination of death extended to the crops and cattle of the deceased. In one village in Chiba Prefecture it was the custom for a family having suffered a death to turn their current crop of potatoes over to another house and receive in return the seeds for a new crop. In Himagashima, an island off the Chiba Peninsula, seeds from wheat or barley growing at the time of a death were replaced by others obtained from a different family.

The same sort of practice is found in the case of cattle. In Takashima County, Shiga Prefecture, if a dying man left a horse, it was exchanged by the survivors for another horse of a different color. Here and there the same applied to dogs, cats, and chickens. On Okinawa it was believed that the cows and horses of a dead person would soon follow him to another world, and consequently such animals were sold as soon as possible. In the event that they were indispensable, they were temporarily sold to a friendly family and then rebought. One supposes that the ancients actually disposed completely of crops and cattle, but that this practice entailed such a great economic burden that it eventually was replaced by merely formal observances. From the very fact that persons other than the bereaved family would consent to receive such property, it can be seen that the taboos on death were not absolute in the more recent past.

2. THE BEREAVED FAMILY AND THE COMMUNITY

When a person died, other members of the community helped his family as much as possible with the funeral, but at the same time there were rules that outsiders were required to preserve in associating with the bereaved, and often in principle no association whatever was allowed. Even in such cases, however, many villages permitted outsiders at least to help with the cremation or burial of the body.

Numerous villages or village subdivisions had organizations for mutual aid with funeral rites. The relatives of the deceased usually took charge of the ceremony itself, but the assembly of family heads in the community often assisted in various ways. In places where the five-man groups of the Tokugawa period continued to exist they often made the various preparations, with or without the assistance of other such groups. The obligation of each family to assist varied with the degree of intimacy with the deceased, and often it was rather firmly fixed. In such cases, a family might be required by propriety to send two persons, or three persons, or more, and in many places the amount of rice sent in condolence was similarly decided by custom.

In large villages families were as a rule divided into a number of cooperative groups of one sort or another, and these performed the various functions involved in the funeral. This was probably the case in more than half of the farming and fishing communities throughout the country.

Assistance of various type was offered. In the first place, when a person died, certain individuals were sent to inform relatives, while others were sent to the local temple. There were names for the persons assigned to do this, and their specific duties were more or less prescribed by custom. In Namekata County, Ibaraki Prefecture, for example; the practice was to send two messengers, who were required to go together and to make no stops or digressions along the way. They had to wear straw sandals of the coarse variety used for traveling.

The practice of sending two messengers together prevailed throughout the country. The messengers were as a rule not subject to the taboos of death, whereas those to whom they made their announcement ordinarily were, and presumably it was felt that two persons could better resist the danger of contamination than one. In Kokonohe County, Iwate Prefecture, it was held that if one person went on this mission, the dead man would follow him, and therefore in the event that the messenger did go alone, he always carried along a scythe for protection. As a rule the objects used in the funeral ceremony were made by the outside assistants, but sometimes the platform on which the casket rested, as well as the implements for digging the grave were community property, kept either in the temple or in a separate hut. This, however, was apparently a relatively new custom, the more ordinary practice being for such things to be made or obtained in a great hurry on the day before the funeral. The older men in the funeral association might come to make the various implements, while the younger ones dug the grave. Gradually it became more and more common for people to buy the needed objects from the towns, but members of the funeral association went to make the purchase. The pall bearers might be either near relatives, members of the funeral association, or hired men, but most often they came from the second group. Because of taboos, the digging of the grave, and for that matter the carrying of the casket, had originally been the work of the close relatives, and this remained true in a number of areas during the Meiji period. More often, however, these tasks devolved upon the association. The latter also helped provide food and shelter for out-of-town relatives and friends, and in many instances it prepared the account of expenses. In short, while the family performed functions directly connected with the burial, the association took care of everything else. In many areas it was customary for outsiders to make a gift of money or rice, but the bereaved family had to give return presents in addition to providing food for all helpers, and the cost outweighed anything received.

When there was no funeral association, neighbours usually helped, this being the ordinary case in towns and cities. In a newspaper for 1886, it was recorded that a professional funeral house, providing all necessary supplies for Buddhist or Shinto ceremonies at low cost, had been established in Tokyo. Subsequently, city people relied more and more on such establishments, which eventually spread to the provinces. As early as 1873 there was a company in Tokyo that even rented rickshas for funeral processions. Under the circumstances funeral preparations came to be made almost entirely by the relatives of the deceased, with possibly a little help from the young people in their neighborhood.

3. THE FUNERAL CORTEGE AND THE FAREWELL CEREMONY

A number of ceremonies were involved in removing the casket from the house. They varied with the district, but almost everywhere there was some sort of farewell meal. Presumably this was originally limited to the nearer relatives, who were subject to the taboos, but gradually more and more people attended, to the point that the meal took on the aspects of a great feast in some places, though in others it was purely symbolic, each person in the family taking only two or three grains of rice.

Generally it was considered that the casket should not leave by the ordinary entrance, and it was usually taken out by way of a side door, but in some districts a wall was broken open for the occasion. Also a temporary gate was often made of bamboo or reeds outside the house, so that the main gate need not be used. In many districts when the casket was taken outside, it was customary to break a teacup on the ground by the gate. All of these various practices appear to have been directed at preventing the spirit of the dead person from returning to his former home.

In some places a fire was built at the house when the casket was being carried out, while in others the leader of the funeral procession or other members thereof carried a flame, and in still others a fire was started at the burial ground before or after interment. The reasons varied. Dependent on the locality, the fire served to guide the way, to fend off devils, to purify the surroundings, to light the funeral pyre, to burn trash, to keep people warm, or to accomplish some combination of these purposes, but in any case fire seems to have been a normal accompaniment to the funeral. A number of dialectical terms suggested that it symbolized the presence of the fire diety. A mortuary tablet bearing the posthumous Buddhist name of the deceased was placed by his deathbed and later sent along with the funeral procession to the cemetery. Usually it was carried by the direct heir and for this reason served to inform the community of the latter's identity—in many places a term meaning "bearer of the mortuary tablet" is synonymous with "heir." In connection with this, we might mention that the wife of the heir was spoken of in many areas as "the bearer of the tray," because it was she who placed an offering of food by the corpse.

In numerous districts women and children of the bereaved family dragged a strip of white cloth before the casket in the funeral procession, and all persons present covered their heads with a cloth, a triangular piece of paper, or a headband. Women sometimes wore the cotton headdress ordinarily reserved for weddings, and in a few areas the closely related women wrapped themselves in white robes, with the left sleeves over their heads. Funeral clothing in general was white.

On the way from the house to the cemetery, rice or coins, carried in baskets, were scattered along the road. In some places it was the practice for the procession to go by a winding route, presumably to hinder the spirit of the dead from finding its way back home.

In principle the grave appears to have been dug by the family itself, but in many villages the chief mourner merely fixed the spot and left the work to outsiders, while in some cases even the location was determined by the funeral association. It was the practice for the bereaved family to give a special feast for the gravediggers, apparently because the work was considered very close to taboo. The task, we might observe, was relegated to the younger members of the association, and they went about it dressed in their dirtiest field clothes.

On the way back from the burial or cremation, the family did not stop at any other house than their own, and when they arrived there they sprinkled salt about to purify the premises, in accordance with a very ancient belief. In villages along the seacoast those who had attended a burial all washed their hands and faces in the ocean and cleansed their mouths with seawater. Often upon reentering their houses, the mourners washed their feet in a basin, without using their hands, and sometimes they discarded the footgear they had worn.

In a newspaper of 1882 a man who had just returned from Shimane Prefecture wrote that in one village, when a person died, professional wailing women were taken along to the funeral, and in 1899 it was reported in the journal *Fūzoku Gahō* (*Pictorial Report on Manners and Customs*) that a similar custom prevailed in the district of Shima (Mie Prefecture). It was added in the latter account that there were distinctions as to the types of wailing and fixed prices for each. Women receiving two *shō* (one-tenth bushel) of rice were expected to be twice as frenzied as those receiving only one. Similar practices were to be found in other communities. The women were generally asked not only to weep but also to make speeches at the grave about the dead person's good deeds and the inconsolable grief of his survivors. The wailers were not invariably professionals. In one section of Kagoshima, as well as in certain villages of the Gotō Archipelago, Nagasaki Prefecture, their function was performed by close female relatives. Apparently, however, the weeping was regarded more as a formal propriety than as a genuine expression of sadness on the part of the bereaved women, and professionals or semi-professionals were considered suitable in most places. By the end of the Meiji period the custom had passed out of existence except for a few derivative practices in very remote regions.

There was a marked tendency during Meiji toward splendid funerals, arising not only out of the desire to impress people, but also from the idea that one day the dead person would have to be confronted again in the other world. Almost everyone desired as big a funeral as possible, and the ceremonies consequently became more and more magnificent, with the number of participants increasing constantly. In the towns the taboos disappeared relatively early, and one not uncommonly saw total strangers standing around to watch large funeral processions. In villages where ancient customs were more or less intact, however, such was unthinkable. On Okinawa, for example, the families on both sides of the street along which a cortege was to pass put stakes before their gates to keep their houses being contaminated. Pregnant women were not supposed even to look upon such a procession, and if they were

unavoidably obliged to attend, they tucked a small mirror inside
their obi to deflect evil spirits.

4. THE SPREAD OF CREMATION

The three known Japanese methods for disposing of the dead
are exposure, burial, and cremation. The first all but disappeared at an early date and traces of it are found only in the
islands of the Okinawa group. The second, burial, was for
centuries the most common by far, but during and after the
Meiji era it was to a great degree replaced by cremation.

The first Japanese reference to cremation is in a passage in
the *Shoku-Nihon-gi* (*Chronicles of Japan, Continued,* a ninth
century text) about a Buddhist priest named Dōshō who requested that his body be burned after his death. The practice spread
among the aristocracy and priesthood of the Nara period, and
in the Heian there were five famous crematoria near Kyoto, of
which two, Toribeyama and Funaokayama, are mentioned from
time to time in the literature of the age. In times of war,
pestilence, and famine, the bodies of commoners were covered
with oil and burned. Aside from such instances, however, the
process whereby cremation was adopted by the lower classes is
not thoroughly understood. Presumably scarcity of land resulting from population increases was one deterrent to burial, and
a high subterranean water level another, but these conditions
do not exist in many of the areas where cremation has been
adopted. The idea has also been advanced that cremation spread
because of the teachings of certain religious sects, but the
results of a survey by Mr. Hori Ichirō do not confirm this.

The people who believe in cremation obviously do not revere
the body of the dead, but they ordinarily pay deep respect and
honor to his spirit. One wonders, therefore, if the most important reason for cremation is not a religious belief in the
non-identity of body and soul, a belief also implicit in the
practice of providing two tombs (*see below*). Those who

interred their dead recognized the independence of the soul by worshiping it in a place remote from the buried corpse, while those who cremated did so by actually destroying the body, but the underlying idea is much the same. As Mr. Hori has pointed out, the double-tomb system represents a combination of burial with the practice of exposing the body to the elements, while cremation lies psychologically somewhere between the two, the function of the elements in this case being performed by humans.

Burial essentially involves only one ritual, that of interring the body, but cremation involves two, namely, the burning of the body and the placing of the remains in an ossuary. In this respect, cremation is similar to the old system of exposure, which entailed not only laying the corpse out in the open but also bathing and entombing it subsequently.

Cremation was more common in cities than in the country, not only because of the lack of land but also for sanitary reasons. In July, 1873, the chancellery prohibited the practice, but this action was nullified in May, 1875, and never again attempted. Crematoria had existed in Tokyo since long before Meiji, but during this era they became much more numerous. In 1889, a huge crematorium was built in the district of Mikawajima. According to a current newspaper, it was capitalized at ¥ 30,000, raised with an issue of 1,200 shares at ¥ 25 the share. Public crematoria directed and operated by officials also appeared, but the smoke and stench around them raised violent opposition in the areas where they were located.

Population movements also contributed to an increasing dependence on cremation. Persons leaving their native villages for other locations usually desired to be taken home after death, and the difficulty of transporting bodies made it virtually unavoidable for their families to cremate them in order to comply.

The exact manner of cremating a body varied with the locality. In some places there was no crematorium, and a temporary shelter was built for each incineration. Often diviners tried by observing the fire and the smoke to determine the direction taken by the soul, that is to say, the state of being into which it would be reborn.

In some districts professional cremators burned the body, while in others the task fell to members of the funeral association. In the either case, the bereaved family usually provided a compensation of food and wine. The bones were usually cleaned on the day following the cremation, and after they had been placed in a receptical they were ordinarily kept on the family altar for the usual forty-nine day mourning period, or in some cases for a year, but in many districts they were sent instead to the local temple. Crematoria began to make arrangements with the temples in various locations for preserving remains, and this eventually led to the practice of dividing up the ashes among Mt. Kōya, the Zenkō-ji, and other famous religious centers.

Cremation was most encouraged in places where land was scarce and sanitary considerations of especial importance, but it gradually spread to the less populated rural areas. Still, there were many, who, emotionally unable to destroy the bodies of those they loved, rejected the practice.

5. TOMBS

a. The Double-Tomb System

For the most part, in modern times a single tomb serves both as a place to bury the dead and as a shrine at which respects are later paid to his spirit, but in certain sections of the country there is a tendency to forget about the actual burial ground as soon as possible and set up a separate tomb for purposes of subsequent ancestor worship. The double-tomb system, as we have chosen to call it here, has in recent years been the subject of many local surveys. In present-day Japan, exclusive of Okinawa and the Amami Archipelago, there are more than sixty known locations where this practice exists, and we may suppose without likelihood of great error that it was more widespread in the Meiji period than it is now.

The origin of this odd custom is uncertain, but it appears to have existed in embryonic form from very ancient times. The prime cause for it was a belief in the non-identity of the body and the soul, which we have mentioned above. The corpse itself, which was considered unclean, was consigned to oblivion, but the spirit had to be ministered to assiduously. As people ceased to consider death unclean, the body of the dead was accorded greater respect, and the double-tomb system was abandoned.

Among the various names for the first tomb—the actual burial place—the most common one is the Buddhist term *sammai*, which means a state of concentration of self-forgetfulness. This is a euphemism indicating that the departed is engaged in meditation leading to nirvana. Other terms for the first tomb usually signify no more nor less than " burial place," or " grave," and one literally means " the tomb where (the body) is thrown away " (*sutebaka*). The most ordinary word for the spiritual tomb, on the other hand, is *rantō-ba*, " the location of the divers sacred pagodas," and many of the variant terms also indicate a place of worship.

Most often the first tomb is rather remote from human habitation, while the second is nearby, usually in the vicinity of a temple or even in the home of the deceased. Still, there are also cases in which the first tomb is nearby and the spiritual tomb distant, and others in which the two are at virtually the same distance from the home. There is therefore no way of knowing what the original practice was in this respect. Often the actual burial ground is the common property of a neighborhood or clan, and in it members of the group have been burying their dead wherever they wished for no one knows how long. Such markers as were used were impermanent—a handy rock or a nearby tree—and it is impossible to tell where any particular person lies, or for that matter how many persons lie in a given place. In comparatively recent times, however, families have taken to gathering together the remains known to belong to their ancestors into a common grave and affixing stone monuments to their plots, a practice that approaches the single-tomb system.

Unlike the first tomb, the second was usually distinguished by a stone epitaph or miniature pagoda, but this too appears to be a relatively late feature. In pre-Tokugawa times this monument seems to have consisted of a mound or a tree or perhaps a grove. Ōshima-mura in Fukui Prefecture employs the double-tomb system, and the old families each perform ceremonies to their ancestors in a particular forest, which they hold sacred. Reports of similar customs have come from other localities. Presumably this was an early form of the practice.

The ancient custom was to abandon the first tomb and worship exclusively at the second. In extreme cases, survivors did not return to the grave after the burial, but in some cases they went once again on the second day, and in others they went throughout the standard forty-nine day mourning period. In any event, after a certain brief interval, they performed all their ceremonies at the second tomb. The people of some villages considered it best to forget where the first tomb was as quickly as possible, but in other villages it was the practice to revisit the first tomb on the first anniversary of the death, or the third, or until such time as a monument was erected at the second tomb. In certain instances ceremonies were held regularly at both tombs. This means, of course, that in the locales in question the double-tomb system was on the way out.

b. Tombstones

The erection of stone epitaphs or miniature stone pagodas over tombs was originally a Buddhist practice. During the middle ages and the Tokugawa period a wide variety of such monuments was employed, but they were all alike in that they were intended as offerings to the dead rather than as markers, and they were not necessarily located at the place of burial. The common people did not use tombstones until fairly late times, and the custom of dedicating one to each person did not spread until the Meiji period. After the Sino-Japanese and Russo-Japanese Wars, it became fashionable to honor the war dead in this way, and the habit developed to the extent that the cemeteries were literally crammed with markers. No doubt a growing attachment of importance to the physical remains of the dead was responsible.

As monuments became more popular, everyone began trying to set up bigger and more magnificent stones than the next person. In crowded city cemeteries the price of plots shot up, and some argued that the cemeteries should be moved out of town.

Still, the tombstone fad, if we may call it that, continued, and continues, apace. Many Japanese are so accustomed to the forest of monuments in modern cemeteries that they unconsciously believe the practice to have come down from ancient times and therefore to be quite proper. But if all the inhabitants of these islands had been setting up individual stones for the dead since early times, the country would have been entirely covered long ago. That it is not is because the common people of the past buried their dead they knew not where and worshiped the spirits of their ancestors collectively at a special "tomb." This was the most feasible way in a land-poor country. In modern times cremation has become widespread, but it helps little if the remains are nevertheless to be buried and covered with a great stone monument, as is now often the case. The day will certainly come when the cemetery problem that Meiji Japan bequeathed us will have to be solved.

Chapter Eight

THE LIFE OF CHILDREN

1. THE CARE OF CHILDREN AND SUPERSTITIOUS PRACTICES

a. Customs Concerning Childbirth

EDWARD Morse, who came to Japan in 1877, made numerous interesting observations on Japanese customs. Among other things he commented that Japanese babies almost never cry, and that he had never seen a Japanese mother lose her temper before a baby. He also stated that no other country cared so lovingly for its children, and that Japanese babies were the best-behaved in the world.

A number of foreigners who subsequently came to Japan considered the country a children's paradise, and while this seems a bit excessive today, the remarks of these visitors are not without value in our studies, since the raising of children in the early Meiji era was far closer to the ancient method than modern Japanese could possibly imagine.

Morse was impressed with the Japanese custom of carrying children about so much of the time. According to him, four out of every five women and five out of every six girls had infants on their backs. Often, he said, the carrier held her hands behind her back to support the child, and the latter put his legs around her waist as though astride a horse.

Actually, the practice was never to leave the child in his baby basket unless his mother and everyone else in the house were too busy to carry him. This last may often have been the case in the country, but in the city there was usually someone handy. As a rule an elder sister was appointed to the task, but when this was impossible, a daughter from another family was engaged. After the spread of schools, one often saw the pitiful sight of a twelve or thirteen year old, no more than a moppet herself, trying to read her lessons and keep an eye on the baby on her back at the same time.

To a stranger like Morse, it must have appeared that the Japanese baby's lot was enviable. One wonders, however, if children in the Japan of those days were really as fortunate as he thought. Miyamoto Jōichi wrote the following of his childhood :

My parents had to work hard, and this certainly told on my mother's health. Her first pregnancy ended in miscarriage, and the second baby died two months after birth. The third one fortunately lived, but the fourth was another miscarriage. I was the fifth child. My father was past 35, and people called me the first child of his old age. After me there was one more boy. Out of six, then, only three lived, and my family was not unusual in this respect. It was that difficult to bring up children before the end of Meiji.

Throughout the Meiji and Taishō eras infant mortality was extremely high. Actually, the writer quoted above lived on an island in the Seto Inland Sea, where natural conditions were comparatively favorable. The situation must have been much worse in areas periodically visited by drought, flood, and other disasters.

Until the Meiji period children were not even protected from smallpox, but the Rrestoration government took strong measures in its early years to see that everyone was inoculated, and there was a tremendous improvement on this score. Among the common people superstition concerning diseases was very strong, and it was generally felt that parents and other interested persons had to resort to all sorts of supernatural means to protect children. There were spells against everything, some of them performed even before the child's birth.

In the northeast region one prenatal ceremony was spoken of with a term that meant literally "bringing up baby." Apparently the idea was that instead of waiting until the child was born to guide it along, it was better, so to speak, to get behind and push. Congratulatory dinners centering around the mother-to-be were given by relatives and neighbors, and everyone seemed to think that they would help insure the child's good fortune. On the other hand, it is quite true that prior to the Meiji period infanticide was widely practiced, but, as is clear from numerous literary references, this was a matter not of choice, but of economic necessity.

In ancient times childbirth was surrounded by taboos, and the expectant mother was forced to live in a separate house of parturition. Although this practice was gradually abandoned, a few customs connected with it were preserved. Immediately after the birth, for instance, the rice served to the mother was prepared separately, in order to limit the member of persons exposed to the food she ate. On the other hand, it was thought that the child's first rice should be shared by as many people as possible for the sake of his future. The placing of rice before the infant marked the opening of the room of parturition, and this rite was combined with a feast dedicated to the god of birth. It is interesting to note that the rice served to the child was the same as that offered to the deity. This is probably a relic of the days when persons making an offering to gods later ate it themselves.

The physical manifestation of the god of birth was usually a small stone. In the villages of the Atsumi Peninsula, the stone was either passed down from earlier generations, borrowed from the midwife, or simply picked up on the premises of the tutelary deity. Devotions before the stone began when the mother was in the fifth month of pregnancy. When being worshiped it was placed on a tray, but otherwise it was kept on the shelf that served as an altar to Ebisu, one of seven popular gods of fortune. After the celebration of the baby's seventh day, when he was named, the stone was returned to the place whence it had come.

The midwife was surrounded by a number of popular beliefs. Throughout most of the country she was spoken of as the *toriagebaba*, or "the old woman who takes up," and there is rather more to this name than meets the eye. Many a country boy, having asserted himself too strongly for his age, has had the embarrassing experience of being reduced to insignificance by the statement "Young man, I took you up." It is clear from this and other dialectical terms employed for the midwife and her function that she was regarded as responsible to a large degree for the child's very existence and was therefore due a great deal of respect. In other words, she was not merely an assistant to childbirth, but a sort of guardian angel who sponsored the child as a member of the society of mankind. In some places the protégé was expected to present her with a gift on New Year's Day, as well as during the *bon* festival, and to invite her to his wedding. Often he was required to stand by her coffin when she died. She was, in brief, a sort of foster parent.

A close examination reveals that children had similar relationships to still other people. There existed, for example, a custom of having a newborn baby suckled at the breast of a woman other than his mother. Often this woman gave milk only the first time, but in places she continued to do so for some time, even though the child was also received by its true mother. In any event, a foster relationship was thus created, and it extended to the other children suckled at the woman's breast.

In the event that a young girl took charge of caring for a child, the child also had a close connection with her mother and father. We have mentioned above the practice of leaving a baby at an appointed place and having him picked up and carried home by a person outside the family. We should add here that his benefactor also was considered a parent of sorts.

b. The Care of Infants

After the ceremonies celebrating a child's birth, the next big events in his life were his first trip to the tutelary shrine and his first step. As a rule, when the baby was first presented to the family deity, someone pinched him just enough to make him cry, and the deity was thereafter supposed to recognize him. This practice apparently spread with the worship of clan deities. In the northeast, devotions to the god of birth, held at the time of birth, were very important, and afterward it was necessary only to bow perfunctorily before the lares of the house, but in the west, where the clan system was very strong, worship before the clan deity was absolutely necessary, while the god of birth had virtually been forgotten.

When a child took his first step, it was often the custom to make an x-mark on his forehead with soot taken from a kitchen pot. More often the mark was modified into the Chinese character for "large" 大 or that for "dog" 犬. In many instances lip rouge or face powder have been substituted for the soot, but the latter, which appears originally to have been taken from the family hearth, was probably once a mark of respect to the god of fire.

When the baby first walked he was often made to cross a bridge, or to pass by either the well or the privy, the action in any case being intended to secure his well being. Ceremonies to the deity of the toilet on this occasion presented a number of interesting variations. Often a bit of clean rice wrapped in white paper, a coin, or some other offering was hung from the ceiling of the room.

In places a pair of chopsticks was inserted in a crack between the ceiling planks. Whatever the particular action, however, the country as a whole recognized a deep relationship between the toilet and the health of the mother and child. There are also examples of the child having been taken to pay respects to the neighbors' toilets, and in such cases the honored household usually presented the infant with a ball of hemp thread intended to help make his future bright. In the islands off Hizen this token was called by a name implying that it lengthened the life of the baby. In later times people of this locale added to the gift a little of bag of money, which was tied around the baby's neck.

There were also various magic practices associated with the preparation of the baby's first meal tray, the appearance of his first teeth, and his first birthday. Spells designed to cure or prevent crying in the night, fits, peevishness, diarrhea, and so on were common.

The various forms of magic were considered particularly important until the child reached its seventh year. During this interval his life was thought to be more or less in the hands of the gods. He was treated with exceptional kindness, and few efforts were made to train him against his will. Funerals for children under seven were quite simple, and the bodies were usually buried just by the house. Whereas elaborate precautions were taken to prevent the spirits of dead adults from returning, it was rather expected that infants would be reborn.

Judging from the prevalence of superstitions, we may readily conclude that the health of the young suffered from lack of knowledge on the part of their parents. People could not care properly for their offspring simply because they did not realize that to do so involved more than magic and indulgence. Moreover, the superstitions were not to be swept away by anything so simple as a dose of enlightenment propaganda.

2. GAMES AND TOYS

a. New Games

Often great changes in the games that children play occur

suddenly, but there are so few records concerning such things that one can but rely on traditions and hearsay. Of these, however, there is an abundance. Some years ago, for example, a newspaper described the following game. The children decided by means of the stone-paper-scissors game who was to be "it," and then the unlucky one had to carry the others around on his back, one by one. The rider chanted "Deer, deer, how many horns?" and the other child had to guess how many fingers his burden had raised behind his back. More than a hundred and seventy letters were sent to the newspaper on the subject of this game, and it is clear that it was a new fashion that had spread in the area around Kyūshū and the Inland Sea. The exact procedure and words, we may note, varied from place to place, and sometimes expressions not seemingly invented by children were mixed in. It is to be supposed from this fact that the game was disseminated after the development of mass communication facilities.

One is astonished at the speed with which this game spread over a wide area and at the many variations it displayed. The suspicion arises that it was in reality a new form of a guessing game that had existed earlier. There is today a popular children's game in which one child stands in the middle of a circle formed by the others, and the latter march around singing a little chant that begins "*kagome, kagome*" (an expression of uncertain meaning) and ends "Who is right behind you?" This is probably the most typical of the guessing games, and an examination of the stages through which it developed indicates that it was at first an imitation of some religious rite, not unlike the mimicking of annual festivals (*tarumikoshi*) by city children of the present day. Until the end of the Tokugawa period the young men and women of a district in what is now Miyagi Prefecture had a similar sport for passing the long winter evenings. One of the less quickwitted of the group was placed in the center, and the others paraded in a circle around him chanting the same thing over and over. Eventually the boy in the center grew sleepy, and then when asked questions he would make all sorts of amusing answers. This game in turn resembles a semi-religious game played by adults in the Meiji era and resembling the so-called Ouija-board game. The participants spread a sheet of possible answers before them and after invoking the help of the god of agriculture, pointed out the supposedly correct answers to various questions with chopsticks. The suggestion of a religious origin is perfectly clear in this.

Apparently after adults of the past lost their religious beliefs, children continued to play guessing games that preserved outward features of primordial divination rites. The origin of the word *kagome* is uncertain, but it may well be a variant of the imperative *kagame*, or ("reveal") altered to coincide with word *kago* ("cage"), which appears several times in the chant that the children sing. There are many other guessing games, but this one continues to be popular, possibly because it moves right along and never comes to a distinct end.

One unusual form of play in the Meiji period consisted of walking up to an unknown person in Western clothing and asking the time. If the latter complied by consulting his watch, there was great mirth, since everyone had guessed beforehand whether the timepiece would be small or large, gold or silver, and so on, and the child most nearly correct won. Urchins who could barely walk alone would approach dignified gentleman and in baby talk ask for the time. One curious feature is that this game did not differ materially from a number of others that were popular in Europe at the same time. New games seem to spread the world over with amazing speed, and yet there is a certain ancient consistency in the world of children. A quality of permanence combines somehow with a tendency toward swiftly changing fashions.

It seems rather a shame when youngsters desert their old games for new ones, but there is usually logic in the shifting fads. "What time is it?" was probably only a new form of the teasing and razzing that villagers of the old days handed out to strangers, particularly those so unfortunate as to appear on a festival day.

There were four classes of group play, distinguished by differences in age and location. Very small children played inside the house, where their parents could keep an eye on them constantly. When they grew a little older they tended to move out under the eaves of the house, or into the garden, where, if they could not be seen, they could at least be heard. As farm houses came to be furnished with glass doors and broad outside hallways this form of play developed greatly (the recess hour at primary schools is rather an extension of it), one unfortunate result being that independent group play was hampered. Children felt that they were under their parents' noses, and they hesitated to act spontaneously. The language of children tended to disappear, and the rhythmical cadences of simple words, repeated over and over, went the way of the songs that adults working together had once sung. City play, in a sense, suffered from the same loss of rhythm as city labor.

The third stage of play was that in which young boys who had "been there only a moment ago" suddenly disappeared. This usually lasted between the ages of four and eight, or thereabouts, and it was a very important part of a boy's social training—the part, in fact, that taught him the fundamentals of equality and honesty. He rejected all interference from his family and went out on his own, but since no one liked to play with disagreeable children, he soon learned to suppress his will for the good of the group. Away from his parents, he learned words and behavior they had not taught him, along with the various games that children had always played. With the coming of schools in the Meiji era, this phase of a child's growth came to be regarded all too lightly, much to the child's misfortune.

During this stage the children walked on stilts, spun tops,

competed at throwing rocks, and played hide-and-seek, tag, hopskotch, or one of a number of variant games. Hopskotch appears to have first become fashionable during Meiji, and there are numerous dialectical terms for it. The novelist Toku-tomi Roka, reminiscing on his childhood in the Meiji twenties, mentioned the game a number of times, and that would appear to be the period when it became fashionable.

The fourth stage of children's play was that in which they gathered on the streets and engaged in competitive sports, occasionally with a suggestion of gambling. The rivalry was often alarmingly fierce, since the winners soon became the leaders, but this was a distinct part of a child's training for manhood.

Changes in Toys

By the end of the Meiji period the principal toys were manufactured on a commercial basis, but in the earlier part of period this was not the case. There were in fact only a few types of toys then and the origin of each could probably be traced back to early times. The Japanese word for toys, *omocha*, comes indirectly from the word *moteasobi*, or *mochi-asobi*, which means "to play with," or simply "to handle," and it originally referred simply to some object with which the child amused himself, possibly something of his own contrivance that would not even be considered a toy today. Children everywhere like to fool with objects that their parents use, and for this reason adults have added to the vocabulary words for toys that mean literally "something to be bad with," "something to break," and so on. Still, the instinct of the child in this respect being nearly uncontrollable, parents have usually hit upon the device of making imitations of their own belongings to give to their offspring. In the Shichitō Archipelago off Kagoshima, the first step in building a house was to make a wooden doll for the children with the carpenter's tools. In

Yamaguchi Prefecture on the other hand, children were given not dolls but simply extra pieces of wood. In any event, however, an attempt was made to let them have something produced with the tools, which they invariably loved. These blocks of spare wood were essentially the same as modern building blocks, and like so many other toys they were designed to give the young a chance to imitate the work of adults.

In the Meiji era toys were bought for children only during festivals and celebrations, and the happiness at receiving a new plaything helped on such occasions to transmit the joyous feelings of the parents to the children. In this way toys contributed to the preservation of ancient customs. The most typical momento of a festival was a mask like the ones worn by the dancers. Children were also given miniature drums and flutes so that they could imitate the music-makers who had contributed to their delights at the celebration. There was a well-known lullaby that began:

Boom, boom, hear the drums and flutes!
If you come to the festival in our village....

Articles held by the dancers, as well as items presented to or sacred to the shrine around which the festival centered, were also imitated and given to the children. Many of the souvenirs for which certain locales are famous today originated in this way. In fact, the general term for a souvenir that one presents to someone else is *miyage*, compounded of *miya* meaning "shrine" and *ge* meaning "container."

Commercially produced toys became a very important item in Japanese industry during the Meiji period. The various toys of Europe and America were imitated with remarkable cunning, and as they became available at low cost, they began to be exported. It is said that in 1883 a workman named Arai Genroku, who lived at Naka-okachi-machi, Shitaya, Tokyo, invented a flywheel that greatly improved toy automobiles, trains, and the like. Then in 1891 the first spring-propelled toys were made.

During the second decade of Meiji, Japanese toys were exported chiefly to Shanghai, Hong Kong, and Singapore, but soon afterward they found their way to America as well. By this time Japanese immigrants in the United States were engaged in many business activities, especially in San Francisco and Seattle, and one among them is said to have made a great success selling toy turtles pulled with a string. Another Japanese did quite well at the Chicago Exposition with a toy butterfly that would actually fly.

3. THE FUNCTION OF CHILDREN IN VILLAGE CELEBRATIONS

a. Annual Festivals

In the ceremonies and festivals that brightened the village year, the children of Meiji played an important part, the main reason being that adults, having lost their simple faith in the old gods, relegated the worship of them to the youngsters. When the latter performed well, their parents, though no longer seriously affected by religious sentiment, took great pleasure and pride. This phenomenon is to be observed all over Japan. Among the ancient rituals or festivals that became largely children's affairs was a variety of observances held on the fifteenth and sixteenth days of the first month in the year, such as the festival of the god of the road (*dōso-shinsai*), the ritual driving away of birds that might be harmful to crops (*torioi*), and the attack on destructive moles (*mogurauchi*). Others were the festival of the god of agriculture in the second month (*hatsuuma*), the doll festival in the third (*hinamatsuri*), the boy's festival in fifth (*gogatsu sekku*), the festival of the star Vega (*tanabata*) and the children's *bon* (*jizōbon*) in the seventh, the chrysanthemum festival in the ninth (*tōkanya*), the festival of the boar in the tenth (*inoko*), and festivals to local mountain gods.

In eastern Japan the festival of the god of the road and that of the chrysanthemum were the most important, but in western Japan they were far outclassed by the children's *bon* and the festival of the boar. To give an example, the following is a description of the children's *bon* celebration in the Usukine district of Ōita Prefecture. The festival came shortly after the regular *bon* season, on the twenty-fourth day of the seventh month in the old calendar. Shortly before that time the children of the community went to each house and asked for contributions of rice and money. The families for whom this was the first *bon* after the death of a member made special gifts of lanterns and artificial flowers. When the great day came, the children set up shops on the streets and sold cookies and cakes, along with candlesticks and other religious implements. They borrowed a statue of the bodhisattva Jizō, who is supposed to be a patron of children, and set it up at an appropriate place for the center of the festival. In the evening priests came and chanted sutras. To add to the entertainment the adults provided the customary *bon* festival dances in the street. After everything was over, the proceeds from the sales were used to cover expenses, and unsold items thrown away or burned.

In Kurima-mura, Kawage County, Mie Prefecture, the festival to the god of the mountain was a great annual event for children. It took place on the sixth or seventh days of the first and eleventh months in the old calendar year. The youngsters covered a stone that represented the deity with red coloring and walked about village singing :

Collection box for the god of the mountain!
A coin, please, or three sheeves of straw.
Your house will be happy and rich.
One coin, three sheeves, a gift to the god—
Yoi, yoi, yoi, the god of the mountain !

Later they erected a bamboo pole and built a great bonfire around it with the straw they had collected. When the fire burned down the pole fell, and the direction in which it pointed was supposed to be blessed with a good crop in the year to come.

In Hayama-mura, Kurita County, Shiga Prefecture, the festival of the mountain deity came on the seventh day of the first month. The children wore headbands and painted five red spots on their faces. Bearing bows, arrows, and a large basket containing a crude wooden image of the deity, they went around singing:

> *This year will be good!*
> *Ear after ear of rice will bud,*
> *And the grain will be measured*
> *Not in pecks put in bushels.*

The procession was accompanied by an adult, who eventually placed the image of the deity in a shrine at the foot of the sacred mountain.

In Toki-mura, Fuwa County, Gifu Prefecture, there was a festival called "seventeenth night," since it came on the seventeenth of the first, fifth, and ninth months. On these days the children went to the shrine of the local tutelary deity and made a pile of stones three feet square, on the top of which they placed a special rock representing the god of fire. Then they went about collecting rice, which they cooked as an offering to the deity. When the preparations were finished they returned, chanting and shouting, to the shrine and, having circled the sacred precinct three times, presented their offering, which was subsequently divided among the villagers. At dawn lots were drawn to determine who would perform the necessary work for the festival in the following year, and when this was decided, it was announced in loud cries. The older villagers say that the sound of the voices seemed somehow mysterious and ethereal as they heard them from their sleeping mats.

In some cases even the all-important festivities of New Year's Eve were left largely to children—a sure indication of weakening faith in the traditional gods on the part of adults. Also, in special children's New Year celebrations, the boys and girls often took charge of various superstitious practices. The classic procedure was for them to go from house to house chanting felicitous phrases. They were probably considered to be taking the place of the gods, for people in the villages were especially concerned over signs and portents on this occasion. Apparently even after adults ceased to hold clear-cut beliefs, they could not help feeling somewhat reverent when their children performed religious rites.

b. The Activities of Children's Groups

There were organized groups of children who took it upon themselves to handle one or the other of the yearly festivals we have been discussing. These were less permanent and fixed than the young people's associations, and in places where adults continued to believe in the gods and maintain the ancient group celebrations, they were not formed. It is interesting to note that where they existed they were strictly hierarchical, the younger members being completely subordinate to the older ones.

These groups usually managed their financial needs by canvassing from house to house as the occasion demanded. The children were from ten to fifteen, and the oldest were graduated into the young people's association each year. The territorial scope was smaller than that of the young people's organizations, usually covering only a part of a neighborhood. The activities of children's groups were greatly curbed when the school system came into being, but in villages where neighborhoods as such retained a good deal of power, such associations often played a larger part in the child's life than the school group.

4. THE EDUCATION OF CHILDREN

a. Education Prior to School

Edward Morse, in his diary of his journey to Japan, praised Japanese children for their knowledge of plants and animals, and indeed it appears that children of Morse's day were quite familiar with the world of nature. After primary schooling became compulsory, however, school life began to occupy a great part of the child's time, and the process by which he became an adult changed completely. Of course, at first a relatively low percentage of young people, particularly girls, attended school, but after the Russo-Japanese War the proportion increased rapidly, and by the end of the Meiji period, the number of schools was comparable to that in the most advanced countries of the world.

The spread of schools unfortunately cannot be taken as an unqualified improvement in education. The new learning tended to exclude such practical elements as the knowledge of nature that Morse had admired, and in many instances it gave the children distorted views of themselves and conditions around them. Formerly education of the young had provided training for life within a group, if nothing else. The group, of course, was as a rule a feudalistic farming village, whose populace was limited by poverty and weakness, and the children naturally suffered from the same limitations, but at least their characters were forged on the anvil of tradition. School education as offered in the Meiji period all too often slighted this phase of a child's development. Naturally there were basic parts of a child's education that could never be furnished by the school, and girls in particular had to acquire much that they needed to know directly from their mothers. It was quite normal, therefore, for the children of Meiji times to stay away from classes to help with household chores, and in most farming villages it was impossible for either boys or girls to lose themselves completely in their studies.

The general aim of home training was to mould the child in a pattern fixed by tradition. The rules being very definite, there was a tendency to place too much emphasis on scolding and punishment, but the rules were the results of generations of experience, and they had the indisputable authority of age. The child was required to imitate and actually to perform tasks for himself. It was recognized, however, that there were distinct levels of development, and until the age of seven there was virtually no discipline. During this period the child's life approached the happy state described by so many foreign observers. When children reached the age of seven, however, the change was swift. Henceforward, cry though they might, they were required to help with the hard work. Girls began first to take care of the family Buddhist altar, and at nine they were put in charge of a younger child. At twelve they began to run back and forth between their weaving and their potato digging.

All of this training was perfectly objective. The adult neither explained nor theorized to the child. The latter simply imitated until he learned. This in many ways was good, since it taught him to consider actual, tangible realities instead of vague abstractions. Adults in farming villages were praised by their fellows when they performed their tasks well, and children worked hard to gain the same approval.

b. Group Education

When the child's home training was complete, he came in for a new type of discipline in the form of constant criticism by his fellow villagers. When the latter gathered together for a meeting of any sort, rumors and comments about individuals made up much of the conversation, and when a young person committed some moral offense or did something silly, he was bound to be talked about. As a rule, he was particularly sensitive to the opinions of the young women's and men's associations. Few youths could hold their own against the opposition of these groups. The latter, for their part, might on occasion go so far as to the expel a member or stop speaking to him, but usually their laughter was sufficient punishment. The Japanese will go to almost any lengths to avoid being laughed at, and education by derision was exceedingly effective.

After the Meiji period young people were deprived almost completely of this type of training. To be sure, the schools were careful to suit material to the age and ability of the children, and to some extent they went in for child psychology, but they suffered from a tendency to emphasize abstract knowledge, and too little attention was given to the actual environment in which the child had to grow up. Much effort went into the improvement of the school system as a system, but an understanding of the everyday lives that the children led was late in coming. Attention was focused on culture and politics in the great metropolitan centers, and important elements of local culture were ignored. As is needless to say, there were many good points about school education, but it erred in failing to incorporate the good features of traditional training. Meiji schools implicitly, and often explicitly, scorned the good as well as the bad features of the past, and the results were in many ways quite unfortunate.

Chapter Nine

THE LIFE OF YOUNG MEN

1. THE OLD AND NEW YOUNG MEN'S ASSOCIATIONS

Since the Restoration abolished feudalism and purported to establish equality among the people, the youth of the nation held bright new hopes for equal opportunities. The word success was engraved on the heart of every young man. In order for a boy to make good, however, the first requirement was an up-to-date cultural background, and unfortunately for many, Japanese society was advancing too rapidly to wait for those who did not have such a background to acquire it. Moreover, whatever the theory, the opportunities for a modern education were practically limited to those young men who were financially able to go to the cities.

In most villages there were few so fortunate. The great majority had to sit at home and hope that their turn would some day come. This was not, perhaps, as bad as it sounds. There was always the possibility that modern culture, or at least elements of it, would reach the rural areas, and even if this never occurred, a job or a change in the family fortune might take a young man to the city. In the latter part of the Meiji period, this happened rather often, but in the earlier half only a small number of youths saw their dreams materialize.

Within the average village the young men were organized into a more or less independent association, the existence of which was sanctioned by tradition. These groups were called by such names as "young men's union" (*wakamono-gumi*), "youths' group" (*wakashū*), and "youths' party" (*waka-renchū*) and they varied somewhat in nature according to the locale. In Satsuma, where they were very strictly organized, a certain amount of deference was probably accorded to social standing, and the same may have been true in certain other areas, but as a rule the older members were the leaders irrespective of their social status. In the seacoast villages of the Izu Peninsula, the youth organizations were preserved long after they had passed out of existence elsewhere. There, the age limits were sixteen and thirty-five, and the principal functions were police duty, fire-fighting, and rescue work in times of calamity, but the group also performed various other services for the community. The upper age limit was rather high in this case, apparently because the police duties were considered very important. As a rule, the top age was about twenty-five. During the first few years, members were required by the leaders to work hard and behave themselves properly, but men over twenty suffered very little interference from the association unless they happened to be in charge of some particular activity.

The youth association had considerable authority in the community. In many places, they could do anything to anybody without danger of criticism from other villagers. Evidently they controlled their organizations so well and worked so hard to contribute to the general welfare that the remainder of the community held them rather in awe. At the same time, they seem to have had plenty of respect for themselves.

In the Meiji period, however, great changes took place. Whereas local officials had formerly relied largely on the young men to maintain the law and fight fires, the new government, by way of organizing provincial administration, put a stop to this. The Meiji leaders attached almost as much importance to the constabulary as to the army, and they were totally unwilling to allow each village its independent police force, no matter how old the custom.

Under the circumstances, the young men's associations

underwent a curious transition. Instead of enforcing of the law, they now became more often than not the objects of law enforcement. They had always been leading organizers of festival dances and such "night life" as the villages afforded, and since these social activities were regarded with suspicion by the new police officials, the youth, sad to say, were constantly under surveillance. Deprived of their customary work and pleasure many of them began to look to the redlight houses in the towns and cities for entertainment.

In a book called *Nihon Dōtoku-ron* (*On Japanese Ethics*, 1886), Nishimura Shigeki passed the following harsh judgment on the youth associations:

> In the towns and villages there are young good-for-nothings who gather together in bands to drink or gamble or run after women. Assuming command of festivals and celebrations, they forswear reason or morality and run rampant over the community. They neither pay heed to the words of their elders nor obey the local laws, and they inflict no end of hardship on others. A good wholesome lad cannot safely walk the streets without joining their organization, and having been forced into it, he eventually becomes so used to its ways that he too becomes a ruffian. The spread of primary schools over the country has done much to curb the activities of these groups, but in many places they are still offending against the public morals and causing harm to innocent people.

This is hardly a fair criticism of the youth groups as an institution, since it is based only on what they became after the central government turned local administration and custom topsy-turvy. Opinions of this sort, however, were rather usual among the critics and polemicists of the day, even those who had originally come from the villages.

It is impossible to describe in a few words the relationship of the old associations to the community, but, at any rate, they constituted an active element of society. They played an important part in annual festivals and administrative affairs, and it was only natural that they sometimes went too far in exercising their authority. From time to time they created a good deal of tension, occasionally culminating in arguments and fights, but usually these could be settled, if necessary, by older persons in the community. The convulsive changes of early Meiji, however, destroyed the respect of the young people for the elder generation as well as their proper judgment of their own importance. They began to rebel against the orderly life of the community, and their pride and recklessness brought further unhappiness to village society.

As one example of the fate of the youth groups, we might cite the case of a fishing village in Niigata Prefecture after the Restoration. Here the group had been very powerful, and the village officials constantly had their eyes on it. Eventually, during one *bon* season, the young men decided to take a holiday for seven days, despite an official decision to the contrary. The authorities thereupon closed the dormitory where the group slept and ordered a fine against those who attempted to stay in it. This action effectively robbed the association of its strength, and it was ultimately reorganized into a spineless youth assembly under the control of the officials.

Until the Meiji era the youth groups had been organized village by village. Now, however, the old villages were often combined into larger administrative units, and an attempt was made to organize the young men on a new basis. Progress was understandably slow. The traditional associations broke down, but the new ones had trouble getting started. There was a blank of several years, and, in some communities, of nearly twenty. The popular rights movement stimulated the formation of new groups in some places, but only for a time.

Finally, the call of a leader was heard. In 1890, the eighteen-year-old Yamamoto Takinosuke, a school teacher in the village of Chitose, Hiroshima Prefecture, published a statement advocating the formation of youth assemblies, and this struck a chord in the hearts of those who were concerned with youth's plight. At the beginning of that year, Yamamoto, disturbed at the torpor of rural young people, had organized a society including more than twenty other like-minded young men, and in the following year, he formed a young people's assembly in his village. In 1896 he published an article entitled "Country Youth," which ran in part as follows:

> They are both youths, but one is coddled and protected, while the other is cast away on the roadside. The latter is the so-called "country boy." He lives in the fields, he has no diploma, he has no certificate of graduation.... Of late the voice of youth has finally come to be heard, but this voice of youth is the voice of the student. We hear of theories on youth, and the like, but these are all in reality theories on students.... The youth of the rural districts are humble and self-effacing, shy and retiring. Discarded by society, they lie down quietly and sleep. They show no signs of the spirit it takes to catch up with the others. As the cherry is the flower of flowers, youth is the flower of mankind, but our young people are wasting the best season of their lives. Each stands off to himself doing nothing, waiting emptily for the chilly autumn winds of old age.

In some villages, the boys who had done well in primary school formed evening study societies in an attempt to satisfy their urge to improve themselves. These were quite numerous in the second and third decades of Meiji, but apparently the young men did not find the broad concepts of statesmanship and national salvation to their liking. Most of them confined their efforts to practical studies, such as arithmetic and bookkeeping, and, in any event, the development of the school system soon rendered their organizations useless. Actually, so long as the teachers in local areas were out of tune with the actual conditions in which their pupils lived, it was impossible to hope for a spontaneous movement on the part of the latter. The youth assemblies organized by Yamamoto Takinosuke, however, were concerned with more than the spread of school learning. They demanded a healthy interchange of ideas among youth as a whole.

The Young Men's Christian Associations of England and America had already established branches in Tokyo in 1880 and were beginning to spread to other cities. The Japanese YMCA published a very dignified journal called *Rikugō Zasshi*, which had considerable influence, and it is possible that the teaching of this group played some indirect part in the formation of Yamamoto's association. The latter, as it happened, was rather vague as to fundamental principles, but it was clearly intended as a replacement for the old-fashioned youth groups, and at first it was organized by the traditional village units. Later the various branches attempted to encompass the legal administrative units, but this on the whole hampered their growth, since the young people were psychologically orientated about their own small communities. The new associations further suffered from the lack of governmental support.

After the Sino-Japanese and Russo-Japanese Wars, the new youth associations came suddenly to be regarded with great favor. In December, 1905, the Ministry of Education issued a statement concerning the leadership and encouragement of young people's groups in the provinces, and in September of the next year the Home Ministry distributed a hortatory pamphlet entitled "Local Autonomy and Young People's Associations." The interest of the government continued to increase, and in March, 1910, eighty-two youth groups were awarded official commendations.

Administrative control by the central authorities was never jeopardized during this era, but by the latter years of Meiji, the national government had begun to recognize the need for giving the provinces leeway to handle some of their own affairs, and the new youth groups took their place among the organs of local self-government. The serious problem that then confronted youth became, and for a long time remained, that of maintaining harmony between their own fresh movement and what the prominent local leaders considered to be autonomy. In 1909 one astute critic, having observed the youth groups in various districts, commented that every time the young people made a mistake the local administrators were ready and waiting to interfere. There was danger, he pointed out, that these healthy independent societies, devoted to the advancement of culture, would be snuffed out.

Before the adoption of the modern system of local administration, the farming and fishing villages were themselves lively self-governing bodies, and the traditional youth associations were conditioned by this fact. The reorganization of local government often combined a number of formerly independent villages into the same official unit, but this did not mean that cooperation among them was immediately extended to all phases of life. It was a difficult task for a youth association based on the new administrative partitions to worm its way into the hearts of people who were still concerned first and foremost with their own little villages. The new groups had little of the atmosphere of the old, and what there was of it was purely formal. Some villages defiantly maintained the old associations until long after the Meiji period, but even when this was not the case, the progress of the new ones was slow. Eventually, however, with help from the government and in response to growing demands for local cultural activities, they were recognized as a valuable means of social education, and their organization, now firm within, was extended throughout the nation.

2. BECOMING A MAN

Modern school education divides young men's lives into such phases as entrance examinations, the beginning of school, promotion, graduation, and the search for a job, but in the past the really important dividing line in a youth's life was his acceptance into the young men's association. As a rule this occurred when the lad was sixteen or seventeen.

One interesting feature was that the person who sponsored his entry into the group was ordinarily not his father, but a temporary foster parent especially enlisted for the purpose. This man was commonly referred to as the "loincloth parent" (*fundoshi-oya*, *heko-oya*), since to symbolize the attainment of manhood the youth began at this time to wear a loincloth. The choice of an outsider indicated that the function of educating and guiding the young man was henceforward to be in the hands of persons other than his true parents.

In many places, there were various initiation rites. In Akita Prefecture, for example, a number of villages required that the youth plow a certain amount of land in a day. On the other hand, in some villages of Nagasaki Prefecture the boy was held by the neck and his breath cut off for a time. In Kagoshima Prefecture, where the youth organizations were very strict, the young man was required to stay shut up in the local shrine for seven days prior to a festival and throughout the final night to sit, or rather kneel, in a formal position. No one who has never sat in Japanese style can appreciate the difficulty of this. One must sit on one's heels with knees, toes, and heels together and body erect. In this case during the test older members looked in on the candidate from time to time to make sure that he did not budge. In various villages on the Izu Peninsula, boys were required to take an oath prescribed by the society and incorporating its rules for conduct. In villages near Kyoto the young man was led to the top of a nearby peak and made to swear that he would maintain the proper rules of behavior. When taking the oath, he had to lie face down with the upper part of his body projecting straight out over the edge of a cliff and his feet held down by an older person. Similar rites were observed in other parts of the country, particularly those where mountain worship was in practice.

In addition to the initiation rites, there were certain physical standards that the young man was required to meet. In the ancient villages, after all, work was largely cooperative, and strength was not merely a question of individual concern. Often the members of the young men's group gathered at the local shrine after the evening meal to test their physical prowess. As a rule they competed at carrying a large stone, which might weigh as much as a hundred and fifty pounds. The standard amount of work that a young man was expected to perform varied with the topography, the quality of the farming implements, and so on. In one village in Kita-azumi County, Nagano Prefecture, a man was required to be able in one day to plow enough land for a yield of three or four sacks of rice (one sack held about two bushels), to transplant enough rice plants to make four or five sacks, to weed about nine acres, to strip six sacks of rice or to mill five sacks of grain. He had also to be able to carry one sack weighing from a hundred and thirty-five to a hundred and forty-five pounds on his shoulder. This last figure may have been higher than usual, since in many villages for which statistics are available, the weight was set at one hundred pounds for men and eighty-five for women.

When a young man was able to meet these requirements, he was allowed for the first time to wear men's farm clothing and carry a tobacco pouch. The standard in fishing villages were somewhat different. Presumably because at work the men were literally all in the same boat, each received a grown man's share of the catch as soon as he entered the young men's association. This is not to say, of course, that everyone's share was equal, since individuals varied in working capacity and were classed in distinct brackets from the kitchen boys up to the captain.

The concept of one man pitching in with the others and performing his proper share of a given task was more or less destroyed by the modern division of labor. Cooperative enterprises passed out of existence, and farming became a one-man activity suited to a money economy. There remained a tendency to work together in the rice-transplanting season, when the work had to be done in a hurry, but even this practice was gradually abandoned.

3. YOUNG MEN AND CULTURE

a. The Young Man's Desire to Distinguish Himself

In a diary of his stay in Japan, under the date 1876, Doctor Bälz commented on the strange attitude of educated Japanese toward their country's past. Students, he said, avowed that Japan had no history whatever. Apparently the young men with whom the German teacher came in contact felt that Japanese traditions were worthless as compared to those of Europe, but if in their contacts with foreigners they were inclined to speak too meanly of their country, certainly they were nevertheless determined to shoulder its burdens, and to this end they pursued their studies furiously despite all sorts of obstacles.

The American teacher, Professor Clark, in his farewell address to the Sapporo School of Agriculture, said to his students, "Boys, be ambitious!" and his words were a slogan for many years thereafter. The students of the Meiji period were in fact ambitious almost beyond the telling. It is difficult to say just how Professor Clark's audience interpreted his words, but to all intents and purposes the common goal of young men was above all to perform some distinguished feat and gain fame for themselves.

The original leaders of the Meiji government were young, and their spirited attempts at sudden reform often turned out to look good on paper but to be unworkable. Political control having become stable after the first decade of the era, there appeared a strong trend toward conservatism. Youthful policies gradually gave way to others designed to maintain the status quo.

At the time of the Restoration the country had been serious-ly divided. Many local territories found it difficult to think of themselves as belonging to the emperor rather than to the old feudal lords. The old fiefs, which had not yet broken up, varied greatly in size and influence. Some were still friendly to the Tokugawa, and others hated them. Age-old customs hampered commercial and economic development, and people in one area had little understanding of or sympathy for those of the others. A result of all this was that the youth of the various provinces differed considerably in their enthusiasm for the new age.

The popular rights movement in the second decade of Meiji was largely an expression of discontent on the part of former members of the warrior class now deprived of political power. In this era, however, young men were as a rule moved to action not so much by being left out as by coming within range of power. A few sons or younger brothers of Tokugawa retainers, imbued more or less with old ideas, achieved some fame in political or literary circles as gloomy critics, but generally speaking the new culture was created not by the people who had formerly had political control but by newcomers from the provinces looking for a chance.

b. The Framework of Culture

After around 1890 the road to success in politics grew nar-rower and narrower, but youthful ideas were rather often re-flected in governmental policies. If a boy had the cultural background of the old warrior class, garnished with some know-ledge of the Occident, his chances of becoming important were rather good.

Two books published around 1885 by Tokutomi Iichirō, later to become a leading progressive, had far more influence on youth than even the author could have hoped. Entitled *Dai-jūkyū-seiki Nihon no Seinen oyobi Kyōiku* (*Japanese Youth and Education in the Nineteenth Century*) and *Shōrai no Nihon* (*The Japan of the Future*), both were brimming with new ideas. Tokutomi, as a liberal, avoided anti-foreignism like the plague, but his heart rebelled against the slavish imitation of the West that he saw around him. A young man whose upbringing was basically that of the traditional military class, he was deeply interested in political and cultural matters and was particularly taken with English and American writings of the periods when those countries rose to power. He felt that such works contained much that Japanese youth needed to know for their own good and that of the nation, and his efforts to stir his fellow young people into action enjoyed wide applause.

Education, as Tokutomi explained it, ought to be of sufficiently broad magnitude to encompass both the Japanese spirit and Western learning, the conflict between which was a serious problem for Japanese intellectuals. The author himself had presided over a school in his native town at the age of eighteen and, though recognizing his own shortcomings, had taught every subject save mathematics. He is said to have believed strongly in the old saying that "teaching is half learning," and to have become a teacher in order to study.

The field of study that most appealed to young men of the era was law, the mastery of which led to an official career. The preference was perhaps natural in a Japan shifting from feudalism to constitutional monarchy, but it unfortunately seems to have been based partly on the idea that the legal profession was the gateway to omnipotence, and that officials were intrinsically better than the common herd. Tokutomi Iichirō recommended history as the most essential branch of knowledge, but he was probably more influenced by the traditional political philosophy of the Orient than others. The Meiji period was almost throughout its course an age of legal studies, and history was studied primarily as an adjunct to law. The second most popular field was medicine, and after that engineering. In other words, practical studies tended to eclipse all others. In the late 1890's the most influential schools in the Kanda area of Tokyo, a college district, were a medical school, the Saisei Gakusha, and a law school, the Hōgaku-in (later to become Chūō University). Each had more than a thousand students.

Youth was also naturally attracted to literature, and in the late eighties and the nineties there was a veritable flood of poetry. At the same time, a journal called *Eisai Shinshi* (*The New Intelligence*) served as the arena for those wishing to compete in the art of polishing prose—a pastime, we might note, not unlike composing legal documents or parliamentary bills. In the early nineteen hundreds, or slightly before, serious social problems arose, but the literary world had only recently become aware of traditional Japanese letters, and it was not quick to take a role in new social movements. Some writers tried to avoid hackwork, then the most popular form of writing, and move on to a higher literary plane, but they did not succeed until they had acquired a new and broader cultural outlook based on the spirit of scientific realism.

4. RELATIONS BETWEEN MEN AND WOMEN

In 1886 Fukuzawa Yukichi wrote *Danjo Kōsai-ron* (*A Theory Concerning Relations between the Sexes*) and tore into his subject with the same vehemence he had displayed in his crusade for national modernization. The general burden was that young ladies of good family were unforgivably oppressed by traditional Confucian ideas and ought to be freed by the adoption of enlightened Western practices. What he said was good advice to Japanese families of the middle and upper classes.

In the Meiji period there were so many new opportunities for young men and women to meet that young ladies of good family were constantly being protected by their parents and teachers. The aim of the latter was of course to teach the girls the self-discipline required in associating with members of the opposite sex, but the interference was too frequent and too great. Girls led such polite sheltered lives that they faced any meeting with a caution approaching terror. Little else could be expected in a class of people who held that boys and girls should be segregated after the age of seven.

Still, both parents and children were vaguely aware that training based on such principles was not sufficient to prepare young people for the relations that must always come. Accordingly many of the youth turned to literature to supplement their knowledge of the relations between men and women. Books, however, dealt with a world of fantasy, and young people, realizing that this had little to do with their own commonplace lives, merely fretted all the more. In any case, literature appealed to only a limited number.

One's eye is struck by the stories in Meiji newspapers and books of lives twisted by the prudish morality of the times, but it is well to remember that this was confined largely to cities. There remained many quiet villages where in the normal course of events young men and women associated together without the restraints of which we have been speaking, and where many a love affair proceeded peacefully and calmly to a happy marriage. The contrast between urban and rural districts in this respect was only one aspect of a general dichotomy that characterized the Meiji period.

To obtain a true picture of relations between the sexes in this era, one must examine not only the books and newspapers, but also the abundant traditions preserved in the country. Folk songs and popular sayings furnish many cases in point. Take for example, the following little song,

The flower may bloom in the field,
But it does not bend and sway unless the wind blows.
I am angry when I think of it—
All he did was treat me kindly,
As he would a plant that's slow to bear.
My name fell from their lips like floods of rain,
Though there was not one drop of love between us.

This is the lament of a country girl who by merely being friendly with a man has become the butt of village gossip. As it indicates, young couples, though free from restraints of the sort found in the cities, were always under the watchful eyes of their neighbors. Boys and girls were particularly free to meet during the *bon* season and at other festivals, but on such occasions they were most frequently in groups and were rarely able to do any serious mischief. Still, meeting in this fashion became the earliest stage of their training for love. Though each of them was first aware of the opposite sex in the collective sense, one person gradually emerged as the most important.

From then on, the fixed ideas, the folk sayings, the folk songs, and village gossip saw to it that the love affair progressed. In places where the young men's dormitory was a firmly established institution, it played a large role. Gathered together in a separate place and free from their families' supervision, boys were able to speak much more openly than otherwise and to draw on the experience of their friends, whose opinions of the girls in the community must have made a much deeper impression on them than anything they would have learned from books or from their parents about relations with the opposite sex. They developed their own ideals of feminine virtues and learned to look for them in the women they met. Since being liked by men was a fundamental desideratum of young women, the ideals formed in the boys' dormitory determined their conduct to a considerable degree. It should be added that the girls also had preferences, similarly formed and similarly influential on the behavior of men.

A typical example of the dormitory system was found on an island in Uwa County, Ehime Prefecture where there were ten men's dormitories for a total of one hundred and forty households. The houses used for the purpose were owned by leading members of the community, and the location remained fixed from generation to generation. The owner was spoken of as the "house father," and indeed his functions were very paternal in nature. The villagers were free to put their children in any one of the dormitories, but brothers were separated. In the New Year season of a boy's thirteenth or fourteenth year his father would deliver him to his new abode, along with his sleeping mats, and request the house father as well as the older boys to see that he behaved properly. From this point on the house father had complete supervision over him and responsibility for his conduct. The boys brought all their clothing to the dormitory, and although they worked at their respective houses during the day they returned to the dormitory to sleep each night. In order to associate with a girl, a young man had to have the house father's approval, and the same was true in the case of marriage. The young men, in return for their quarters, performed services for the house father once or twice a year. After marriage, they left the dormitory and were referred to as " middle-aged."

In the cities, young people did not work together as in the country, and their chances to evaluate one another were largely confined to the sitting room. After the middle years of Meiji one of the favorite occasions for men and women to judge each other's character was the annual New Year gathering for the purpose of playing *karuta*. This is a type of card game. The cards, on each of which a poem is written, are spread out before the players, and when a reader recites the first line of a poem each player attempts to find and pick up the card on which it is written before anyone else. The one with the most cards at the end wins. The game is not as simple as it sounds. It often becomes rather tense, and something of a person's nature can be seen from the way he reacts while playing. While this may have furnished some information, however, it was a very limited form of association and provided much less assurance than the more liberal practices in the rural areas. In all fairness, however, we should note that Tokyo, Osaka, and the other Japanese cities still retained many bucolic features during the Meiji period, and for that reason boys and girls had more chances to associate in the natural fashion than in the later times. With the rapid increase in urban population there were fewer and fewer opportunities for them actually to judge each other's true merits.

5. GOING OUT TO WORK

During the Meiji period, Japanese labor and production were completely reorganized. The farm ceased to be the center of industry, and young men other than eldest sons flocked to city factories. As a consequence many people complained that the factories were undermining the agricultural labor force, but actually this was only one side of the problem.

Even before the end of the Tokugawa period many farm communities had begun to be drawn into the economy of nearby cities, and with the revision of the tax system and the expansion of the monetary system, farmers everywhere ceased to be able to supply their own needs, as they had done in the past. They now looked to the cities, or at least to urban factories for their fuel, their clothes, and a good deal of their food. This was particularly true of the new villages that appeared as the result of the many rural development projects carried out during Meiji. Farmers as a result felt it wasteful to keep their younger sons on the farm, where the tasks they had once performed no longer existed, and instead these young men were sent out to earn money.

During the Tokugawa period in slack seasons people had often left the farm to find temporary work elsewhere, but the government, considering this detrimental to the economic organization, tried in various ways to prevent it. Still, it was said that during the winter people from the snowbound northern provinces would come to Edo to do any sort of work whatever, and tradesmen or artisans from various other sections of the country, such as the sake brewers of Niigata, the roofers of Aizu, and the medicine salesman of Toyama, were famous throughout the nation.

Since the laborers who left the farms in the Meiji period cannot by any stretch of the imagination have been considered as professionals, they of course found it difficult to establish independent organizations. No skilled artisans, but simple working men, they were naturally lacking in the qualities necessary for organization. Often they were literally indentured to employers or labor bosses. As early as 1888 alleged cruelty in the treatment of miners at the Takashima Colliery was mentioned in the press, and there was a widespread feeling that similar instances among the miners and new settlers in Hokkaidō were, by the simple fact of their being far from their homes, never brought out into the open.

The tragic history of the female laborers in spinning and textile factories can readily be understood against the background of this system of bond-laborers. At the end of the Tokugawa, there had already been a case of such a system in operation in Kiryū in Jōshū (Gumma Prefecture). During periods of no work, the girls were sent back to their homes. Female laborers in the mid-Meiji period never really managed to become anything more than seasonal help seeking a means of income outside the home. Their basic weakness lay in the fact that both economically and socially they never were able completely to sever their ties with the agricultural villages and hamlets from which they came. How pitiable they must have been, working in their factories, with no recreation facilities available to them, either in the factories or in their vicinity. In their rare moments of leisure, they had nothing to do but gather in lonely little groups and talk about their homes. Such gatherings and such conversations were the only amusement they had to look forward to, day after day.

Fishing villages and those in the mountains saw an even more drastic change in the labor situation than did the agricultural villages. Changes in fishing and forestry techniques tended toward both the accumulation and the dispersal of the labor force. It is generally thought that the population of mountain villages tended to decline from the early part of Meiji on, but actually there was a certain period, from the middle of Meiji to Taishō, when they showed instead a growth due to the need for men in lumbering. As the lumber-supply situation ceased, however, this growth also fell off.

More girls from fishing villages went out seeking work than from mountain villages. At first, of course, this was simply a seasonal activity, for which there was a variety of dialect expressions. The girls were especially active during the busy autumn harvest period as helpers in farmers' homes. Their wages tended to be somewhere in the neighborhood of one *shō* (1.59 quarts) of rice a day. A more advanced stage was observed in Western Honshū, where girls hired themselves out as maids in the splendid metropolitan homes of the cities around the Seto Inland Sea. This became so common that a girl who did not have such experience to her credit would, it was said, have difficulty finding anyone willing to marry her. The same thing began to be true in the villages around such cities as Tokyo and Osaka, but while to a certain extent non-economic factors were motivating causes in some cases, by and large the major reason for seeking such employment was of course the profitable utilization of surplus labor.

Another great phenomenon of the Meiji period was the exodus of those seeking their fortunes overseas. From the early Meiji period on, emigrants left Wakayama and the Seto Inland Sea areas for Hawaii and the Pacific coast of North America, and since in many cases the trip was made at the urging of and with the help of friends who had already gone, it was not viewed as such a serious step as it might otherwise have been. A booklet of instructions for going overseas was printed some time around 1897. Actually, most of those who went overseas in this fashion had not the least intention of settling permanently, and many planned only to accumulate a large sum of money and return one day to their native villages, dressed in rich finery. It is painful to have to add that these last were the ones who were pointed out abroad as "typical Japanese."

6. YOUTH AND CONSCRIPTION

a. Society and Conscription

The Meiji government maintained a conscripted army and from time to time increased its manpower, but with notable lack of enthusiasm from the general public. Some people in the early years of the period felt that if their sons were called up, it was the fault of the village headman for not writing up his report on men eligible for the draft in such a way as to ensure that such a thing would not happen, and accordingly a son's call to the colors was often celebrated by storming the headman's house.

All this completely changed with Japan's victory in the Sino-Japanese War. The war taught the people just how valuable a standing army was. Until it occurred, persons entering or being discharged from the service were hardly ever given a proper send-off or welcome-home. They disliked going so much that they clung to their parents until the last minute before leaving for the barracks. The militaristic spirit simply did not exist, except perhaps among elementary school children, who thought soldiering something splendid. But once Japan had been victorious over China, all this changed overnight, and the Japanese public's enthusiasm for the military climbed to fever pitch. A splendid triumphal arch was built in Tokyo to welcome returning soldiers, and every town and village was quick to build its own replica.

It gradually came to be considered a great distinction for a young man to be conscripted, and more attention was paid to the spiritual and material needs of the troops. It was, of course, extremely difficult for a family to get on financially when the wage earner was called up, but in such a case friends and relations would come to its assistance. The soldier in the meanwhile actually enjoyed a somewhat higher standard of living than most other people. The camps were in the big cities, and when on liberty, he could enjoy the glamour of the metropolis. Hence his pay never went quite far enough, and it was not at all uncommon for him to have additional money sent to him from home. A soldier's life in those days was something like that of a college student in a dormitory.

At the time there were few indeed who ever went beyond elementary school, and for most men the standard three years of military service served also as an education for life. Barracks life provided those rational organized elements missing in traditional Japanese education and had as a result a tremendous effect upon the men. After three years of training they found it easy, upon returning to their farms, to assume positions of leadership. All that was needed to be called up was a physical examination and a winning number in the lottery by which recruits were selected. This meant that the great majority of the young men who were to form the backbone of village life benefited from the education of the barracks.

b. War and Life on the Home Front

With the advent of the Russo-Japanese War, the new rural youth associations became active, manufacturing things to sell in order to make money for soldiers' families and engaging in similar pursuits. They were still unofficial bodies—people drawn together out of a burning desire to work together with the soldier on the front lines and to make things as easy as possible for those left behind when friends and neighbors were called up. Unfortunately, after the war, the government made political capital of the youth associations, praising them for their splendid display of patriotism, and making provision for their nationwide organization.

The military spirit hardly sprang up overnight, but it must be admitted that in the typical village there did exist the conditions and the background which made it possible for propaganda and education aimed at militarizing Japan to succeed. Military experience had great influence upon the soldiers, and when later on they applied in social situations the principles they had learned as soldiers, the results were often very profitable. In many areas, an investigation of the background of leaders and planners in many kinds of activities will show the great importance of the years spent in the service.

Chapter Ten

THE LIFE OF WOMEN

1. THE FUNCTION OF THE GIRLS' ASSOCIATIONS

a. The Evening Work Group

In the past, when a young girl reached the age of puberty she ordinarily joined with the other girls of the community in a group similar to the young men's association. Often this organization had a special dormitory, under the supervision of an older person, and parents entrusted their daughters to the latter in very much the same way as in the case of boys.

The girls gathered in the evening to mend clothing, make thread, or perform similar tasks. There was a certain light-heartedness at these meetings, but the work itself was also important, and in general it was highly valued in farm communities. In places where cooperative effort was the rule, the young girls' association took charge of hulling and milling rice as well as of other farm work that contributed much to the economic life of the community.

Participation in the association was considered a necessary part of a girl's education, and it was felt that those who remained outside it were likely to be spoiled by their parents. At the same time, however, parents sometimes objected to having their daughters stay away from home all night, and in many instances they complained that the leader of the girls' group was not seeing to it that the younger members were properly trained for their future married life. Still, belonging to the group was most often thought an essential stage in attaining maturity.

b. The Girls' Dormitory

When the village girls gathered to work in the evening and spent the night together, they were often, if not usually, visited by the young men of the community. In early times the girls' associations were most probably centered about dormitories as were the young men's groups. In very rare instances it appears that both sexes shared the same dormitory, and there are other cases in which the effect was the same.

In Eshima, Nagasaki Prefecture, the boys and girls slept in separate dormitories under the supervision of elder persons. Each evening after they finished their dinner at home they went to the dormitory, paid their respects to the supervisor, and obtained his permission to go out for the evening. When a young man first visited the girls' dormitory, he had to be introduced by the supervisor of his. Once he began to associate with a particular girl, he was expected for a time thereafter to call on her each night rain or shine, but the relationship was not necessarily permanent, and as a rule boys went with several different girls before finally marrying one. When a young man had no steady companion the other boys in the group found one for him. It was essential that the young man associate regularly with a girl for a time before marrying her. When he decided he was ready to marry, his family, in conference with persons from the dormitory, appointed go-betweens to make the necessary arrangements. Once the marriage took place, the young people left the associations and ceased to go the dormitory. Marriages not recognized by the dormitory group were likely not to succeed.

In other parts of Nagasaki Prefecture, the young girls of the community spent their nights in the house of some influential person instead of in a separate dormitory. In this area until the middle of the Meiji period the girls were considered to be under the control of the young men's association and could not refuse visits from the latter. As a result the two sexes virtually shared the same sleeping quarters.

On the island of Iki, boys and girls alike spent the night at some place of their own choosing, often the home of a newly married couple. The girls met in the evening to sew or mill flour, and later the boys came to see them. Nominally they slept separately, but this was not actually the case.

In the Gotō Archipelago the young people gathered at the house of some elderly couple, bringing their mats and night clothes with them. At first no one had a fixed companion, but in the course of time couples paired off together, and eventually marriages were arranged by the leader of the young men's association or the group as a whole. Around 1920 men who had come from other areas to seek work began to visit the places where the girls slept, and the principal of the local primary school insisted upon a reform. The old sleeping arrangement was abolished and a new association of young women formed, but the girls themselves were much opposed on the ground that this made it difficult to find suitable husbands.

c. The Decline of the Girls' Organization

The girls' dormitory disappeared earlier than the boys'. With changing social conditions, parents ceased to put much faith in the institution, and gradually the young women were left only with get-togethers devoted to working, or learning etiquette, or something of the sort. The right to choose husbands passed from the girls themselves to their parents, and the girls' association as such lost much of its authority.

The original organization was in effect a kind of school for brides. Younger girls were more or less under the control of those who were older and had more experience. The latter were careful to criticize the young men of the community and to protect the younger girls from boys whose conduct was improper. In one sense the young men were at the mercy of the girls' group, since they had to depend on it to see that its members married within the community instead of looking for husbands in other places. In effect, membership in the group gave girls a large amount of freedom in choosing a husband. Collective action enabled them to make their opinions felt in the community. Separately a young girl was often deprived by her parents of her authority to choose her own mate, and in the Meiji period the tendency was more and more toward family-arranged marriages. The matrimonial alliance became a political or economic agreement between two households, and the wishes of the bride, or for that matter of the groom, ceased to count for much.

The unfortunate result was a great increase in the number of young women faced with the prospect of such distasteful marriages that they committed suicide. There were many more who went through with the wedding, but ceased in their hearts really to live. During the wedding festivities, when brides dressed in beautiful kimonos and occupied the center of attention, they were the envy of other young women, but the first years of their married life were often anything but enviable. As a rule they could expect to be treated little better than slaves, and their very status as wives was precarious.

2. THE BRIDE'S LOT

The old system of village marriage had been based on a spirit of mutual cooperation among the members of community, and since women as a group had performed important tasks, their position had been relatively strong. During the late Tokugawa and early Meiji periods, however, there was pronounced tendency for each family to become a separate unit, dependent solely on its own efforts for survival. As this occurred, the position of the head of the house became much more important, and his authority virtually absolute. Herein lies the basic cause of the miserable existence led by so many young brides in this epoch. After going to live at the house of a father-in-law, a young woman had to be moulded to fit his idea of what a wife should be. Her conduct had to convince him that she would be a credit to his house. She was directly under the control of her mother-in-law, and the latter was usually blamed for her sufferings, but in a broader sense, the bride's basic difficulty was that her marriage was subordinated to what her elders conceived of as the benefit of the tribe. The relationship between herself and her husband became a thing of secondary importance. Often a young bride would be sent back to her home before there had been time to tell whether she and her husband would be compatible or not. The divorce rate in the middle years of the Meiji period was scandalous, and while there were numerous other reasons, one of the main ones was certainly that marriage arrangements were transferred from the hands of young people to those of their parents.

Ironically, wedding celebrations became more festive than ever, and the bride was increasingly beautiful and doll-like. There were no doubt many young women who realized that their married life would not be as joyful and splendid as their weddings, but there were few who did not prefer to submit to the accepted conditions rather than to remain spinsters. The fear of not being married at all or of being discarded after marriage was a great weight on young women's minds.

The Restoration was supposed to have brought equality and enlightenment to all, but the unfortunate fact is that many of the common people squandered their new freedom in an attempt to ape the prestigious military class. The Confucian ideas of marriage held by the latter were widely accepted, and the heads of houses assumed all control over matrimonial matters. Sons or daughters who did not conform to their will could do little other than leave home or commit suicide, and brides who did not produce a child for two or three years after marriage were often returned to their parents. Not infrequently wives were divorced on the vague grounds that they did not fit in perfectly with family life in their new homes. Of course, many girls did manage somehow to suit their parents-in-law, but the sacrifice was often very great.

3. THE WORK OF HOUSEWIVES

If a bride survived the ordeal of living under the watchful eyes of her husband's parents for a sufficient number of years, she became mistress of the family in her own right, and her condition improved immeasurably. She now had the responsibility of feeding the family, keeping them in clothing, and in general caring for the household finances, and she was likely to have her hands busy at sewing, cooking, and cleaning much of the time, but the work was rewarded with appreciation and respect.

The following description of a housewife was written by Ema Mieko in a book entitled *Hida no Onnatachi* (*The Women of Hida*):

I went to a very small mountain village in the upper region of the Akao River (Ono County, Toyama Prefecture) and visited a farm house where three families lived together. The mistress of the house not only looked after her eighty-year-old parents-in-law, but also directed her son and daughter-in-law in their work and helped train their children. This woman was about fifty. Her forehead was rather broad, and her hair had a slight wave. There was an air of great tenderness about her, but one also received the impression that she was alert and diligent. I had dinner with her family and watched her as she sat by the hearth and ladled out the food to them. As I looked at the scene, I became aware that this women, with her simple, brisk, and efficient manner had a sort of majestic dignity difficult to describe fully. It was not merely a personal dignity, but the traditional dignity of a matriarch presiding over her clan at table. Sitting there quietly and unperturbed, she was truly beautiful.

During the Meiji period the mistress of the house usually had such dignity and authority. In later times people often said that in comparison with the past housewives lived as queens, but as the work that women contributed decreased, the authority that they had possessed also tended to disappear.

4. WOMEN AT WORK

a. Women and Production

The women in Meiji literature generally seem modest and reserved, if not actually servile and ineffectual. In this respect they accord with the prevailing conception of Oriental womanhood, but the literary picture of wives totally dependent on their husbands was hardly valid. The average woman did her share of the family work, and her contribution insured her the respect of society. However, a number of people under the influence of Confucian ideas considered it proper for women to be entirely subordinate to men and were shocked to see women of the modern era taking up new work and attempting to advance their social position. This attitude unfortunately became common, though there was little basis for it in fact.

Even in city shops women performed much of the daily work, and in the rural districts they were much more actively connected with the production and circulation of goods. All over the country the annual transplantation of rice shoots was considered a woman's task, and in many areas women were held responsible for the original seeding. The harvest was usually brought in by men and women together, but in many places the women threshed the grain, and in almost all instances they hulled and milled it. Tasks like this were more and more carried out with the help of simple machines, but the division of labor between men and women was maintained.

In mountain communities of the past, forestry and hunting

were the exclusive province of men, while the same was true of the various work involving boats and nets in fishing communities. In such places, however, women took complete charge of gardening and farming, and at times they maintained fields up in the mountains at a considerable distance from their homes. Sericulture was carried on entirely by them, and since most fishing villages became more and more reliant on farming, the part played by women became increasingly important. Most fishermen took little interest in household affairs and simply left the management of finances to their wives. During the Meiji period agriculture grew so vital to the economic life of the islands in the Seto Inland Sea that women gained much authority with regard not only to household economy but to village economy as well. In some cases the money that a man retained for his personal needs was called by the name now ordinarily used for the small change that wives of salary earners pilfer from the household money.

In fishing communities where women worked all day as divers, men were little more than accessories. The reputation of a woman rested on the question of whether she could provide her husband's keep or not, and as a consequence the social standing of women was very high. In most fishing villages it was left up to the women to sell the fish, and often they traveled as merchants to nearby farming villages.

b. The Public Activities of Women

Despite the large part played by women in production, they were surprisingly inactive in public life, simply because they were largely confined to their houses and had little chance to associate with outsiders. Even the most domineering shopkeeper's wives in the Asakusa district of Tokyo—on the whole a rather terrifying class—were forced to take a back seat to their husbands in public. Still the women of many communities maintained organizations, usually of a religious nature, which gave them a chance to express their views on a number of public questions.

In the Meiji period a few women began against almost overwhelming obstacles to perform welfare work for the benefit of the many people who had become destitute as a result of the prevailing social confusion. As a rule the efforts of these ladies were directed primarily at providing protection and education for unfortunate children. Such work was exceedingly rare before the Restoration, and it appears to have owed much to the influence of Western women, but the inspiration was not entirely from without. A woman named Uriu Iwako established a school and welfare agency for children in the earliest years of the Meiji period, before foreign ideas of charity work had been imported to any appreciable degree, and we might note that a statue was later erected to this lady in Asakusa Park in Tokyo by her admirers and helpers.

A number of women educators appeared on the scene, but instead of advocating a common education for men and women, they usually were interested only in the domestic training of girls, and aside from a few who promoted Western-style learning, most of them retained the traditional strong emphasis on ethics and household virtues.

There were some who advocated increased political rights for women, but as a rule they eventually settled down in conservative movements for promoting women's education. During the third decade of the Meiji period, a number of feminine writers became prominent. Also, around the same time newspapers began to include columns on domestic matters, and the first women's magazine appeared. Around 1900 people were discussing such questions as whether women ought to be allowed to climb Mount Fuji, hitherto reserved for men, or to ride bicycles in the public streets. In 1910 a society called the Seitō-sha or Association of Bluestockings began promoting equal rights for women, and there was much talk of "awakened womanhood."

5. WOMEN AND RELIGION

a. The Woman's Part in Family Worship

Women were usually left out of the public rituals during festivals, but often they played the principal role in family worship, and in general, they were considered to be in relatively close spiritual contact with the gods. Japan has always had a good number of mediums and sorceresses, and there appears to have been a general belief in the past that women possessed great religious powers.

It is clear from examples found around Okinawa, for example, that the gods were considered far more likely to speak through women than through men, and it is possible that the men of the past in general relied on the spiritual strength of their wives or sisters to protect them from harm. Many of the customs that ostensibly indicate scorn for the feminine sex may be seen upon further study to be based on an ancient fear of women's supernatural powers.

During the Meiji period household worship underwent many changes, but the *bon* festival remained one of its most important aspects. It was considered that the spirits of ancestors, particularly ancestors not long dead, returned to earth in this season, and despite the exegetical reasons offered by Buddhists for the *bon*, it was largely a non-Buddhist form of ancestor worship by individual households. As spiritual mentors of the family the mistress of the house and her mother-in-law waited on the dead almost as though they were still alive.

b. Clairvoyants

Prior to the Meiji period, female clairvoyants occupied a fairly important place in Shinto shrines, but when the Meiji government reorganized the shrine system, they were either turned out or given purely formal positions. The government also tried on occasion to suppress independent sorceresses, who commanded a considerable following, but no sooner than old ones disappeared, new ones took their place. These women took a large part in local religious festivals and exerted much influence on household religion. The average housewife, if told by one of them that she was not paying sufficient attention to the spirits of her family's ancestors, trembled to the depths of her soul. Local religious societies of women often sought the teaching and guidance of such people, and two religious groups, Tenri-kyō and Ōmoto-kyō, both of which believed in them, spread throughout the country during Meiji because of the adherence of country women to them.

Around 1910 a number of women who claimed to be clairvoyant caught the public eye. As they competed among themselves for supremacy, scholars pronounced some genuine and others fraudulent, while the general public listened avidly, if not always credulously, to the various predictions. The flame soon died, but the phenomenon as a whole illustrates the deepseated Japanese belief in the spiritual powers of women.

6. THE CONCEPTION OF WOMEN'S WORK

a. From Old to New Work

As we have seen, women of pre-modern times played an important part in production. Both in the country and in the cities, however, most of them did little work outside the home, and most of those who did were actresses, music teachers, hairdressers, or midwives. In addition a number of young girls served as maids, and a few of them continued to do so throughout their lives.

During the middle years of the Meiji period new forms of

employment became available to women. They began, for instance, to be hired by large textile mills, and before long they held between seventy and eighty per cent of the jobs in this industry. They were employed largely because they were content to work hard for a small salary, and their working conditions were often miserable. Many of them lived in extreme poverty and contacted serious diseases, in particular turberculosis. Almost invariably they quit working when they married, at the latest, and there were very few who were interested enough in a career to attempt to improve their position as workers.

As time went on, however, a number of women gained a place for themselves as public servants, most notably as telephone operators. Women were first hired for this work in 1899, and they performed so creditably that in the next year they were also employed in other phases of communications work. They were made to work in different rooms from the male employees, however, and were not put in charge of tasks that involved direct contact with the public. Obviously, the practice of hiring them was still regarded with considerable caution.

As time went on, they were accepted by more and more businesses. In 1903 they began to work in the Bureau of Railway Operation, the Tokyo Electric Light Company, and Shimbashi Station (as ticket sellers). The Mitsui Clothing Store went so far as to set them to work selling goods to the public. In 1907 the Ministry of Communication attracted some attention by making female employees eligible for promotions hitherto reserved for men. The consensus at the time was that the ministry, cognizant of their ability, diligence, and tractability, as well as of the fact that they would work for less money than men, took this measure in order to keep them from transferring to private companies and banks. People who held high hopes for the emancipation of the feminine sex read the ministry's action as a sign of the times and predicted that one day women would even be able to serve the public as lawyers and judges.

Women also took up intellectual occupations, the number of them engaged as school teachers being particularly large. Twenty-five hundred were employed in primary schools only ten years after the establishment of the school system in 1872. To be sure, this number represented only three per cent of the total number of teachers, but considering that the only women hitherto engaged as educators had been a handful of Buddhist nuns working in temple schools, the figure is quite remarkable. Many young women began to go to normal school, and various prefectures established new institutions of this type especially for them. High schools for girls also increased notably in number.

Music schools attracted quite a few young ladies, and in 1899 a women's school of medicine was established. In the same year, we might note, laws governing midwifery were enacted, and modern practices introduced into this ancient profession.

The current conceptions of women's work remained old-fashioned. Though young women were being employed in increasing numbers, few people devoted much thought to the special new provisions needed for their health, education, and discipline. The employers, the employed, and even the latters' parents usually considered women's working careers as only temporary. Young women with no more than a high school education were not equipped to consider the larger economic implications of their position, but they usually were dimly aware of inconsistencies between home life and the office, and they preferred the former. As a consequence, they did not often seriously consider trying to advance in their working careers.

7. WOMEN AND EDUCATION

a. House Work and School Training

Prior to the Meiji period only a few ladies of the upper class could read and write to any appreciable extent. Therefore, in 1872 when Tsuda Umeko and four other young ladies agreed to be taken abroad by an American lady to study in the Western style, they aroused much interest and admiration. It is pleasant to note that they all subsequently became prominent and worthwhile members of society. Still, the feeling of the average person was that women did not really require book learning, and even after the establishment of modern educational facilities for women, the number of girls attending school was disappointingly small. At first many of those who did attend were saddled with their infant brothers or sisters, and when the latter began to wail during class there was nothing to do but go out into the hallway and wait till the crying ceased. Around 1905 the number of girl students began to increase quite noticeably, but even so few advanced beyond the required first six years.

Though the traditional education for women was meager, it at least provided them with ample knowledge of household affairs. The women of the past were largely responsible for handling finances, and the prosperity of the family rested on their ability to manage. This fact underlay the practice of requiring brides to serve a period of apprenticeship under their mothers-in-law. This training, like that for boys, was of a very practical nature and consisted mostly of imitation. The discipline was often cruelly strict, but girls were brought up to expect this, and many of them had the experience of seeing the brides of their elder brothers scolded time and time again. Some may actually have added their bit to the nagging, but more often they watched in silence and made mental notes of what they should and should not do when they themselves became daughters-in-law. We might add that all the girls in a family had specific tasks that varied with their age, and by the time they were grown they had learned to do all the divers household chores.

The establishment of public schools caused much of this

practical training to fall into neglect, but for many years it continued to take up much time that young women might otherwise have spent on literary studies. As far as most house-wives were concerned, academic learning was a sort of attractive veneer, and the training that really came in handy was received in the home. Society in general was fairly well satisfied with this attitude.

At the time when schools appeared, people in the cities were very much in the habit of employing young girls to tend babies, and often these girls grew up with no book learning at all. The responsibility for their training was too heavy for their employers to accept, and their own families usually did not give the matter much thought. Finally, however, people began to take pity on them and to organize special schools where they could study for two or three hours each day.

b. Women and Classical Education

It was generally considered proper for a young lady to acquire a classical Japanese education rather than a Western one. Nevertheless, a few women by virtue of exceptional ability and perseverance progressed from the former to the latter. The novelist Higuchi Ichiyō, for example, used her training in the Japanese classics as a basis for a new approach to political and economic questions, and went so far as to express her opinions in newspapers, where incidentally they attracted considerable attention. Most women, however, were too occupied merely with traditional literature and arts to bother with social problems. After all, they looked forward to becoming respected wives and mothers, and a traditional education was helpful in this respect, whereas an excess of modern learning might well have proved a hindrance to finding a husband.

In 1901 the first women's university was opened, and girls of superior intelligence were given a chance really to display their ability. Still, aside from welfare work, education, and the arts, there were few fields in which they could expect to succeed. The braver ones experimented with a variety of other occupations, and although a few gained respect and admiration, many others failed miserably.

Though women's schools increased in number and prestige, they were prevented by public opinion from relaxing the traditional limitations placed on women's conduct. In 1909 a group of women educators in Tokyo held a discussion and agreed on ten "musts" for female students, but the list was so conservative that the newspapers laughingly called them "must-nots." Fukuzawa Yukichi's progressive *Shin-onna-daigaku* (*The New Women's Colleges*), published in 1898, was immediately banned by many women's schools, but it seems to have been read to some extent, since it proved necessary for several of the schools to reiterate their ban some ten years later.

It was difficult to draw or define a new symbol of womanhood that satisfied both the general respect for traditional learning and the needs of modern times. Schools for women were caught between the old and the new, and the same was true of home education as well, since the ancient requirements of housewives were giving way to newer ones.

Chapter Eleven

ANNUAL EVENTS AND CELEBRATIONS

1. THE OLD AND NEW CALENDARS

a. The Calendar Reform

In the course of its many reforms, the Meiji government replaced the traditional lunar calendar, adopted from China many centuries before, with the solar calendar in use in the Occident. By a decree of the ninth day of the eleventh month of Meiji 5 (1872) it was decided that the third day of the succeeding twelfth month would become the first day of 1873. The decree added: "On this day a ceremony for revising the calendar will be held, and the emperor will inform the sun goddess and the imperial ancestors of the change. Pursuantly, the solar calendar will be promulgated, and days of worship and celebration provisionally fixed. The day will be divided into twenty-four hours instead of twelve two-hour periods, as hitherto."

The *Tokyo Nichinichi Shimbun* for the fifteenth day of the same month reported on the sales of the issue in which the promulgation had been printed. Customers, it said, came to the head office and newstands "like clouds and mist." The sales for the tenth and eleventh days amounted to more than ten thousand. On the twelfth day the article was reprinted, and sales through that day came to almost twenty-five thousand copies. Now, the editor stated with satisfaction, people would be more grateful for newspapers.

Calendar revision had many precedents in both the East and

the West. The Japanese calendar had been changed any number of times, and several alterations had been made even in the Tokugawa period, of which the most famous were those of 1684 and 1798. The calendar of the latter year, with minor corrections, remained in effect until Meiji. It was based on the moon, of course, but an extra month was added every three years to compensate for differences with the solar year. We might note in passing that the Tokugawa-period scholar Ōtsuki Gentaku, along with several other students of Dutch and Western science, celebrated the first day of the solar year 1795, which happened to fall on the eleventh day of the inter-calary eleventh month of the Japanese year, and which was spoken of at the time as the "Dutch New Year."

The Meiji revision of the calendar raised considerable doubts among the people. One large question was that of monthly salaries for government employees. With regard to this matter, the chancellery decided to retain the same monthly salaries as before, which represented something of a loss to employees, there being five days more in the new year than in the old. Yano Fumio in *Dōkei Kanwa* (*Quiet Talks of Dōkei*, 1924) quoted Ōkuma Shigenobu as saying that the new calendar was adopted to avoid expenses incurred in years having intercalary months. The Tokugawa shogunate had made its payments on an annual basis, but the new government was paying by the month, and by the old calendar there would have been an extra payroll every three years. Over a period of time, this would have added up to a tremendous sum.

When the Gregorian calendar was adopted, the number of the year was counted from the supposed founding of the Japanese empire by the Emperor Jimmu in 660 B. C., and 1873 was therefore numbered 2533. To provide for leap years, the government simply stated that every year divisible by four would be lengthened by one day, and since 660 is divisible by four, this rule worked. It did not, however, take care of 1900, and for that year the government was forced to issue a new provision, the wording of which throws an interesting light on official attitudes of the times:

Reckoning from the time of the Emperor Jimmu's accession, every fourth year has an intercalary month (i. e. February). This notwithstanding, after subtracting six hundred and sixty from the number of the year and dividing the reminder by one hundred, if the result be not divisible by four, the year in question is to be an ordinary year.

People had trouble appreciating the reasons for changing the calendar. They considered the new system inconvenient, and they argued that it did not agree with the traditional seasons. The most unpopular feature was that by the solar calendar the moon did not seem to shine at the right time. There was a saying that "when whores are faithful and eggs are square, the moon will come up on the last day of the month," but now the moon did sometimes come up on the last day of the month. A number of satirical poems were written on the subject:

The moon is not shining
On the fifteenth day of the new calendar.
Shall we wait for it to come up
Pail and wan in the morning light?

And:

The moon shone on the last night of the month,
And it was not too dark to read the calendar—
Not even in villages where no one knew how.

Some people took an extremely nationalistic viewpoint. The new calendar, they said, violated the "national polity" and made Japan a colony of the hairy barbarians. A few were particularly angry about the acceptance of "Jesus Christ's New Year." In common parlance the new New Year was spoken of as the emperor's and the old one as the Tokugawa's, and the latter was generally preferred even by non-extremists. Ogawa Narihara wrote the following criticism:

We had come along thus far with the traditional calendar,

and it had caused no trouble to anyone. Why did the government suddenly decided to abolish it? The whole thing is disagreeable. The old system fitted in with the seasons, the weather, and the movement of the tides. One could plan one's work or one's clothing or virtually anything else by it. Since the revision, the New Year and the *bon* come at crazy times. The cherry trees bloom in the sixth and seventh months, and the summer storms come in the tenth. In the fourth and fifth months snow and frost are still on the ground.... Nothing is the way it should be.—*Kaika Mondō*
(*Questions and Answers on the Enlightenment*.)—
As a matter of sober fact, the cherry blossoms bloom in March and April, the typhoon season comes in August and September, and snow is virtually unknown after April, but the exaggeration illustrates the prejudice with which some persons regarded the calendar revision.

b. Adoption of the New Calendar by the People

The calendar revision, then, was the object of much opposition, and the question even became involved in anti-government riots by conservatives. Customs connected with the old calendar continued to be observed for a long time. According to newspaper accounts, for example, none of the laborers employed by the bureau of railroads came to work on February 17, 1874, on the grounds that that was the lunar New Year's Day. Still, modernists like Fukuzawa Yukichi defended the new calendar, and it was adopted more and more by public organs. After about forty years it had been accepted to the extent that the dates of the lunar year ceased to be included in ordinary calendars alongside those for the solar year. Nevertheless in some out-of-the-way places the new calendar remained completely unknown, and in most agricultural communities it was used alternately with the old. Even after the Russo-Japanese

War, Inoue Enryō wrote that villages he had visited near Mount Yoshino were largely ignorant of the new system, and a history of the village of Yatsumoto in Saitama Prefecture, printed in 1913, commented on the stubborn local opposition to calendar reform. According to this source, two or three sections of the village had finally begun to adopt the solar calendar in 1909, and the other sections had agreed to adopt it in 1913. Actually there are still many places where the old calendar is in constant use. In 1946 the Minister of Education conducted an investigation of this question in three typical primary schools, one in a city and the other two in farming and fishing villages, respectively. The sixth-year students were asked to find out whether their families still used the old calendar, and the answers were as follows:

	Still Used	Did Not Use
City	26%	74%
Farm Village	52%	48%
Fishing Village	59%	41%

The manner of measuring time was changed at the same time as the calendar. The Japanese had formerly divided the day into twelve two-hour period which were either named after the animals in the Chinese zodiac or numbered in descending order. Henceforward the Western method was used, but it did not gain immediate acceptance. The old divisions even appeared on occasion in announcements made subsequently by the chancellery.

The seven-day week was introduced by foreign merchants in Yokohama and later gradually incorporated into Japanese life. It was adopted into the Japanese school system in 1874 because of foreign teachers who wished to have Sundays off, and on March 22, 1876, it was decreed a day of rest for Japanese in general. Still there are many today who work on Sundays.

2. HOLIDAYS

a. National Holidays

Even before the Meiji period there were national holidays, but they were not necessarily the same for nobles, warriors, and common people alike, and they varied somewhat from era to era. In the Tokugawa period, the feudal lords were required to pay their respects at the shogun's palace on certain great days, among them the first of the eighth month, called *hassaku*, and the sixth of sixth month, called *kajō*. Both of these had been days of celebration in earlier periods, but *hassaku* was particularly important to the Tokugawa since it happened to be the day on which Tokugawa Ieyasu first entered the castle of Edo, and *kajō* was a special favorite of the military class. When the Meiji government reformed the calendar, they also changed the holidays. By an order of January 4, 1873, five traditional holidays (the seventh of the first month, the third of the third, the fifth of the fifth, the seventh of the seventh, and the ninth of the ninth, all of which were connected with lunar calendar astrology) were abolished, and on October 14 the following established: the imperial New Year celebration of January third, the day of the imperial New Year banquet on January fifth, the anniversary of the former emperor's death, the anniversary of the legendary founding of Japan on February 11, the anniversary of the Emperor Jimmu's death on April 3, the thanksgiving offering to the sun goddess on October 17, the imperial thanksgiving on November 23, and the Emperor Meiji's birthday, which happened to fall on November 3. Later, in June, 1878, the spring and fall equinoxes were decreed sacred to the memory of the imperial ancestors and raised to the status of holidays. On the emperor's birthday in 1873 the practice of flying the Japanese flag on holidays was instituted. All of these changes aroused considerable dissent. An article by

Hayashi Wakaki entitled *Kaireki no Eikyō* ("The Influence of the Calendar Revision," in the periodical *Shūko Kaishi*, 1915), made the following comment:

The government abolished the age-old holidays, such as the five annual celebrations and the *bon*, and instead appointed days like the emperor's birthday and foundation day, which mean nothing to the people, as national holidays. Ask any child, and he will tell you that the eighth day of the fourth month is the Buddha's birthday, and that during the *bon* festival the boiling caldrons of hell are opened for the condemned souls to escape. But even an old fellow like myself will not be able to tell you why the foundation day and the emperor's birthday need to be commemorated. To exalt these days that the people care nothing about, the government makes everybody put up lanterns and a flag that looks like an advertisement for red pills. The old holidays were celebrated because the people felt them to be festive occasions. It is asking too much to make the people celebrate days they do *not* feel to be festive.

Many years later, however, the painter Kubota Beisen, wrote as follows of the emperor's birthday:

This holiday was originally declared thirty-four years ago today, in the first year of Meiji's reign. In those days people did not hang out flags, and ... since the capital had been moved to Edo only shortly before (in the tenth month), Kyoto had become very lonely. Still, something of the spirit of the capital remained, and the command to celebrate the holiday was the first of its sort after the emperor's removal to Edo. Kyoto people being fond of festivals in the first place, the celebrations turned out to be quite lively. Of course, there were no magnificent congratulatory services such as the one today, but the stores closed, put their best screens out in front, and hung lanterns. ... Floats were carried along the streets, and people invited their friends and relatives to feasts. This was at the time the usual fashion for celebrating the most important festivals, and we were all happy to observe this fine new holiday.

Apparently the abolition of the old holidays was none too effective. It was reported in the *Tokyo Nichi-nichi Newspaper* for September 9, 1875, that women on the street were dressed in their best, as for the old celebration on the ninth day of the lunar ninth month, and that other practices associated with that festival were also being continued. In 1872 the government forbade New Year celebrations and the customary exchange of gifts, stating that even if New Year gifts were presented to one's family and were intended for practical purposes, they represented a wasteful use of money. The order seems to have had little effect, since people still exchange New Year gifts today.

b. Revision of Holidays

When the national holidays were revised, many local customs were also attacked. In various prefectures, for instance, the common practice of decorating the front gate of the house with pine saplings during the New Year season was abolished he the pretext of conserving forests. Many local authorities also abolished festivals to the god of the road and had the innors of that deity combined with that of the local tutelary god. The god of the road had often been worshiped with bonfires, and the government was in this case no doubt trying to reduce the risk of conflagrations. The measure was first adopted, it might be noticed, in the densely populated city of Edo. Frequently seasonal celebrations to local deities were abandoned with no prompting from the government, because with the changing of the calendar the traditional date became incompatible with the season. Offerings of particular types of food had usually been presented, and sometimes these became unavailable at the proper time.

Before the adoption of the seven-day week the sixteenth of the month was the usual holiday for working people, but it is not certain why. At the beginning of the Meiji, there was considerable variation, and letters to editors of newspapers often requested that the government set a particular day for everyone. Sunday was the day of rest for schools and official bureaus, and it gradually became more or less standard, but not by any means universal.

Since the ancient past, the first, fifteenth, and twenty-eighth days of the month had been considered holy to the gods, and they had often been observed as holidays. Presumably the first and fifteenth were regarded as special because they were the days of the new and full moon. On the other hand, the reason for the inclusion of the twenty-eighth is uncertain, but at any rate it was the appointed time in many places for worshiping the god of the hearth. The first and the fifteenth continued to be observed after the beginning of Meiji even in Tokyo, and on these days quite a number of school children carried in their lunch boxes the mixture of rice and red beans reserved for special occasions.

Among the city tradespeople holidays had been fixed by guilds, and eventually these were confirmed by labor laws. Such holidays, incidentally, were days for worshiping the deities connected with particular trades, but this does not apply to enterprises that have sprung up since the Meiji period.

In farming and fishing villages, where work could not always be halted once each week, the tendency was to observe the old seasonal holidays. As a rule, rural villages enjoyed forty or fifty days of rest each year, and special holidays were declared on occasions when the work had been particularly heavy for several days. In such cases the young men who bore the brunt of the labor decided on a day, and on their request the local authorities issued official orders. Days of rest were more or less sacred, and in some places sanctions were applied against persons who did not observe them.

Summer vacations for students and workers began earlier than one would have expected. The government started granting them as early as 1873. At first the vacation period was from June 8 to June 13, but later this was changed to some time in August. Sick leaves were also granted as the occasion demanded.

3. THE URBANIZATION OF HOLIDAYS

a. Holidays in Tokyo

With the development of cities, annual celebrations changed greatly and for that matter are still changing. There was a general tendency to abandon old holidays and adopt new ones, but in some instances the cities took up some ancient fete and made it more lively than ever before.

The traditional Japanese celebrations were centered about the cultivation of rice and had little meaning to the urban population. The tendency to abandon them appeared even in the Tokugawa period. A book called *Tōto Saiji-ki* (*Annual Events in the Eastern Capital*, 1838) lists many of the same festivities that were observed in farming communities, but by the time Edo became Tokyo, only a few of the more important ones, such as New Year's Day and the *bon* festival, were still observed. At the beginning of the Meiji period people still celebrated the eighth days of the second and twelfth months, which were considered the first and last days of work in the year, but this practice soon disappeared. The first of eighth month, which as noted above was particularly important to the Tokugawa government, was dropped, as to a large extent was the day of the horse in the second month, which had been sacred to the god of agriculture, Inari.

The latter holiday, however, was still quite an occasion in the early years of Meiji. The following description is taken from the *Tokyo Nichinichi Newspaper* for February 7, 1874:

Today being the first day of the horse in the second month, the streets and alleys resounded with the drums of the festival to Inari, and the city was quite excited. Unfortunately, after the old custom urchins from the slums gathered in groups and went around drumming on boards and crying for money. . . . They clamored outside people's houses, and if the inhabitants refused, heaped unspeakable abuse on them. Our evil customs do not improve even though we are now under the emperor's very eyes. The parents of such children perhaps do not know how shameful this is. The children of beggars are now as good as anyone else in the sight of the law, and they must not be allowed to practice at being beggars.

Even when the ancient holidays connected with farming and fishing were retained in the city, they lost their original meaning. New Year celebrations, for example, continued to be held, but the relation between them and the success of the year's planting, so important in rural communities, was forgotten. Ebisu and Daikoku, formerly gods of fishing and agriculture, came to be regarded as protectors of trade in the cities. In the days when people wore raincoats made of straw, there had been a lively fair in Asakusa each year when these were brought to market. By 1873, however, this custom had vanished, together with the bulky coats. Similar developments, resulting from changes in the demands of buyers were not unusual.

In the old days the articles used in celebrations, particularly the dolls for the girl's festival in March and the boy's festival in May, had often been very shabby, and the practice in many places had been to throw them away when the festival ended. Now, however, entrepreneurs began popularizing elaborate, richly decorated dolls, and city people bought them. The department stores contributed to the general excitement of certain festivals by having sales of the items associated with them.

One holiday that became very colorful after the beginning of Meiji was that known as *shichigosan* (seven, five, and three). This falls on November fifteenth, and like so many other Japanese festivals, is centered around children. Boys aged three or five and girls aged three or seven are dressed in the best clothing possible and taken to the local shrine. The reasons for celebration at these particular ages are that odd numbers are generally regarded as auspicious, and that these years are supposed to be pivotal points in the child's life. The holiday was not unknown in the Tokugawa period, and Edo merchants celebrated it so lavishly that the Tokugawa government issued sumptuary prohibitions against it, but the general populace was not nearly so concerned as they are now.

Though there were few Christians, Christmas was introduced by foreigners and encouraged by tradespeople to the extent that it was accepted in the towns as an occasion for gaiety, if not for worship. The following account appeared in an essay by Togawa Zanka:

Hara Akitane founded the Hara school for Women... in 1876, and this appears to have been the first Christian girls' school established by a Japanese. Lady missionaries from abroad served as teachers, and there was a cheerful Christmas celebration every year. Nowadays the churches on the Ginza have huge Christmas festivities, and stores like the Kame-ya and Meiji-ya put up splendid decorations. Apparently all this began in Mr. Hara's School.

At first gifts were exchanged only by Christian believers, but in 1877 the Maruzen Department Store imported a number of items to be used as Christmas presents, and in 1888 Christmas cards were introduced from abroad. The custom of giving gifts, however, did not become general until after 1900.

b. Old and New Celebrations

The majority of the really new celebrations were associated

with schools. Among these the most usual were sports meets, picnics, and cultural assemblies attended by parents as well as students and teachers. In rural communities such events took on the stature of annual holidays. In this connection we might also mention that around 1887 primary and middle schools began to provide their graduating classes with inexpensive trips to one or another of the famous scenic or historical locations, and these jaunts, though usually lasting only three or four days, became exceedingly important in the children's lives. Often they represented the only chance the poorer boys and girls ever had to see any place other than the one where they were born.

Another type of celebration developed in connection with the new conscripted army. Recruits entered camp on December 1 each year (later changed to January 14, in order to permit the boys to be at home during the New Year festivities), and since going into the Army was considered a great honor, the soldier's family held a feast for relatives and friends, who ordinarily gave parting gifts of money. On the day of departure relatives, youth organizations, and so on, gathered at the station with drums and other musical instrument to send the boys off. Similar celebrations were held when the soldiers, having finished their required service, returned home.

Annual meetings of clubs and other organizations began in many cases to take on the aspect of festivals. Tokyo was the most popular place for conventions, but they were held in other places as well. The annual meetings of the Red Cross and the Ladies' Partriotic League were especially famous. These attracted committee members from all over the country. The Red Cross was organized in 1886, and the Ladies' Patriotic League in 1901. The former held its first national convention in 1893 and the latter in 1902. Both conclaves were usually held in May or June, and the first meeting was invariably attended by the empress. Ordinarily she also delivered a command, which was gratefully received by the presiding officer. The meetings were held in Hibiya Public Hall.

4. PRODUCTION AND FESTIVALS

The ancient festivals were almost invariably linked with agriculture and particularly with the production of rice. They marked the times for plowing, planting, harvesting, and so on, when it was the custom to pray or give thanks to the gods. With changes in agricultural methods and the introduction of new products, the old holidays lost much of their meaning, but they were still important enough in many areas for people to insist upon observing them in accordance with the old calendar instead of the new, in which the traditional dates often disagreed with the actual farming seasons. In some instances, new industries led to the development of new celebrations. This was particularly true in the case of sericulture.

Strictly speaking, of course, sericulture was not new, but although it had been practiced all over Japan since early times, it did not assume its modern proportions until around the middle of the Meiji period. By this time silk had become the principal export to the United States, and a sudden change in the American demand had a definite effect on farmers throughout the entire country, particularly in the central regions. The new importance of silk wrought a number of changes in rural lives. Many farmers added a second floor to their houses in which to raise silkworms, and in the process they also built chimneys and extra windows, since smoke was not good for the insects. The new emphasis on this industry created new busy seasons, and in the two or three months beginning in May, farmers, and more particularly farmers' wives, hardly had any rest at all. Traditionally silkworms had been raised only during the spring and summer, but after the around 1887 a fall season was added. By the late Meiji period there was a growing number of farmers who actually specialized in sericulture.

The summer crop of silkworms was ready for spinning just at the time for the seventh-moon festivals of the old calendar

(i. e., *tanabata* and *bon*), and as a result, a number of places changed these to August or September by the new calendar.

The new industry affected not only the dates of holidays but the manner of celebrating them as well. For example, one of the customs during the children's New Year had been to cut a branch from a tree and decorate it with rice cakes in the form of rice flowers, but now, while the practice was in essence retained, the cakes took on the shape of cocoons. The spring festival to the sun, held in many places, came to be regarded as the time for requesting the gods' protection for the silkworms.

In the region of Oku County in the province of Mikawa (Aichi Prefecture) it was the custom in the past to celebrate the day of the full moon in the eighth month of the old calendar by eating young soy beans especially prepared for the occasion, but by 1892 or so, sericulture had become so important in this region that the people no longer raised beans, and the celebration disappeared. Also it had been the custom on the seventh and thirteenth nights of the seventh moon to hold a large all-night Buddhist celebration, during which everyone went about chanting sacred invocations on the streets and in the cemeteries, but these dates coincided with the summer silkworm season, and after about 1882 the celebrations were abandoned.

Sericulture, which was so intimately connected with commerce, was a more speculative enterprise than ordinary farming, and farmers engaged in it tended to be greatly concerned with their luck. They not only employed superstitious means of improving it, but began in some places to hold fairs or festivals dedicated to deities of fortune.

As old methods of production fell out of use, celebrations connected with them were forgotten. Formerly, the fifteenth day of the eleventh moon, for instance, had been the day for celebrating the end of the season for producing rape-seed oil, which farmers had until modern times used for lighting and other purposes. Now, however, the oil was no longer made in the home, and the festival was virtually forgotten, although there were still some communities in which it was the custom to serve something cooked on oil on this day.

5. CELEBRATIONS BY FAMILIES AND NEIGHBORHOODS

a. The New Year Celebration

Aside from the national holidays, there were others observed by individual families or neighborhoods. The most important was the New Year celebration, which lasted at least three, and often more, days. The government, as we have observed, attempted to discourage extravagance during this period, but had very little luck with its efforts. The season was celebrated in a variety of ways, but it was almost invariably marked by the practice of serving *mochi* (cakes made by pounding glutinous rice), and that of erecting a pine branch outside the gate to the house. It is interesting to note, however, that some families or neighborhoods traditionally avoided the *mochi*. Most often they explained, quite speciously, that when their ancestors, fighting in the medieval civil wars, first settled down in their village, they had not had time to pound the rice, and that even if they had had time, they could not have pounded it because blood from their battle wounds would have fallen into it. Other houses and neighborhoods avoided the pine branch, offering equally dubious explanations for this peculiarity. In the past, old families often held a number of private celebrations every year, and many of these are described in detail in historical records. Such celebrations were sometimes maintained over long periods and through times of social change, and even today in some villages one or two houses have very special customs.

In the Meiji period, however, these tended to disappear because of the expanded scope of social life. When young men educated in modern schools succeeded their fathers as heads of families, they often ceased to observe old-fashioned customs that were meaningless to the community as a whole. Still, in the northeast region, where the organization of large clans some-times remained firm, ancient clan celebrations were preserved, particularly in those districts where the clan traditionally did its farm work as a unit. Celebrations by private families were as a rule displaced by neighborhood festivals, and the latter tended to become the responsibility of only one house or even of the official head of the local shrine.

The most typical ceremonies held during the New Year festival were designed either to protect the coming year's crop or to give thanks in advance for a good crop. Many of these observances had no meaning to urban dwellers and consequent-ly were largely abandoned in the new era. In particular, cele-brations that involved group chants in local dialects came to be regarded by many adults as foolish and embarrassing and ac-cordingly were either dropped altogether or relegated to chil-dren. People who moved to the cities usually forgot the chants, and in any event they sounded strange when uttered with urban-ized accents.

During Meiji, in areas where clans still remained to some extent intact, and branch families were closely connected with the main house, the former invariably called on the latter in the New Year season. As a rule, however, this fashion changed greatly. Now the people of the community began instead to gather at the public school or some other government building to pay New Year's respects to each other and exchange name cards.

b. The *Bon* Festival

Aside from New Year festivals, the most important celebra-tion of the year is the *bon* festival. This commemorates the annual season in which, according to Buddhist lore, spirits of dead persons are released from hell to return and roam about the earth. Accordingly, in Japanese houses various offerings are made at this time to the dead, particularly to those who have died during the preceding year, and lanterns are hung to lead the way for their return.

By the old calendar, the *bon* fell on the fifteenth day of the seventh month, and despite the calendar revision, the old day was abandoned only gradually. To give an example from Kumamoto Prefecture, in one area the *bon* was held by the old calendar until 1897, but by 1907 was beginning to shift to the new. At the end of the Meiji period the new date was fixed officially, but the old continued to be observed in various houses. Then, in 1916 or 1917, when sericulture became a flourishing secondary occupation for many farmers, the new calendar date was generally accepted. On the other hand, merchants in the towns, avowing that they could not take a vacation at this time, selected August 15 of the new calendar for their celebration. In some areas of south Fukuoka Prefecture which maintained the old calendar for all dates, people observed the *bon* as many as three times each summer.

During the *bon* festival the custom in most places was to hold a series of dances in which everyone participated, but the new government regarded these as detrimental to public morals and interfered with them in many instances. In Kurakawa Village, Kita County, Ehime Prefecture, it was a practice until around 1897 to have ten or more *bon* dances, but around that time the prefect banned them, and they virtually fell out of existence. Still the dances were among the greatest annual delights of the common people, and even where they were forbidden, they were often continued surreptitiously or revived later.

In the past one of the regular entertainments associated with the *bon* was a tug of war, but in most places this has ceased to be a particular feature of the *bon* and has become instead merely an ordinary game for children.

The industries that most distinguished the Meiji period from previous ages were commerce and manufacturing. The people involved in such occupations, however, instead of inventing new festivals held nearly the same ones as ordinary city residents. They looked forward most to the New Year, the *bon*, and the annual neighborhood festival. Until the adoption of the modern system of vacations, factory workers and the like often returned to their home towns during these seasons, and this custom still exists in many places.

6. AMUSEMENTS AND THE SEASONS

a. The Excitement of Festival Days

Everyday life is intimately bound up with the weather and with the change of seasons throughout the year, and this intimate relationship continues to a certain extent regardless of what changes may transpire in society or in the world around us. Nevertheless, during the Meiji period there was a notable tendency for annual festivals or observances and pleasure excursions to fall off. This became true to a striking extent first of all in the cities. In earlier days, there had been a clear-cut distinction between the humdrum, drab existence of everyday life, and the spirit that existed on festival days. Today this distinction has been all but obliterated. In the cities there is to be found a wealth of amusement facilities. People seek strong stimulation every day of their lives, and hardly any occasion remains for making much of the excitement and sense of thrill that was once provided by festival days. In earlier days everyday food and clothing were plain and simple in the extreme. Now everyone drinks sake every day and wears fine clothes as a matter of course.

Much of the change can be seen by considering the pleasure excursions of Tokyo citizens. Today people in Tokyo still make seasonal excursions to view cherry blossoms in the spring, or to gather autumn leaves, and these pleasures are essentially the same as they were in the past, but in most cases the excursions take people a considerable distance away from Tokyo. In the Meiji period such excursions could be carried out within Tokyo itself, and also in this period, the "sense of the season," i.e. a feeling for the particular time of year at which the excursion took place, was much stronger than it is today. The first clear waters of the Sumida River, so splendid a place for a pleasure excursion, were the boast of Edo residents. The wisteria of Kamado Tenjin, the irises on the edge of the palace moat, the chrysanthemum dolls of Dango-zaka, and the azaleas of Ōkubo all were celebrated. Throughout the year from season to season they attracted great crowds. Nor were such seasonal places of celebrated beauty confined to Tokyo, for rural areas too had their share. Cherry blossom viewing in the spring was almost a symbol of Japan itself, and countless places throughout the country were famous as cherry viewing sites.

But in earlier times even these seasonal pleasure excursions did not exist solely for purpose of amusement. Nowadays we realize that such amusements are to a certain extent essential to human life, and with this realization has come the adoption of the English word "recreation" to describe this concept. In earlier times, however, there always remained a certain element of religious faith in such things. The seasonal observances punctuated man's life, they gave him that stimulus necessary for his continued activity. This will be understood by anyone whose youth was spent in the Meiji period, especially if he was reared on a farm. Any such person can remember experiences like the following account of the New Year's observances given by Sakai Toshihiko in his *Autobiography:*

New Year's eve was certainly a time fraught with importance, and only a somewhat old-fashioned expression like "fraught with importance" can really do it justice. First we lit a certain number of lamps and set them on the shelf containing the representations of the tutelary gods of our home. As I gazed at them, my child's heart was purified to its very bottom by their bright gleam. Next we placed more lamps in a number of places, inside and outside the house, in the decorative alcove, on the kitchen range, on the mill, on the well, and in the privy. These were not like those on the shelf for the tutelary gods, but were of a special temporary construction. What we did was to take a large white radish, cut it into one-inch lengths, hollow one end of each of them out a little, pour in oil, and add wicks, which we then lit. I will never be able to forget the feeling of a kind of supernatural mystery and of a solemn grandeur, which I would experience when coming into a room illuminated with these radish-lamps. My feelings were especially marked when I went into the kitchen, or the mill, or to the well, or to the privy surrounded by the pitch-blackness of night. As we sat quietly in the kitchen, the lights all over the house gleamed and shone; it was a feeling of a very special kind of illumination. The impression which festivals, seasonal observances, and the like made on people was especially strong because of the extremely drab and simple mode of everyday life.

Another example may be cited from Imaizumi Mine's *Dreams Remaining*:

When I was a child, our diet was always rigidly fixed. For breakfast there would be a thin soup and at noon dried sardines or strips of fried radish, and this was about all there was to it. . . . Thus even in the household of a direct feudatory of the shoguns, food was always exceedingly simple and plain. The aim was that each day be the same as every other day, and surely there were many who even though born like myself in Edo cannot remember ever having tasted fine Asakusa sea-weed. This was my situation, even though I was an only daughter. But particular attention was paid to observances of special days. At meal times we felt that what was really vital was the offering to the gods, but when this was completed, we were permitted to help ourselves, as it were, to what was left.

Thus even in what was at the time a comparatively well-off family, everyday fare was extremely plain, and special foods were prepared as a rule only on days of special religious significance.

After the Restoration, a reactionary movement eventually set in among many of those who had abandoned the old observances in their pursuit of new things from the West. Baba Kochō wrote in his *Tokyo in the Meiji Period:*

> From about 1881 on, a certain intellectual reaction began, which expressed itself among other things, in a gradual revival of old observances. More and more, things which had been discarded at the beginning of the Meiji period because they reeked of old-fogyism and backwardness, came back into use. The public had rejected its old tastes, but now it found that it had nothing new to take their place. There was nothing to do but to revert to the old.

In other words the progress and advancement brought on by the Restoration were in the main a triumph only for relatively few persons, and the rest of society, once the situation had calmed down, gradually went back to its old habits of behavior.

Fondness for antiques and the revival of older observances were met on every hand. Fencing, archery, jūdō, and other military arts also were quite widely revived, and a kind of archery which could be engaged in equally well by young and old was quite the rage, so much so that around 1887 there was hardly a section of the city without its archery hall.

b. Outdoor Exercise and Amusements

Though the old observances and the military arts were revived, great numbers of people turned their attention to new amusements and sports. The school athletic meet became a fashion of such proportions that the magazine *The Japanese* in its issue of December 5, 1896, attacked the practice as being in too many cases indistinguishable from a theatrical performance.

Most of these sports were new ones imported from abroad. At first few were concerned save the students, but as time went on the games more and more caught the public attention. Baseball and boat races became practically a seasonal observance and even developed in popularity to the stage where newspaper's carried tips on favorites. The article in *The Japanese* had attacked the charging of admission fees to these contests, but gradually the public began to accept these charges as a matter of course. Even so, in the Meiji period there was nothing like today's major sporting events or nationwide contests, nor was public interest in sports anything like what it is now. The skill of the contestants was none too highly advanced, and spectators went to matches in a leisurely, sightseeing mood.

Excursions to the mountains were common in the Edo period, but their scope broadened in the Meiji period. Mountain climbing and swimming in the summer became new fads. Both of these had existed in Japan from early times, but in a different sense. Mountain climbing had been considered no mere sport, but rather an expression of religious faith. This aspect has to some extent survived even today, but in the Meiji period a new spirit of travel for adventure was born. Many people went climbing on as many different mountains in as many different parts of the country as possible. Soon there was no peak that had not been scaled, so great was the fascination of the unconquered mountain.

Western-style mountain climbing was encouraged by such persons as Aston, who named the Japanese Alps, but the sport would have developed even without this stimulus from abroad. As mountain climbing became increasingly popular the annual list of disaster victims grew larger, and some of these remained deeply impressed on the popular mind, a few especially pathetic instances being immortalized in song.

Swimming had been widely practiced as a military accomplishment, and there was a traditional method of swimming, but it remained for the introduction of the crawl-stroke from the West for it to gain popularity as a sport. Bathing in the sea had been carried out since antiquity as a kind of purification ceremony, with specified days of the month throughout the year for entering the water, and in addition the beneficial effects to the health of bathing in sea water were recognized. Still, it was not until the Meiji period that the practice became widespread. There are many conflicting opinions as to where the first sea bathing beach in Japan was, but there is evidence for one at Ōiso as early as 1885. Even earlier, in 1871, foreigners reported observing Japanese ladies bathing in the sea and there is evidence of sea bathing at Atami in 1874. Naturally these beaches were attacked by some quarters, and there was especially strong feeling about women bathing publically. The *Chōya Newspaper* for August 17, 1890, took note of the presence, among the throngs of people streaming from Tokyo to escape the heat and spend a few hours in some cooler spot, of groups of ladies who braved the surf and salty waves, disporting in Western-style bathrobes and straw-hats, without, it would seem, a thought either to their own safety or to the proprieties. All this the *Chōya* found " most amazing."

In 1888 an announcement of the Kanagawa Prefecture office ordered that the sexes be segregated on all bathing beaches in Kanagawa Prefecture and further stated that any violations of this rule would be punished as infringements of the law. In this case the officials were probably concerned with an area specifically used for bathing purposes, rather than with recreation facilities, and were applying to them the same regulation that obtained in the public baths. Thus the problem of public morals and sanitation, which have yet to be completely solved even today, have plagued the bathing beaches ever since their inception.

Chapter Twelve

CONSUMPTION OF GOODS

1. THE DECLINE OF HOME PRODUCTION

Prior to the Meiji period most families in farm villages produced everything they needed either by themselves or with the aid of the community. Only a certain number of items or services were secured from professional tradespeople, and the exchanges most often took the form of barter. As mentioned before, the dyeing of cloth was usually the task of a professional or semi-professional craftsman, but the latter most often received his pay in grain. Pure fishing communities had to rely on trade to obtain rice, vegetables, and other edibles, and farming communities were similarly dependent for fish and salt, so that there was a certain amount of exchange between coastal and inland areas, but the quantity was insignificant in comparison with what it was to become in the Meiji era.

Most dependent on the outside world were communities that produced only rice, for farmers in such places had to secure fuel and fertilizer from other areas. Villages possessing communal forest lands were fortunate in this respect, but they apparently dealt highhandedly with outsiders who had to rely on them, and the latter greatly disliked them. Traditionally fertilizer was not a great problem. Farmers simply spread leaves on the rice paddies and allowed them to rot, or in later times prepared various composts. Nightsoil was not ordinarily used on rice fields in pre-modern times. Increased production of vegetables in the Meiji period, however, led to a much greater need for fertilizer, and suburban villages that sold vegetables to the cities began to rely greatly on the latter for nightsoil. In the Meiji period the farmers paid for it, but nowadays they are paid to take it away.

Farmers also bought sardines and the waste from sardines after the oil had been taken, and after about the middle of the Meiji period chemical fertilizers were adopted. The latter, however, were expensive, and many farmers regarded them with distrust. As a result, they were not quick to find favor.

The situation in many farm villages during the earlier part of the Meiji period was much the same as is indicated in the following passage, taken from a description of a village in Saitama Prefecture:

> The farmers in the past usually made their own bean paste and soy sauce, but in recent times many of them have begun purchasing these items. Until 1887, very little oil was used, and a few houses made what was needed by boiling and compressing rapeseed. This practice has completely disappeared.

> Formerly people grew cotton, and there were professional willowers. Virtually every house had a spinning wheel and made its own clothes, but this is no longer the case. The manufacture of indigo has also ceased. Rice and other grains were formerly hulled and milled by hand, but now people are beginning to use machines run by horses or electricity.

All this must have made farm work easier, but it meant that a larger amount of money had to be spent by the agricultural populace. Furthermore, the spread of urban ways of living brought on a change in people's sense of values. Things that had formerly been thrown away became necessary, whereas others that had been regarded as valuable became useless. The price of rice straw, for example, increased greatly during the Meiji period, largely because of a new demand for straw ashes to make fertilizer in the gardening belt. Ash markets appeared here and there, and eventually a whole new business developed.

In addition there was a great increase in other straw products. People who had been wearing straw sandals in many cases changed to *geta* or shoes, as we have stated above, but on the other hand, many others who had been barefoot began to wear straw sandals.

There was also a large demand for straw in cities, where it was used in floor matting, and as time went on even country houses began to boast rooms with matted floors. Furthermore, there was an increased need for straw to make paper, and the military required it for fodder.

As more and more cheap manufactures from cities became available in rural areas, agricultural families were relieved of the necessity of providing their own commodities, but while new mass-produced articles were convenient and pleasing to the eyes, they rarely lasted as well as hand-made goods. Still, ease and the ability to pick and choose compensated for loss in quality.

When the tax system was revised and farmers began to submit their land taxes in money instead of grain, rural economy was completely transformed. Land was often assessed unfairly, and many farm communities abandoned their formerly invaluable common property for fear of excess taxes. It is said that persons who held land not under cultivation would actually give it to anyone who would take off their hands. In 1882 there was a depression, and land often sold for much less than it was worth. Later, many people regretted having disposed of their property, but there was little they could do about it. Until the last of the Meiji period the switch to a money economy was incomplete in rural areas, and tenant fees were still often paid in rice, barley, or beans. Farm products could not quickly be converted into cash, and money transactions tended to be long and inconvenient. Still the prevailing trend was inexorable, and the conclusion foregone. Farmers gave up home production of commodities and with it their independence from urban markets and factories. Their younger sons ceased to be needed as farm workers and were instead sent out to work for money. The old system of self-supply and communal effort entered the final stages of collapse.

2. THE DEVELOPMENT OF CONSUMER GOODS

a. Stores and Purchases

Even in the old days country people had gone to market in nearby towns to transfer their produce for certain necessities. The markets were usually held on a fixed day each month, and some towns still bear names such as Yokkaichi (fourth-day market) and Mikkaichi, (third-day market). The largest markets came at the end of the year and before the *bon* festival, when semiannual supplies were purchased. Aside from the New Year's edibles, these included such things as tobacco, paper, ink, porcelain ware, metalware, and so on. There was usually a god of the market, and the market day was sacred to him. It was apparently regarded with a certain amount of wonder, and people said for instance that at the market place one would often see a face similar to one's father's.

There were fairs in the cities, and the townspeople loved them, but attended them more for pleasure than for business. The goods sold were usually luxury items or playthings for children and were often of a very perishable nature.

In the towns and cities during Meiji most housewives formed the habit of going out daily to buy food and other necessities. At the same time tradespeople began to send employees around each day to solicit orders from regular customers. Bills were often collected by the month instead of at the time of purchase. In the country, however, there were still places that maintained the old system of collecting twice a year—that is, just before the *bon* festival and at the end of the year.

Peddlers of various kinds had plied the city streets during

the Edo period, and now their number increased greatly. In particular, each neighborhood had its bean curd man, fermented soy bean (*nattō*) man, and so on, and each of the salesmen had his own particular cry. The availability of a number of prepared dishes made housekeeping considerably simpler for small families.

People shopped more and more, and often they made the mistake of buying things they did not need. The custom of buying by the month led many of them to buy in excess. There was a general feeling that if one had the money handy, one might buy anything one might happen to want, and not a few lived too luxuriously.

Until the middle of the Meiji period, to go shopping usually meant only to walk around to the neighborhood stores, but as the economy developed, many stores acquired reputations that attracted customers from far and wide. The shopper's field broadened, and often shopping became something of a pastime. Many people began to go out to the stores with no intention of buying anything at all.

b. The Development of the Department Store

The appearance of department stores, most of which were clothing stores that had gradually grown, gave a new impetus to buying. The famous Mitsukoshi Clothing Store was converted into a department store in February, 1904, and afterward Shirokiya, Matsuya, and Matsuzakaya followed suit. All these now catered to the general public rather than to a select clientele, and they brightened the public streets with large show-windows designed to attract ordinary customers. Various new sales methods were devised. In 1908 Matsuya held its first "bargain day," and since the idea proved to be a thumping success, the other stores soon adopted it. All of them held particularly large bargain sales in midsummer prior to *bon* and at the end of the year. The success of the department store took much business away from smaller businessmen. The big stores were able to provide things that their less powerful competitors could not afford to stock. They had attractive window displays and a constantly changing array of goods that people did not necessarily have to buy in order to see. Moreover they could and did run huge advertisements in the newspapers.

Historically speaking, the department stores were outgrowths of emporia, the first of which appears to have been established in 1877, when articles that had been displayed at a national industrial exhibition were put on sale. At this time the metropolitan government built an emporium in the center of town and lined it with small shops of various sorts. Subsequently, a number of private enterprises of the same kind appeared, but though popular for a time, they soon gained the reputation of selling inferior goods, and they were easily put out of business by the new and better organized department stores. We might note that the practice of putting price labels on articles began in the emporia. Until then prices had not been fixed, and customers had usually haggled over each item with the dealer. If the latter had insisted on his own asking price, incidentally, he had usually fallen into disrepute. The attachment of price tags came as a result of the unification of trade guilds, and it contributed much to the standardization of prices.

Many hitherto unknown sales practices were instituted, among which an important one was the holding of lotteries. The first of these appears to have been in 1898, when the Japan Industrial Bank (*Nihon Kangyō Ginkō*) issued bonds with special premiums attached. Later the practice of giving prizes was started by the newspapers to drum up circulation, and it gradually spread to other businesses. By the late years of Meiji, lotteries were a standard feature of bargain sales.

Restaurants were among the most flourishing of the new businesses. Meat, which had hitherto rarely been eaten at all, became a favorite dish, and Western foods or Japanese concoctions with Western names were to be found everywhere. Coffee, black tea, beer, and other Occidental items of the sort became an inseparable part of many Japanese lives.

Nowadays we consider ice water and ice as ordinary as plain water, but they are comparatively late innovations. In early times ice was presented to emperor on the first day of the six month each year, and the Tokugawa shogunate at times received contributions of snow stored up by the lord of the northern province of Kaga. As a rule, however, ice was exceedingly rare. Then around 1870 a man from Yokohama named Hasegawa Kahei launched the modern refrigerating industry by putting on sale ice that he had obtained in Hokkaidō. (Even before that a small quantity of ice had been imported from Boston.) In Tokyo ice water was first sold in Asakusa, whither ladies and gentlemen of the middle class or above came happily to drink it. After 1877 the ice business was firmly established and thriving.

3. HOUSEHOLD PROPERTY

Every family has a number of possessions, such as furniture, kitchen utensils, dishes, and so on, that are kept over a long period of time. The quantity and quality vary with the family means, but in a given area and economic class, these articles tend to be very much the same in any house. In the Meiji period standard household possessions changed considerably, primarily because the family ceased to be a self-sustaining unit. Farm houses, for instance, ceased to require looms, spinning wheels, and the like, since cloth was no longer made at home.

Prior to the Meiji era, most people had among their treasured belongings a number of items that were used only on special occasions. It was felt necessary, for example, to own a set of good dishes for use only when guests were present, despite the fact that this was exceedingly uneconomical. Similarly, the special clothing and other articles required for marriages, funerals, and festivals, were numbered among the standard household possessions. In the Meiji period, however, it became possible to buy such supplies as needed or even to borrow or rent them, and the average family ceased to bother with them. At the same time, however, new things now became necessary. As an example, we might mention particularly the changes that have taken place in the articles that a bride is expected to bring to her new home. In former times she ordinarily brought a clothes chest, a mirror stand, a wash tub, a needle box, and a variety of smaller items needed for housework. Nowadays, however, she most often furnishes first and foremost a cabinet for Western clothes, which has become a necessity. We might note that a number of other items, some of them rather amusing, are substituted in some locations. In many of the islands off Izu, for instance, the bride brings a pole and bucket for carrying water. In Ōshima on the other hand, a bicycle trailer is considered better. In all of the seacoast villages where women engage themselves as divers, brides take along a bucket, goggles, and other articles needed for this work.

Among the ordinary household possessions peculiar to Japan are the altars for the Shinto deities and the Buddha. The Shinto altar is usually simple and inexpensive, but the Buddhist altar is often quite elaborate, particularly in the case of those owned by the numerous members of the Shin Sect. Often a poor house has a Buddhist altar seemingly all out of proportion to its means. This usually results from the fact that when there are several family branches only the main one maintains an altar, but the others all contribute to buying it. Nowadays in the cities there are many families, especially those who live in rented houses, who do not keep altars at all, and they are generally regarded as cumbersome.

During the Meiji period many former necessities became obsolete, but at the same time a number of new articles, particularly imports from the West, became necessities. Uneconomical though it was, people began to have Western clothes, shoes, and stockings alongside their kimono, *geta*, and *tabi*. Often they found it impossible to maintain both a Japanese and a Western wardrobe and had to be satisfied with a good deal less than the best in each. In the Meiji period Japanese clothing remained predominant, but Western apparel grew ever more popular, and it is now the more common.

During the third decade of Meiji a report on conditions in the village of Kaneda, Kanagawa Prefecture, stated that every house had a national flag, while one in three houses possessed a study desk, a clock, and a thermometer. Each house had two *kake-mono* and almost every family had a tobacco tray, a brazier, cushions, and cups for use when company came. Seven or eight houses in ten had a bath tub and virtually all families possessed a *haori* with family crest. Most of them had at least one Western umbrella, and about half of them a Western hat. One person in thirty households had an overcoat. Everyday wear was ordinarily made of cotton, while good clothes were silk in seventy per cent of the cases and a mixture of silk and cotton in the rest. The usual footgear was the straw sandals, but on special occasion *geta*. Shoes were very rare.

It appears that most people were able to buy flags, clocks, lamps, thermometors, and umbrellas—the implements of Meiji culture—but a number of items now found in the most ordinary farm houses were missing. Most conspicuously absent was the bicycle, which is now almost as necessary as arms and legs. Bicycles were used in Tokyo just after the Restoration, but twenty years later only a few were to be found even in nearby villages. In Ogi County of Saga Prefecture, for example, the vehicle was first used in the second decade of Meiji, and there were many villages where it did not appear until ten or twenty years later, but by the Shōwa period there were six thousand bicycles in the whole county.

4. IMPORTS AND JAPANESE PRODUCTS

a. The Craze for Imported Articles

After the Restoration, foreign products enjoyed a tremendous vogue in town and country alike. The very word for "imported article" was uttered with a feeling approaching reverence, and to be able to use foreign things was a source of great pride. As a rule foreign commodities were expensive, but they were of superior quality, and they lasted well, so that they were usually preferred to Japanese imitations, which in the early part of the Meiji period, were still fairly primitive. Actually Japan had always depended on foreign countries for many of the material accoutrements of culture, and the fad for Western commodities was not completely new. It is interesting to note moreover that there was an old tendency to give superior Japanese devices a name implying that had been brought from China, and in the Tokugawa period, when Holland was the only one of the European nations allowed to trade with Japan, the Japanese word for Dutch carried considerable commercial prestige. In the Meiji period Western food, Western clothing, Western anything was eagerly adopted. The chief consumer's goods brought from abroad were writing equipment and mechanical implements of one sort or another. Umbrellas were among the most prominent items of the latter class. They were first imported by an Englishman in 1859, but at the time anti-foreign feeling was strong, and so few people bought them that the shipment had to be returned. After the Restoration, however, the demand went up sharply. In 1872 alone fifty thousand dozen were imported at a total cost of three million yen. A Japanese imitation soon appeared, and eventually local manufacturers captured most of the market. In the early years of the period umbrellas were still so rare that people often held them when posing for formal photographs, but after three decades there were few farm houses that did not own two or three. In some places, an umbrella became part of bride's prescribed trousseau. The umbrella-man became an institution in many villages.

It was much the same with clocks and watches. In the early Meiji, a number of Japanese attempted to produce Western-style clocks, but failed. During this interval imported time-pieces increased in popularity, and the profits went primarily to foreign traders. Finally in 1899 a man named Yoshinuma Mataemon produced a successful imitation. At first only pocket watches were made, but later wall clocks were perfected, and after a short time they were to be found in every house.

Foreign pencils became very popular, and while there were Japanese imitations, people complained that the lead broke too easily, and that one could not write clearly with them.

b. The Encouragement of Japanese Products

Despite the fashion for foreign products there was strong opposition to them in some quarters. During the second decade of Meiji, when nationalism was very strong, there were movements to boycott them. One foreigner wrote in a news-paper about the refusal of people in Akita Prefecture to buy wares, and in Matsumoto, Nagano Prefecture, an organization called the Ethical Society attempted to prevent people from buying non-Japanese goods. A similar situation prevailed in certain other locales.

In 1878, Motoyama Hikoichi, later president of the *Mainichi Newspaper*, made the following criticism:

Although imported goods appeared only ten years ago, one sees them in the house and on the person of every member of the urban upper classes. People want anything foreign, whether it is of value or not.... Some method of preventing this would be most welcome. Now finally people have begun to recognize the harm of this fashion and are forming societies to promote Japanese articles. This is cause for rejoicing. In the rural areas, however, the craze for foreign goods is truly amazing. Conservative tradesmen are selling them, and stubborn farmers buying them. . . . The quality is not necessarily good, but prices are twice what they are in the cities. . . .

The Japanese imitated all the more useful of the foreign innovations, and a good number of the copies were on display at the National Industrial Exhibition in 1877. One observer, Yano Fumio, was greatly pleased with the array of chairs, eyeglasses, surgical implements, handkerchiefs, gloves, and so on, and he predicted that one day the Japanese products would replace imports. Of course, some of the imitations were at once inferior to and more expensive than foreign goods, but by the end of Meiji, Yano's prediction had to a large extent come true. The Japanese imitations of foreign goods were in many ways a credit to the nation, but imitative skill led to a few undesirable results. One of these was that cheap or inferior products were in many instances passed off on the customers as the genuine article. This was true in the case of purely Japanese commodities as well.

Chapter Thirteen

RELIGIOUS LIFE

1. TUTELARY DEITIES AND PARISHIONERS

a. The Revised Administration of Shrines

The Meiji government claimed in principle to be reverting to the golden age of the Emperor Jimmu, and in the first month of 1870 it issued a promulgation which exalted the great way of the ancient native gods and stressed the importance of ceremonies and festivals dedicated to them. Officials in charge of religion were given ranks nominally superior to those of lay officials, and in December, 1873, a project to purify Shinto of Buddhist elements was launched.

In the fifth month of 1871, the chancellery issued a decree stating the qualifications of Shinto shrines, and in the next year the Bureau of Religion ranked shrines as to whether their parishes included metropolitan prefectures, regular prefectures, towns, or villages. A large number of local shrines were recognized as places of worship, but excluded from the system of ranks, and countless tiny shrines in mountain forests were not even recognized.

In deciding the qualifications and ranks for shrine, the government ostensibly followed ancient custom, but in fact it often failed to do so. This gave rise to many problems in rural areas, where the shrines were closely connected to village life, particularly since the government also undertook to fix the size and boundaries of parishes. This latter step had considerable connection with the shrines' financial status, and when village shrines were classified as town shrines or vice versa, as was sometimes the case, much discontent arose. Until now there has been no fixed rule as to which shrine a person would attend, the matter having long since been decided by custom, and when objections to the new system were brought up, the Home Ministry merely issued, in 1882, a vague statement to the effect that each shrine presumably had a fixed parish, and that the religious officials and parishioners ought to settle such questions them among themselves amicably. This solved nothing.

The persecution of Buddhism was one of the most famous acts of the early Meiji period. An extreme example of its enforcement is found in the case of the former Matsumoto fief in Nagano Prefecture. In 1870 the hereditary lord of that district issued an order to the effect that all temples should be destroyed, all Buddhist statues and implements of worship burned, and all priests returned to agricultural work. As the first step, the personal temple of the Lord of Matsumoto was destroyed, along with the epitaphs of his ancestors. Nevertheless, a few people, at the risk of their lives, managed to save a number of other temples. The main effect that the Buddhist persecution had on ordinary people was that it put them at a loss when the need arose for funerals, which traditionally required the presence of a Buddhist priest. In Matsumoto the farmers were given a book of instructions for rites wherewith they might bury their own dead. For the larger part, the ceremonies were derived from those of Confucianism.

We should remark that the purge of Buddhism did not begin in the Meiji period. The famous Lord Tokugawa Nariaki of Mito, disturbed by corruption among the clergy, had outlawed Buddhist funerals and substituted burial for cremation in his fief many years before. Actually, in Mito there was some justification, since the priests do actually seem to have been guilty of lewd conduct and gambling, and Buddhism had declined to the extent that a number of temples had been completely abandoned.

After the Meiji period began, the nation as a whole was encouraged to hold Shinto burial services. On the fourth day of the eighth month, 1869, Doai Prefecture, in which the Ise Shrine was located, issued a set of instructions for an abbreviated funeral ceremony with no trace of Buddhism. Later, in 1877, the shrine held a Shinto service for the men from the vicinity who had died in suppressing the Satsuma Rebellion. In one sense this was propaganda for Shinto funerals, and it appears to have worked, since the whole town of Yamada, where the shrine is situated, began to favor the Shinto ceremony.

In the course of the separation of Shinto and Buddhism, other Buddhist ceremonies were either banned or given non-Buddhist names. In June, 1873, for example, fireworks, dancing and other activities connected with the *bon* festival were forbidden in Doai Prefecture, but later a new prefectural order permitted the celebration of *bon* with fireworks, but no dancing, at the shrines of various tutelary deities. Later the Ise Shrine area came under the jurisdiction of a different prefecture (Mie), and the old orders went out of effect. Now with the permission of the police, the dance festivals could be held, provided they did not involve masquerading as ghosts or engaging in other activities that might suggest Buddhism or in any way damage public morals. The following was written concerning the abolition of the festival of the Buddhist divinity Jizō:

Recently the festival of Jizō was abolished in Shiga Prefecture, and all the stone images of that deity were collected and piled on carts to be taken away. As they passed through the town of Ōtsu, old people and women went ahead of the carts making offerings of incense and fruit and bowing to the images. Some with tears in their eyes chased along behind shouting praises to Jizō. It was too laughable (Translator's note: Sic !) for words.

One other step taken to encourage Shinto should be mentioned. In 1870 the people in general were ordered to register their names at the shrine of the god of birth in their particular locality and to receive from the shrine the impression of its official seal, which they were to carry with them at all times. When a child was born, it was to be taken immediately to the shrine to receive this certification. In 1873 this rule was suspended, and it was never again enforced, but one still comes across the seal impressions from time to time.

In 1906 a very important development in shrine administration occurred. The then Home Minister, Hara Kei, decided that there were too many shrines throughout the nation and issued an order to the effect that, barring special circumstances, there should be only one in each town, and that other existing ones should be combined with it. There were in fact quite a few shrines of questionable character here and there, but the mechanical way in which the government set about carrying out this order aroused the opposition of intellectuals and became a very heated issue. The government's heedlessness is well illustrated by what occurred in Wakayama Prefecture, where the opposition to the measure was very strong. Until this time the worship of tutelary deities had taken a very primitive form in rural parts of this district. In many cases a large tree represented the deity, and there was no shrine building at all, but now the officials tried even to annex such places to the town shrine. In places thirty or forty shrines were joined into one, and the sacred forests cut down, so that people had to journey in some instances as much as eleven miles and back to the approved shrine. The disappearance of many shrines caused a number of people whose work had been connected with them—such as the dyers who made festival banners, and the fruit vendors or confectioners who catered to worshipers— to go out of business. To make matters worse, certain former officials invited traders from other prefectures to come and cut forests, an abuse that eventually led to lawsuits. Vagabonds took up where the merchants left off and turned the wooded lands into a desert. Many plants that would be valuable to botanists today were destroyed.

The merger of shrines was carried out most rigidly in the following prefectures:

Prefecture	Shrines still in existence	Shrines destroyed
Mie	942	5547
Wakayama	790	2923
Ehime	2027	3349
Saitama	3508	3869
Nagano	3834	2997

(From the *Osaka Mainichi Newspaper*, June 25, 1911)

This measure was eventually abandoned, and in some prefectures it was not carried out to any appreciable extent. In others, moreover, shrines that had been destroyed but were still regarded as sacred places, were later marked with shrine buildings.

b. The Privilege of Worshiping the Tutelary Deity

In pre-Meiji days the privilege of carrying on worship services and celebrations to the tutelary deity in many villages belonged to a limited number of old houses, who often formed a guild for the purpose. People who were not supposedly related to the deity genealogically were outsiders at these festivities, and this applied even to former retainers of guild members who had split off and formed separate families. An interesting development of the Meiji period was the loss of the distinction between those who had the privilege of worship and those who did not. The change came as the result of the social and economic rise of new families, and it often caused serious social conflicts. The opening of the shrine guilds to all members of the community came around the middle of the Meiji era. At this time the old members still had considerable political authority in their various districts, and their prestige was an effective force in village life, but in contrast to the past one could now buy into a guild and even become head of it with a sufficient outlay of money.

The guilds did not suddenly open their doors to everyone. Even after outsiders were taken in, they were usually distinguished in one way or another from the older families, whose prerogatives were slow to vanish. Eventually, however, all members of the guilds became equal. A good example is found in the district of Honda in the village of Sentō, Kumamoto Prefecture. Here a shrine called the Saisei-kyū was controlled by a guild of forty-four houses. At the first of the Meiji period only the names of the eleven most important families appeared on the roles of the shrine, and the other thirty-three, who were small farmers, had little influence on shrine affairs. On the shrine roles for 1888, however, the names of all forty-four were listed for the first time, apparently because the small farmers had increased in strength. In 1912 the guild was divided into upper and lower sections, which took turns running the annual festivals. The privilege of belonging to the guild was negotiable, and between 1888 and 1912 seven shares changed hands, which signifies the disappearance of old social barriers. In 1934 all members of the community were admitted on an equal basis. We should mention in this connection, however, that a number of local guilds remained exceedingly exclusive, and others were opened to new people only after a struggle. In the village of Nogami, Tochigi Prefecture, the guild that controlled the Utsunomiya Shrine was composed of twenty-six families who managed all ceremonies and festivals. Outsiders were allowed only to cook or do odd jobs connected with the celebrations. In the Meiji period, however, the outsiders began to feel that the system was unfair, and between 1882 and 1884 a serious dispute arose between the two groups, at the root of which lay the fact that the former underlings had gained possession of the land attached to the shrine, thus causing the angry guild members to go to court in an attempt to preserve their rights. It is clear that in this village, shrine affairs were closely connected with political and economic rights.

The tradition in some places had been for the head of the chief clan to hold the right of directing festivals exclusively, but in the Meiji period this privilege was gradually extended to others.

2. CEREMONIES AND FAITH

a. Changes in Ceremonies

In April, 1875, the government decided upon a system of shrines and prescribed the ceremonies for public processions and worship services. At the same time, it made an effort to wipe out the heterogeneous popular religious festivals, which even beforehand it had condemned as deterimental to public morals. In particular it deplored festivals in which people dressed up as members of the opposite sex, as was the practice in some locations.

Many of the festivals that centered around the smallest shrines went on as before, but in shrines large enough to merit a governmental representative at their annual observances, the festivals became very formal affairs carried on almost exclusively by officials. In such cases the traditional festivals were often carried on separately, but they were officially regarded as distinct from the real worship services, and were not uncommonly proscribed in time of war or disaster.

Throughout the Meiji period changes in social conditions led to the spontaneous abandoning of old religious ceremonies in many places. This phenomenon is only partly explained by the general weakening of faith in the old gods. It was also due to a widespread inclination to change everything, and often simply to the instability of the times. We should note, however, that a number of the festivals abolished or abandoned during this period were later revived. In the vicinity of Lake Suwa, for example, there was an old belief that cracks in the ice covering the lake in the winter were made by gods walking across, and that they indicated the prospects for the harvest in the ensuing autumn. Each year they were the object of a divination ceremony, which appears to date back to the Heian period. In the early Meiji era this custom was dropped, but in 1892 the shrine at Suwa decided to begin observing it again.

After the revision of the calendar, many ceremonies and festivals were observed in accordance with the solar calendar, but for a variety of reasons the lunar calendar was still followed in some instances. A curious conflict arose in the case of a festival at the Fuwa Hachiman Shrine in the village of Naka-mura, Kōchi Prefecture. There the annual festival fell on the fifteenth day of the eighth moon by the old calendar. After the beginning of the Meiji period, therefore, a representative from the prefecture was sent to the shrine on August 15th each year, but there were no festivities among the general public on this day. The reason was that the customary festival involved taking a portable shrine up the nearby river in a boat to the shrine building, and this could be done only at full tide, which occurred on the old day for the festival. Thus, the prefectural dignitary to the contrary notwithstanding, the festival was held by the lunar calendar as before.

In the cities the portable shrines carried about during festivals became more elaborate and beautiful than before, and many new types of entertainment were devised, but one is inclined to doubt that the gods were especially pleased, since much of the new gaiety and clamor was clearly intended to entertain not them, but the celebrants. There were many more people in the festival parades in the cities, but they evidenced little religious feeling. The village celebrations carried on solely by the traditional worshipers of the tutelary deity displayed far more concern for the god himself. Even the heads of shrines in the cities failed to observe the traditional ascetic practices associated with annual festivals, but in the rural areas the devotees of a deity would often fast or, if the custom demanded, bathe in the frigid water of a river in the dead of winter to purify themselves.

The modern lack of religious feeling in festivals is illustrated by the manner in which the traditional food offering to the gods is handled. In the old days those in charge of the shrines made elaborate dishes that required considerable preparation, but now in many instances the deity had to be content with some vegetables or a fish or something that could easily be obtained and presented by a shrine official, to whom the task of making the offering was relegated.

Prior to the Meiji period the families who took charge of festivals brewed special sake as an offering, and the other worshipers were allowed to sample its flavor. Villagers were very critical on such occasions, and if the beverage was the least bit unsavory, the reputation of the brewers was bound to suffer, and their qualifications as leaders of the celebration to be questioned. In 1872, however, the government forbade private brewing, and henceforward sake for the gods was simply purchased from a dealer.

b. Faith in the Gods

In modern times personal religious beliefs differ greatly, and there are many people who hold none at all, but this has not always been the case. In the past, religion occupied a place in everyone's life, and in a given area, although individual fervor might have varied, everyone had very much the same faith. The customary annual festivals were closely connected with the common religion, and the decline of the former is directly due to that of the latter.

It is often stated that the Shinto religion is the national Japanese faith—the spiritual force that binds the society together. In a sense, of course, this is true, but it is a mistake to consider that all the various facets of popular religion are encompassed by the single term Shinto. It would perhaps be better to say that, with certain exceptions, the country as a whole worships the native gods, whatever other religious beliefs it may hold simultaneously, but there is a pronounced element of eclecticism. This can be seen in the concrete expressions of popular belief and in the changes that have occurred in them since the beginning of the modern period.

Practically every house in Japan has a miniature shrine to the Shinto gods, and in the late Tokugawa and early Meiji periods it was customary for people to bow before this each morning. This practice, however, cannot be traced back to pre-Tokugawa times, and it is virtually certain that the shrine in its modern form was not originally a Shinto device. Indeed, the ancients appear to have made a shrine whenever the need arose, just as people today prepare special shrines during the New Year and *bon* seasons. Most probably the modern shrine was inspired by the miniature Buddhist altars kept by members of the pietist sects.

One interesting form of Japanese worship is the widespread habit of bowing to the sun each morning. It is difficult to say when this practice began or whether it represents sun-worship pure and simple, but in any event it was exceedingly common in the Meiji period. A harvest celebration held each year in many villages was called *himachi*, which was probably derived from *himatsuri*, meaning "festival of the sun," but many people, interpreting the term as "waiting for the sun" (*hi-machi*), thought the celebration involved waiting up all night to pay respects to the rising sun. In some villages on festival days people arose early in the morning, went first to the shrine farthest to the east and then, following the sun westward, visited the others in order, and completed their pilgrimage before sunset.

In 1943 Mr. Miyamoto Jōichi recorded the beliefs of his grandfather, which were very likely typical of those held by villagers in the early Meiji period. The old man considered the sun as the physical manifestation of the sun goddess Amaterasu

Ōmikami, and regarded it more highly than anything else. Next to the sun he respected the deity of Izumo most. He regarded the imperial family as descendants of the sun and the hereditary chief priest of the Izumo Shrine as the descendant of the god of Izumo. He also believed that the sight of the emperor would blind the eyes of ordinary people, and that the highest hope anyone could have was to travel to the shrine of the sun goddess at Ise and on the way back bow before the emperor's palace in Kyoto.

3. SPECIAL RELIGIOUS ORGANIZATIONS

a. The Ise Pilgrimage

There is almost no town or village in Japan that does not have a cooperative organization called a *kō*, which is composed of persons who have contributed to a mutual fund intended for one of a variety of purposes. In recent years the number of *kō* has declined, but in the Meiji period they still existed in abundance. Their activities varied little from place to place. On certain days they met at the house of one of the members to eat and drink together, and once a year a few of the members went to pay respects to the shrine of the deity worshiped by the group. When they returned they were greeted by others with a party, and in return they distributed charms from the shrine to everyone. They ordinarily made their pilgrimage by the same route each year, at least until the coming of new transportation facilities in the Meiji period. Every five or seven years the whole group went at once, and after the beginning of the Meiji period they frequently did so more often.

The most widespread organizations of this type were those known as *Ise-kō*, which were dedicated to visiting the great shrine of the sun goddess at Ise. While at the shrine, travelers of the Edo period had usually stopped at the house of one of

1869, which was the day for a meeting of the *Ise-kō*, a charm from the Ise shrine was found in a certain person's house, and as soon as word spread, everybody gathered to celebrate. Breaking an almost sacred tradition, they wore shoes into the lucky house, and amid the plunking of *samisen* (three-stringed musical instruments) and the beating of drums, kept repeating an odd little song:

In Edo's Yokohama stones fall—now isn't that fine !

Hereabout the gods descend—now isn't that fine, isn't that fine !

Amid the hubbub a number of persons started out for Ise just as they were, without a bit of money and in some cases still carrying their farm implements. Along the way people gave them food, shelter, and money. The same phenomenon occurred in other parts of Wakayama Prefecture at the same time. It became evident later that at least some of the charms had been planted by professional soothsayers, a number of whom were arrested.

1890 was the customary year for pilgrimages of this sort and although there was little of the clamor described above, a fair number of people actually did make the journey. The following appeared in a contemporary newspaper:

> This is the year for sudden pilgrimages to the Ise Shrine, and despite the biting cold, many people from the Tokyo area set out by train or ship in January. The steamship companies have given each pilgrim a hand towel with a special commemorative design, and so far one thousand have been donated.

Aside from the *Ise-kō* there were numerous similar organizations designed to provide for various celebrations or for mutual aid in times of trouble. A number of these groups were composed of women. On certain occasions, usually once during the New Year celebration and once during the *bon* festival, the ladies gathered together and spent the night gossiping or making hemp thread. After the latter ceased to be produced in the home, the women formed the habit of inviting the principal of the primary school or a similar functionary to make a talk on home education or agricultural improvement. It was customary for the *kō* to erect a small stone pagoda with the names of members engraved on it.

4. TABOOS

a. Decreasing Fear of Taboos

In order to worship the gods properly, a Japanese must cleanse his body and spirit in a number of different ways. Often this involves staying in a separate house, eating over a separate fire, and avoiding certain foods, particularly the flesh of fish or animals. Aside from these special means of purification, there are certain taboos which no one is supposed to be able to violate with impunity, and when one involuntarily infringes upon them, one must take steps to "decontaminate" oneself. The most common taboos still in the popular memory are those connected with funerals, birth, or menstruation, but in the past there was a variety of others. For instance, one was contaminated when one's house burned or when one saw blood.

The various ancient restrictions on the conduct of persons in mourning were intended to protect outsiders from contamination by contact with death. During the Tokugawa period, relatives of a dead person were required by law to stay in mourning for a fixed number of days, dependent on the rank of the deceased and on the degree of kinship with him, but in the Meiji period these rules were gradually were relaxed. In 1868, at the time of the formal accession of the Emperor Meiji, persons in mourning for their fathers or mothers were ordered to refrain from attending the palace ceremonies, but in 1872 it was decided that the rules for attending shrines should be relaxed to the extent that those having attended a funeral, but to the letter, it would have been necessary for men and women to live separately, but that being unfeasible, a compromise was made. The tops of mountains and certain other locations were set aside as places for abstaining, and women were forbidden to enter therein, not because they themselves were impure, but because their presence increased the danger that impure acts would be committed.

The prohibitions against women largely disappeared during the Meiji period, and eventually even the sacred Buddhist mountain Kōya ceased to remain inviolate. The following appeared in the *Tokyo Asahi Newspaper* on July 2, 1906:

For more than eleven hundred years after Kōbō Daishi founded his monastery on Mt. Kōya, in the province of Kii, women were forbidden to climb the mountain, and priests were forbidden to eat meat. However, the present abbot of the monastery, Mitsumon Yūhan, considering that these prohibitions were out of step with modern society, recently assembled the monks of the various temples, as well as laymen in the neighboring towns, at the Kongō-ji to discuss this matter, and it was agreed that the abbot was correct.

There were minor taboos on various phases of everyday life. Indeed, if one counted all the things one was not supposed to do, they would probably have come to two or three thousand, though of course no one paid any attention to most of them. Virtually everyone brought up in the Meiji period was taught not to cut his nails at night, or to step on the rail of a sliding door, or spit in a toilet, but even these common taboos have almost passed out of existence. A number of words homonymous with the word for death (*shi*) were often replaced in conversation with a euphemism, an example being the common term for salt (*shio*), which was often replaced by the expression "flower of the waves." Curiously, many of the tabooed words were avoided particularly at night. Some stores refused to sell salt in the evenings even if the customer used the euphemistic term.

There was a large variety of taboos connected with particular days of the month and the various directions of the compass. Formerly these were observed with particular rigidness on farms, but they are now largely forgotten. Still, few people today will move into a building without holding ceremonies at the northeast corner of it to ward off devils, who are thought to come from this direction, and funerals are never held on a number of days in the old calendar which are called *tomobiki*, or "leading a friend," for obvious reasons. Both of these superstitions, incidentally, are based partially on imported Chinese ideas. Some ages were considered particularly unlucky, and people in the past took various special precautions to protect themselves in those years, but this practice too has gradually declined. Still, in the Meiji period shrines and temples were often requested to say special prayers for individuals during their unlucky years.

5. SUPERSTITIONS REGARDING EVIL SPIRITS

a. Foxes

In central Japan and Shikoku, the belief that people can be possessed by foxes was exceedingly strong, and after the beginning of the Meiji period it seems to have grown even more so. In 1907 the Educational Society of Shimane Prefecture issued a statement against the superstition, but the results of this effort to destroy it were questionable. The underlying reason for the attempt was that the families supposedly possessed had grown so numerous that they constituted a large faction, and the opposition between them and the "unpossessed" houses had become an important factor in local government. The concept of possession, which had given rise to the conflict, was in turn nurtured by it. Being possessed was in effect the badge of membership in a particular group. Another reason for the spread of the superstition, however, was simply that it was fostered by religious charlatans, who made their sustenance by going to various places and "healing" those who were afflicted. Sometimes these faith healers told their patients specifically which (imaginary) fox from which family was troubling them, and the maligned household was henceforth classed among the possessed. In many places the superstition did not spread until the Meiji period, and in some it continued to cause serious social problems in the Shōwa period. Siebolt's and Bälz's comments on the Japanese beliefs concerning foxes are well known in the West, and since the publication of Kadowaki Masae's *Kitsune-tsuki-byō Shinron* (*A New Theory Concerning Possession by Foxes*) in 1902 the various psychological aspects have been clarified to a considerable extent. The Ainus have a similar superstition, and indeed all other countries, particularly those of Asia, have the same sort of idea, though the animal varies from place to place. Although the fox is most often mentioned in Japanese legends, the animal referred to appears to have been in reality a small ermine-like creature. In China and Korea, one also hears of people possessed by foxes, but the various superstitions concerning them differ to some extent from those of Japan. The most unique feature of the Japanese belief is that it includes the idea that possession is hereditary and is transmittable through marriage.

In the northeast region a little goblin who rides on a fox is widely worshiped, but the superstition with regard to the animal has not proved as harmful there as in central Japan. Belief in foxes spread together with the cult of Inari, a god of agriculture now worshiped over the entire country. Foxes are considered messengers of this deity, and they share his supernatural qualities. In the beginning Inari was most probably worshiped only in agriculture communities, but nowadays he is respected in fishing communities and cities as well. In the latter he is regarded as a god of riches, and in urban department stores there is always a small shrine to him, which supposedly insures profits. In relatively modern times the practice of worshiping gods at places other than their original shrines has become very common, and Inari, like various other deities, has gained a very wide following, partially because of active propaganda issued by Fushimi Shrine, which is the center of his cult. In many houses he has been substituted for the former tutelary deity.

Since foxes are the object of so much superstitious belief, it is not surprising that professional soothsayers went about claiming to have received revelations from them. These people frequently aroused disturbances of one sort or another, and the Meiji government tried to suppress them, but was not throughly successful.

b. Foxes and Faith

The reason for attributing supernatural qualities to foxes was probably simply that they are beautiful, quick, and clever. Furthermore, since they appear most frequently in Japanese rural areas, it is no accident that they are regarded as messengers of the god of agriculture. At the same time, however, since wild foxes actually did a good deal of damage to farmers, it is equally natural that there was an inclination to regard them as sources of superhuman mischief. The things they were supposed to have done were very much the same in every locality and this applies in the case of badgers, which were also supposed to have supernatural powers. One interesting point is that the tales about these animals clearly show the flavor of the historical period in which they were invented. In the Meiji era, for instance, one heard of foxes and badgers knocking at doors and saying they had come to deliver a telegram. They were also said to stand on railway tracks and stop trains, and the fact that they were occasionally run over lent credence to this. In places where damage supposedly done by foxes was particularly great, people sometimes petitioned the government to take steps to control them. The following is from one such petition:

From the Farmer Kagami Shinjirō   Age 46

The aforesaid Kagami Shinjirō, being in any case poor has been suffering from various illnesses since the middle of the seventh month of last year. He has tried various cures and even prayed at the great shrines to the gods on high, but has not received relief. Recently foxes on the prowl in this village have further burdened this ailing man. He is so desperate that his life is in danger, and he is most sorely troubled in spirit. Therefore, at this time, it is most humbly begged that the government will graciously exercise its authority to the end that foxes no longer roam about this community.

Signed: Kagami Shinjirō
His Relative: Ōkura Kitarō
In Association With: Ōhara Matsutarō

The above is certified to be true and valid.

Assistant Village Head,   Hamako Chihei
Village Head,   Ikeda Fusajirō

To Fuchibe Kōshō, the Adjutant of Hōjō Prefecture

Disposition: Those who are in charge of affairs will see that people do not complain of damage by foxes and badgers.

(Seal)

3rd day of the 3rd month

(The above document is in the possession of Mr. Watanabe Junji.)

On Shikoku, where there are no foxes, dogs are supposed to be able to possess people. A well-known story has it that the great priest Kōbō Daishi, who lived in the eighth and ninth centuries, shut up all the foxes in a cave and effectively rid the island of them, but that later, in violation of his command, the cave was opened. Inside, nothing save a picture of a dog was found, but since that time, it is said, dogs have acted like the foxes in other parts of the country. Some Tokugawa-period writers alleged that soothsayers in Shikoku buried dogs in the ground up to their necks, put food before them, but out of reach, and when they had starved to death, used their heads as magic charms. There is no real proof of this, but it is thought in the area that if a person possessed by a dog is hungry, even rice newly prepared for him will sour before he can eat it. Possession by dogs was also transmitted through marriage, and superstitious dread of it has caused considerable social harm.

In certain villages there existed two rather vague hereditary strains which were considered incompatible, and which prevented marriages between members of opposite types. In parts of Tokushima Prefecture, for example, certain families were considered to be of a "broad strain" (*hirosuji*), while others belonged to a "narrow strain" (*semasuji*). Members of the one could not wed members of the other, and since the same area also believed that some families were possessed by dogs, marriage arrangements were exceedingly difficult to make. These distinctions probably originated in some early religious difference long since forgotten. Though in the Meiji period the new education sought to root them out, they proved very resistant to change.

6. RELIGIOUS FADS AND THE CASTING OF SPELLS

When society changes at a rapid pace, there often appears a spate of new religions, the majority of which are little more than heathen. This is happening in present-day Japan and it occurred in the Meiji period as well.

According to newspapers of around 1887, a number of people were claiming to have received revelations from the gods, and in particular from the sun goddess. Many of these persons attracted quite a few believers, and while most of the new religions that they established gradually faded away, some thrived for many years.

In this connection we might mention that a number of local deities gained nationwide popularity during this era, and occasionally very small shrines expanded into large institutions. A shrine of Inari in the Haneda district of Tokyo is a case in point. Until the early 1800's this area was a barren marsh, but around that time a person named Suzuki Yagoemon began to open up the land, setting up this little shrine to protect his possessions. Many years later, in 1885, an old fox that had long lived in a godown belonging to the Suzuki family acquired the reputation of having cured an ailing man, and thereupon people began to flock to the shrine. According to the *Hōchi Newspaper* for January 7, 1897, it boasted by this time 2700 *torii*. A similar case was that of a little shrine to the Buddhist deity Jizō at the Hōsen-ji, a temple in the Nakano district of Tokyo. The statue of this deity had lain on the ground for years without anyone noticing it, but around 1892, it allegedly appeared to a certain sick person and promised to cure him if he would build a better shrine for it. He did so and was immediately healed, so we are told. After that worshipers came in droves.

With the spread of modern scientific knowledge, the movement to do away with superstitions grew stronger, but it is not always easy to say where religion stops and superstition begins, and many out-and-out superstitions are still in vogue. One supposes that there were many more during the Meiji period.

Japanese have probably always believed in amulets of one type or another, but the modern printed charms now given out by shrines and temples first became popular in the Tokugawa period or later, and the practice of wearing miniature charms on one's person is also new. The latter custom is particularly common in cities, where sickness, fires, theft, and traffic accidents are relatively frequent, and it has tended to expand with the advance of time. Today by the driver's seat in every Tokyo bus or streetcar there is a religious charm designed to protect the vehicle in traffic. It would be difficult to say that all the people who carry charms of this sort really believe deeply in the gods they are supposed to represent, but many feel uneasy without them. The amulets are in one sense a product of the modern practice of worshiping deities at places other than their original shrines.

The development of modern transportation not only expanded the cults of various shrines and temples, but also caused the spread of certain superstitions and popular myths. A similar effect resulted from the new and enlarged system of communication. People had always made certain requests to deities in writing, but now they began actually to send them on postcards. In the Shōgyō-ji, a temple in the Hongō district of Tokyo, there is a stone statue of Jizō which is thought by many to have the power to cure coughs. The old custom was to make written supplications to this deity, and in the new era the Hongō post office began to receive no end of postcards addressed to him. The temple had to make special arrangements to take care of its mail. An example:

To: Jizō   Komagome, Hongō Ward
From: Koike Matsuzō   8, Nishi-Torigoe-chō, Asakusa
January 6, 1900

Koike Matsuzō suffers from a cough. He hopes that you will cure him within three days. When he recovers, he will come to pay thanks.

The number of people who still govern much of their daily conduct by divination is surprisingly large, particularly among the agricultural population. Farmers are particularly careful to consult diviners or fortunetellers before building a house or changing residences, and many do the same when they must make an important decision, as, for example, whether or not to adopt some new method of agriculture. Once one acquires the habit of relying on fortunetellers, it is difficult to break it, and whether the prophecies prove correct or not, people who believe in them feel more assured when they take the precaution of hearing them.

During Meiji magic spells were used all over the country for curing illnesses, but a great number of them seem to have originated no earlier than the middle of the Tokugawa period. Those in the country were very different from those in the cities. Farmers, for example, had many spells for curing arm ailments and warts around the eyes, which rarely troubled city people. On the other hand, spells for tooth ailments seem to have developed in the cities, where sweets became popular at a relatively early date. Many city residents wrote supplications or made offerings of money to deities in an effort to cure their toothaches.

When epidemics of colds or measles broke out, even people who had grown accustomed to consulting doctors hung various mystic objects on their front gate to keep the disease out, and spells calculated to prevent or cure smallpox were so highly regarded that they interfered with the government's campaign to inoculate the whole population. Even among the residents of Tokyo there were people who preferred magic to vaccination. After vaccination became compulsory for primary school students, the incidence of smallpox was greatly reduced, but from time to time it was imported by persons returning from foreign countries, and it occasionally breaks out even today. On the other hand, the old spells have not been completely forgotten. People still fear the smallpox deity and in times of epidemic perform a ceremony designed to keep him away. Sometimes parents do this when their children are first vaccinated. Thus, scientific knowledge does not appear to have completely killed the old customs.

INDEX

INDEX

A

abandonment of the special mourning house 184

adoption 120, 121

Afternoon Naps in the Eastern Capital 61

agriculture 73

agricultural
—gods 129
—policy 84
—society 100

aguranabe (安愚楽鍋) 40

Ainu (アイヌ) 310

air tires 139

Aizu (会津) 33

ajichi (アジチ) 107

akagetto (赤毛布) 20

Akita (秋田) Prefecture 95, 124

altars 286

Amikake (網掛) 村, Sarashina (更科) County, Nagano (長野) Prefecture 98

amulets 314, 315

Amami (奄美)
—Archiperago 195
—Ōshima (大島) 183, 161

ancestor(s) 31

ancestor worship 248

ancestral names 106

animal husbandry 38

Aogashima (青ガ島) 34

Aomori (青森) 21, 124, 172

apartment buildings 65

apprentices 93, 149

aprons 19

arabiake (荒火明け) 186

arame-ya (あらめや) 25

Arashiyama (嵐山) 147

arguments against foreign trade 98

Arita (有田) County, Wakayama (和歌山) Prefecture 303

arm coverings 17

army 12, 21, 34
—personnel 139

artificial eyebrows 24

artisan 86, 88, 89

Asaake (朝明) 郡, Mie (三重) Prefecture 25

Asakusa (浅草) 144

Ashikaga (足利) period 38

ashiire (足入れ) 162, 163

assembly laws 147

Association(s)
—of Bluestockings 247
—of young people 167

atotori (アトトリ) 118

atotsugi (アトツギ) 118

Atsumi (渥美) Peninsula 201

automobiles 148, 150

auxiliary; eaves 60, 80
—foods 35

O

This book was set by hand and printed by the Hinode Printing Company in Tokyo. The typeface is Century Catalogue.

CENTENARY CULTURAL COUNCIL SERIES

JAPANESE
MANNERS AND CUSTOMS
IN THE
MEIJI ERA

Published

by

ŌBUNSHA

for

THE CENTENARY CULTURE COUNCIL

First Impression 1957

For information regarding reproduction of translation rights, address
Hidaka Daishiro, Executive Secretary
The Centenary Culture Council
147 Kamifujimae-cho, Komagome, Bunkyō-ku
Tokyo, Japan.

For information regarding the purchase of additional copies, address
Ōbunsha Publishing Co., Ltd.
Yoshio Akao, President,
55 Yokodera-cho, Shinjuku-ku,
Tokyo, Japan.

PRINTED IN TOKYO, JAPAN

CENTENARY CULTURAL COUNCIL SERIES

(* Already Published.   Other books not yet in print.)

A CULTURAL HISTORY OF THE MEIJI ERA (1868-1912)

(Where the translator is not indicated it means that the Council has not yet selected anyone for the task; however, all of the volumes will be translated.)